NATURAL ALLIES

MCGILL-QUEEN'S/BRIAN MULRONEY INSTITUTE OF GOVERNMENT STUDIES IN LEADERSHIP, PUBLIC POLICY, AND GOVERNANCE

Series editor: Donald E. Abelson

Titles in this series address critical issues facing Canada at home and abroad and the efforts policymakers at all levels of government have made to address a host of complex and multifaceted policy concerns. Books in this series receive financial support from the Brian Mulroney Institute of Government at St Francis Xavier University; in keeping with the institute's mandate, these studies explore how leaders involved in key policy initiatives arrived at their decisions and what lessons can be learned. Combining rigorous academic analysis with thoughtful recommendations, this series compels readers to think more critically about how and why elected officials make certain policy choices, and how, in concert with other stakeholders, they can better navigate an increasingly complicated and crowded marketplace of ideas.

5 Government
Have Presidents and Prime Ministers Misdiagnosed the Patient?
Donald J. Savoie

6 Cyber-Threats to Canadian Democracy
Edited by Holly Ann Garnett and Michael Pal

7 The Canadian Federal Election of 2021
Edited by Jon H. Pammett and Christopher Dornan

8 CETA Implementation and Implications
Unravelling the Puzzle
Edited by Robert G. Finbow

9 Multilateral Sanctions Revisited
Lessons Learned from Margaret Doxey
Edited by Andrea Charron and Clara Portela

10 Booze, Cigarettes, and Constitutional Dust-Ups
Canada's Quest for Interprovincial Free Trade
Ryan Manucha

11 NORAD
In Perpetuity and Beyond
Andrea Charron and James Fergusson

12 Under the Weather
Reimagining Mobility in the Climate Crisis
Stephanie Sodero

13 Rethinking Decentralization
Mapping the Meaning of Subsidiarity in Federal Political Culture
Jacob Deem

14 Natural Allies
Environment, Energy, and the History of US-Canada Relations
Daniel Macfarlane

Natural Allies

Environment, Energy, and the History of US-Canada Relations

DANIEL MACFARLANE

McGill-Queen's University Press
Montreal & Kingston • London • Chicago

ISBN 978-0-2280-1759-2 (cloth)
ISBN 978-0-2280-1760-8 (paper)
ISBN 978-0-2280-1807-0 (ePDF)
ISBN 978-0-2280-1808-7 (ePUB)

Legal deposit third quarter 2023
Bibliothèque nationale du Québec

This book has been published with the help of a grant from the Canadian Federation for the Humanities and Social Sciences, through the Awards to Scholarly Publications Program, using funds provided by the Social Sciences and Humanities Research Council of Canada.

Funded by the Government of Canada | Financé par le gouvernement du Canada | Canada | Canada Council for the Arts | Conseil des arts du Canada

We acknowledge the support of the Canada Council for the Arts.

Nous remercions le Conseil des arts du Canada de son soutien.

Library and Archives Canada Cataloguing in Publication

Title: Natural allies : environment, energy, and the history of US-Canada relations / Daniel Macfarlane.
Names: Macfarlane, Daniel, 1979– author.
Series: McGill-Queen's/Brian Mulroney Institute of Government studies in leadership, public policy, and governance ; 14.
Description: Series statement: McGill-Queen's/Brian Mulroney Institute of Government studies in leadership, public policy, and governance ; 14 | Includes bibliographical references and index.
Identifiers: Canadiana (print) 20230159184 | Canadiana (ebook) 20230159214 | ISBN 9780228017592 (cloth) | ISBN 9780228017608 (paper) | ISBN 9780228018070 (ePDF) | ISBN 9780228018087 (ePUB)
Subjects: LCSH: Canada—Relations—United States. | LCSH: United States—Relations—Canada. | LCSH: Environmental policy—Canada. | LCSH: Environmental policy—United States. | LCSH: Energy policy—Canada. | LCSH: Energy policy—United States.
Classification: LCC FC249 .M33 2023 | DDC 327.71073—dc23

This book was typeset by True to Type in 10.5/13 Sabon

Contents

Tables and Figures

TABLES

FIGURES

Acknowledgments

This book has several different wellsprings, so to speak. The first was a course on the history of US-Canada environmental relations I created and taught over a decade ago while a postdoc at Carleton University – *Natural Allies* is the direct descendant of the lectures created for that class. The second wellspring has been my experiences crossing, living, and teaching on both sides of the Canada-US border. Another wellspring has been my previous research projects on various aspects of US-Canada environmental, water, and energy relations. The final wellspring was the COVID-19 pandemic, which prevented me from taking research trips during my sabbatical but also gave me the time and motivation to write this book.

Norman Hillmer, my postdoctoral supervisor at Carleton, made it possible for me to teach that course on US-Canada environmental relations. He also read and commented on a draft of this book and has remained a supportive mentor and friend. The same is true of Serge Durflinger, my doctoral supervisor. Stephen Azzi, Andrea Olive, and Ruth Sandwell read earlier drafts of this book. I am deeply thankful to all of them, as well as the anonymous reviewers arranged by the press, for their incisive, helpful, and generous comments and suggestions. The usual caveat, however, is in order: any mistakes of fact or interpretation remain my own. At McGill-Queen's University Press (MQUP), I want to thank acquisitions editor Kyla Madden and managing editor Kathleen Fraser. They were both a pleasure to work with, as were Lesley Trites and the rest of the MQUP staff. I need to extend my gratitude to the copyeditor, Alicia Hibbert, for improving the text. Colin Duncan provided indexing and proofreading. Jason Glatz once again came through with custom maps.

Internal funding as well as a year's sabbatical leave from my home institution, Western Michigan University (WMU), gave me the resources and time to write this book. My home department, which recently became the School of Environment, Geography, and Sustainability, has been a fruitful incubator for ideas and interdisciplinarity. I've been lucky to have many excellent colleagues and students at WMU. Lynne Heasley, my office neighbour, frequent collaborator, and friend, has been a constant font of support, encouragement, and happy hours.

In addition to my two years as a postdoctoral fellow at Carleton University, this book also benefitted directly and indirectly from other past positions. These include my time as a Banting postdoc with Nancy Langston at Michigan Tech University, as a visiting scholar in the Canadian Studies departments at Carleton and St Lawrence Universities, and as a Fulbright Visiting Research Chair in Canadian Studies at Michigan State University. Though I wasn't able to take advantage because of COVID-19 restrictions, the Water Center in the Graham Sustainability Institute at the University of Michigan provided a visiting fellow position during my sabbatical.

As always, my friends and colleagues at the Network in Canadian History and Environment (NiCHE) provided encouragement, comradeship, and opportunities to work out some of the ideas in this book. While writing *Natural Allies* I was the president of the International Water History Association and had several different roles with the American Society for Environmental History; both of those organizations have provided valuable support and inspiration. The Bill Graham Centre for Contemporary International History at the University of Toronto, where I am a senior fellow, has provided a similar milieu for Canadian international history scholars. Parts of this book are highly synthetic, which reflects both the wide-ranging nature of this study and the reality of writing a book during a pandemic. Consequently, this book relied on the published work of many scholars. Though there isn't room to list them all here, they will find themselves in the notes and bibliography. I do especially want to acknowledge Greg Donaghy, who passed away in 2020. His serendipitous advice while I was a PhD student gave me a new dissertation topic, which led to an enduring interest in Canada-US environmental relations. After I completed my PhD, Greg continued to support my research and challenge my thinking. It is hard to find a historian of Canadian international relations whom Greg didn't help.

Thanks to Asa McKercher and Philip Van Huizen, the editors of the book *Undiplomatic History*, for including my chapter, which served as a sort of outline sketch for what *Natural Allies* would become. I appreciate the feedback on my chapter provided by the editors and other contributors to that volume, as well as by Kurkpatrick Dorsey. I thank the *American Review of Canadian Studies* for their permission to reproduce parts of "Hydro Diplomacy: Canada-US Hydroelectricity Exports and Regulations Prior to the NEB," *American Review of Canadian Studies* 51, no. 4 (2021): 508–32. *Natural Allies* draws upon the research and ideas in many of my other previous publications, including those co-authored or co-edited with Andrew Watson, Murray Clamen, Noah Hall, Lynne Heasley, Norman Hillmer, and Michael Manulak. Many of the archival sources I cite were initially consulted during research for previous books, so I again thank those archivists and librarians who assisted me. In some cases, I have opted to cite FRUS or DCER sources since those are more easily accessible for the reader than an archival source.

My aforementioned sabbatical started in the fall 2020 semester, during the first year of the COVID-19 pandemic. During that sabbatical year, our two children, Elizabeth and Lucas, attended school virtually, which meant that I was at home with them (and with my wife, Jen, who worked virtually from home for much of that period). Thus, rather than the grand plans I had for my sabbatical, it turned into a sort of part-time "visiting teaching professor of elementary school at living room state university." Consequently, it might be more accurate to say that this book was finished in spite of my family, not because of them. Regardless of whether they made this book better, they undoubtedly have made my life immeasurably better. I thank Jen for her love, patience, and sense of humour. I thank Elizabeth and Lucas for distracting me and preventing me from taking myself too seriously. I also need to thank Becky Macfarlane, Bob and Vivian Thomson, and many other relatives for their continued support.

Abbreviations

ANWR	Arctic National Wildlife Refuge
AOC	area of concern
AQA	Canada–United States Air Quality Agreement
AWPPA	Arctic Waters Pollution Prevention Act
BWT	Boundary Waters Treaty
CEC	Commission for Environmental Cooperation
CFCs	chlorofluorocarbons
CITES	Convention on the International Trade of Endangered Species
CUFTA	Canada-US Free Trade Agreement
DEW	Distant Early Warning
EEZ	exclusive economic zone
FERC	Federal Energy Regulatory Commission
FPC	Federal Power Commission
GATT	General Agreement on Tariffs and Trade
GLWQA	Great Lakes Water Quality Agreement
GLSLRBSWRA	Great Lakes–St Lawrence River Basin Sustainable Water Resources Agreement
GRAND	Great Recycling and Northern Development
HEPCO	Hydro-Electric Power Commission of Ontario
IRS	International Rapids section (St Lawrence River)
IJC	International Joint Commission
JBNQA	James Bay and Northern Quebec Agreement
MOIP	Mandatory Oil Import Program
MOU	memorandum of understanding
NAFTA	North American Free Trade Agreement
NAWAPA	North American Water and Power Alliance

NAWMP	North American Waterfowl Management Plan
NEB	National Energy Board
NEP	National Energy Program
NOP	National Oil Policy
NORAD	North American Air Defence Command/North American Aerospace Defence Command
PASNY	Power Authority of the State of New York
PFAS	perfluoroalkyl and polyfluoroalkyl substances
PFOA	perfluorooctanoic acid
POPs	persistent organic pollutants
RAP	remedial action plan
TFM	3-trifluoromethyl-4-nitrophenol, a fish poison
UNCBD	United Nations Convention on Biological Diversity
UNCLOS	United Nations Convention on the Law of the Sea
UNFCC	United Nations Framework Convention on Climate Change
USMCA	United States–Mexico–Canada Agreement
VOIP	Voluntary Oil Import Program
WTO	World Trade Organization

NATURAL ALLIES

Introduction

It probably comes as a surprise to most Americans when they learn that their largest trading partner has long been Canada. Canadians, conversely, are generally well aware of this fact. Crossborder trade between Canada and the United States is normally worth around $2 billion per day. Indeed, until very recently, Canada and the United States carried on the largest bilateral trade in the world. Much, maybe most, of that involves natural resources. And it has been that way for a considerable time. Almost a century ago, in his classic *The Fur Trade in Canada*, Harold Innis lamented Canada's dependence on exporting natural staples, describing the country as a "hewer of wood, drawer of water." This cliché – or aphorism – has remained a common refrain for framing the American appetite for Canada's resources.

This book is a study of that wood and water – and a host of other resources – in Canada-US relations. More broadly, it is a study of the role of the environment and energy in that relationship. I am concerned with the nature of bilateral diplomacy: that is, the actual *nature* (trees, fish, oil, minerals, etc.) involved in diplomacy (state-to-state relations at an official level). The central conceit of this book is that understanding the history of Canada-US relations requires comprehending the importance of environment and energy. Yet historians of Canadian-American relations usually neglect or downplay the natural elements of the bilateral entanglement. There are some exceptions: natural resources with strategic or economic value, such as uranium or oil, and the environmental and energy aspects of Arctic diplomacy. Nevertheless, these are ordinarily reduced to just "natural resources," stripping them of their vitality and turning them into passive, one-dimensional objects bereft of any materiality or agency, mere statistics on paper. Furthermore, there is little recognition that diplomatic decisions have enormous repercussions for landscapes across the continent.[1]

Environmental history as a discipline revolves around studying human-environmental interactions in the past, looking at how society and the natural world have mutually changed and shaped each other. It draws on sources and approaches (e.g., ecology, science, technology) that foreign affairs historians might find, forgive the pun, foreign. An environmental history perspective insists that the nature of natural resources makes an enormous difference – whether it be smelter smoke or zebra mussels, fluctuating rivers or a changing climate. Inherent in that perspective is the belief that nature is a powerful historical actor with its own forms of agency.[2] By this, I do not mean the intentionality, foresight, or rationality associated with human agency – but the extent to which human actions are rational is greatly exaggerated anyway, plus humanity often unintentionally causes historical change. Similarly, non-human nature is a driver of change regardless of whether intentionality or foresight is involved. Pollution, fish, and other mobile aspects of nature insert themselves into binational predicaments by disregarding the border. Inanimate resources can be co-creators of history: many of the defining features of modern North American history, and contemporary twenty-first-century society, are only possible because of resources such as fossil fuels, electricity, plastics, metals, and fertilizers.

In the Canadian-American context, energy diplomacy chiefly revolves around hydroelectricity, fossil fuels, and uranium. Energy history, for its part, is a rapidly growing field of North American scholarship.[3] In my opinion, the most exciting approaches to energy history are those that engage with environmental history or political ecology. Drawing from some of these approaches, it becomes clear that any bilateral trade in foodstuffs, whether it be meat, fish, or grains, is also a type of energy diplomacy and exchange since food generally ends up being converted into caloric energy. In many respects, the American and Canadian states and economies were at base primarily concerned with governing the liberation of energy, whether it was in the form of directly trading electricity, fossil fuels, or caloric energy (e.g., foodstuffs), or the energy embodied in all the materials that were exchanged across the border.

Depending on how it is framed, energy diplomacy can be either separate from environmental diplomacy (when only the economic, security, or political aspects are stressed) or an overlapping form of it when the ecological dimensions are recognized or foregrounded. Indeed, energy production and environmental protection are usually at odds – a common dilemma for Canada and the United States, as this book demonstrates. I conceive of energy statecraft as both a distinctive type of diplomacy and a type of environmental diplomacy. For that reason, I will often refer collectively to Canada-US environmental and energy diplomacy in this book but will at times address energy diplomacy on its own.

This book is equally an exercise in international history. I will consider those environmental and energy aspects that were the matter of direct relations between the Canadian and American governments (and, until Canada fully held the reins of its diplomacy, the British government). That means I am concentrating on issues that run through governance institutions and the diplomatic machinery: the federal governments and their relevant departments (usually the US State Department and Executive branch and the Canadian Department of External Affairs and Cabinet) and bilateral institutions such as the International Joint Commission and numerous other offices, organizations, and agencies. Difficulties in getting treaties through Congress and Parliament is a common theme in this book; in particular, the US Senate frequently blocked bilateral agreements. By extension, this points to the influence that special and regional interests have on foreign policy aims in each country.

Dealing with natural resources shaped bilateral diplomacy in another decisive way: it necessitated giving subfederal levels of government – especially the provinces and states – a partial role in policymaking. Both countries have federal systems in which provinces and states exercise constitutional jurisdiction over many aspects of natural resources. Consequently, these aspects generally drove the evolution of early subnational diplomacy efforts, such as in the realm of border waters and hydro power. Moreover, there are far more states than provinces, which can create greater political hurdles south of the border. For example, only one Canadian province touches the Great Lakes, while eight states do the same. It is not hard to imagine how this scenario complicates water diplomacy.

I have opted to use the word *diplomacy* while hoping that the reader will leave any semantic baggage that this term might carry at the door. That term has become déclassé for many because of its "great (white) men of the past" approach. Other terms like *international*, *transborder*, *transnational*, *geopolitics*, or *ecopolitics* – which I will also use – have found favour because they are more encompassing and inclusive of different types of actors beyond just heads of state, foreign ministers, and diplomats. After all, by drawing attention to the environment, this book inherently seeks to privilege some non-traditional diplomatic "actors." At the same time, this book also focuses on governmental and state-sanctioned actors conducting formal relations – the traditional bailiwick of diplomatic historians.

Some bilateral environment and energy issues were of the punctuated variety: disputes, crises, and negotiations that grabbed headlines and caused major concerns or controversies within the bilateral relationship. The St Lawrence Seaway, Columbia River Treaty, Arctic sovereignty, oil exports, and acid rain are examples of such punctuated events. These tend to make it into general histories of Canada-US relations, or at least get mentioned in passing. But many environmental and energy issues seem so mundane that they are left out, even though they become crucial parts of the background infrastructure that facilitates the smooth flow of transborder relations. The two nation-states have a predisposition for working out modi vivendi, ways to compromise or productively agree to disagree, and I would argue that this tendency stems from dealing so persistently with these types of issues.[4]

Those seemingly ordinary and constant environmental subjects take up much of the time of US and Canadian diplomats and are cumulatively very consequential.[5] In the 1970s, Henry Kissinger opened a meeting with Canadian ambassador Marcel Cadieux with the sarcastic query: "I hope you have not come to talk to me about the sex life of the salmon."[6] Not long after that interchange, while writing about the constant fish negotiations in fin-de-siècle Canadian-American relations, historian C.P. Stacey quipped that "[t]here is a certain tiresome iteration about the question of the North Atlantic fisheries."[7] These remarks are indicative of the minor importance many esteemed political actors and commentators put on crossborder issues like fish and timber, compared to national security and global diplomacy matters. But the trade in natural materials that makes up much of the transborder relationship has a considerable ecological impact over time. Indeed, if we took stock of all the goods that have moved across the US-Canada border, the environmental repercussions of producing, manufacturing, and transporting them all would be astronomical. Despite Kissinger's aspersions, the collapse of fisheries, to pick just one example, may well prove to be of more long-term historical significance, both for the planet and the people that inhabit it, than the high politics that the famed American diplomat deigned worthy of his attention.

I am not only arguing that environmental history helps us better understand Canada-US relations, for the reverse is also true: we cannot fully comprehend the environmental history and ecological impact of either country without reference to their international history. More so than most G-20 countries, Canada's prosperity has historically been linked to sending resources abroad (primarily to the United States), with all the attendant national anxieties that doing so dredges up. The desires and vagaries of US markets shaped Canada's engagement with its natural resources. Many Canadian landscapes at, or even far from, the border were altered or impacted by the United States; really, we should refer to *borders* in the plural since, in addition to the "main" border, the two countries also share northern and maritime borders. Clearly, the history of northern North American interchanges had a profound impact on the continent's ecosystems.

ENVIRONMENTAL DIPLOMACY

The history of environmental diplomacy combines the approaches of the fields of environmental history and diplomatic history. Environmental historians have long been more "international" in their outlook than diplomatic historians have been "environmental" in theirs. Beginning in the 1990s, several American historians wrote pieces that explicitly sought to define and promote "environmental diplomacy" as a field of North American historical inquiry.[8] American scholars have since authored a number of works on the history of environmental and energy issues in that nation's foreign affairs.[9]

Yet political scientists and international relations scholars have produced more research explicitly on international environmental relations than have historians – both globally and in the North American context.[10] While the result has been a great deal of valuable work, a side effect is that non-historians have largely determined the agenda for studying past environmental relations. Scholarship on contemporary environmental protection, which tends to focus on multilateral protection agreements such as United Nations climate change efforts, is the dominant strand in environmental diplomacy.[11] As a result, scholars typically view environmental diplomacy as contemporary (post-1970) environmental protection.

Table 0.1
Major Canada-US environmental and energy diplomacy issues since 1900

1900s	International Waterways Commission and border waters (Chicago diversion; Milk–St Mary, Niagara Falls, etc.)
1900s	Niagara power developments and exports
1907	Fluid and Electricity Export Act
1908	Inland Fisheries Treaty
1909; 1937; 1985; 2002	Salmon treaties
1909	Boundary Waters Treaty & International Joint Commission
1910	North Atlantic Cod Fisheries Agreement
1910	Passamaquoddy Bay Treaty
1911	North Pacific Fur Seal Convention
1916	Migratory Bird Treaty
1923; 1930; 1937; 1953; 1977	Halibut treaties
1927–41	Trail Smelter Dispute
1929	Niagara Convention
1930s	Canada-US trade agreements
1932 & 1941	Great Lakes and St Lawrence agreements
1940s–present	US bases and infrastructure in northern Canada
1940s–present	Canadian nuclear and uranium exports
1940s–present	Canadian fossil fuel exports and pipelines
1941 & 1943	Ogoki–Long Lac diversions
1945–present	Post-Second World War eastern border waters: Richelieu, Champlain, Passamaquoddy, Saint John, etc.
1945–present	Post–Second World War western border waters: Garrison, Devil's Lake, Red River, Skagit, etc.
1946 & 1954	Great Lakes Fisheries Convention
1950s	St Lawrence Seaway and Power Project
1950s–present	Expansion of Canada-US electric grid and electricity exports
1950s–present	Law of the Sea and maritime boundaries

1950	Niagara River Diversion Treaty
1961	National Oil Policy
1965	Canada-US Auto Pact
1969	The *Manhattan* Affair & Arctic Waters Pollution Prevention Act
1970s	Reciprocal fisheries agreements
1970s–present	Electricity exports from northern Canada
1972 & 1978	Great Lakes Water Quality Agreements
1977	Pipeline Transit Treaty
1977	Natural Gas Pipeline Agreement
1979	East Coast Fisheries Resources Treaty
1980s	National Energy Program
1980s–present	Softwood lumber disputes
1980s–present	Ozone and greenhouse gas discussions
1985	The *Polar Sea* affair
1986	North American Waterfowl Management Plan
1987–present	Great Lakes areas of concern and remedial actions plans
1988	Canada-US Free Trade Agreement
1990s–present	Tar sands exports and pipelines
1990s–present	Climate change negotiations
1991	Canada-US Air Quality Agreement
1994	North American Free Trade Agreement
2008	Great Lakes–St Lawrence River Basin Sustainable Water Resources Agreement
2011–21	Keystone XL Pipeline
2016	North American Climate, Clean Energy and Environment Partnership
2020	United States–Mexico–Canada Agreement
2021–present	Line 5 in the Straits of Mackinac

Note: In this chronological table the left column indicates date and/or time range and the right column lists the issue or agreement.

But a concentration solely on agreements in the last half century about environmental conservation is too temporally rigid and excludes diplomacy that is not aimed at protecting the environment. Moreover, while there has been a proliferation of multilateral environmental protection treaties since 1970, Canadian-American treaties to conserve wildlife and resources actually stretch back to the nineteenth century. In fact, the two countries have made more than fifty bilateral arrangements that concern the environment in some way. Furthermore, in the realm of international environmental law, the Canada-US relationship has frequently been a global trendsetter through the creation of accords and settlements such as the Boundary Waters Treaty, the Trail Smelter case, and the Great Lakes Water Quality Agreements.

I contend that the field of historical environmental and energy diplomacy should not only include agreements and relations aimed at preserving wildlife and stopping pollution. Rather, any form of past diplomacy dealing with natural resources, including their exploitation, is an appropriate subject for inclusion as environmental diplomacy. Otherwise, we miss out on a large part of the historical process. Hence, for the purposes of this book, I define historical environmental diplomacy as the study of past international relationships and negotiations that directly involve the management or usage of natural resources, including those forms of diplomacy that result in both environmental protection and environmental degradation.

Since this book examines energy and environmental relations, I concentrate on the period when both the United States and Canada were sovereign or semi-sovereign nations, from Canadian Confederation in 1867 until the present. Environmental diplomacy has been central to Canada working out its role as an independent nation caught between Britain and the United States. Natural resources are apparent in the evolution of the so-called North Atlantic Triangle, the construct some Canadians employed to claim a linchpin, or translator, role in trilateral American-Canadian-British relations. After all, many, even most, of the earliest diplomatic forays by Canadian officials in conjunction with, or mostly separate from, the British foreign service involved natural resources. As will be shown, the localized knowledge required to conduct environmental diplomacy effectively helped Canadian officials carve out a role increasingly independent from Britain, while also enhancing Canada's status as a sovereign nation and Ottawa's ability as an able negotiator in the eyes of Washington.

Tied up in such conceptualizations are imperialism and continentalism. In the Canadian context, both have unique meanings that have changed over time and have both positive and negative connotations. Continentalism refers to an approach favouring closer ties with Uncle Sam, often directly or indirectly at the expense of a stronger connection to Britain. Continentalism has often been at odds with various forms of Canadian nationalism, and the question of closer integration versus greater autonomy could be said to be a founding, and perennial, debate on par with the English-French question. Similarly, imperialism has varied meanings in Canadian international history. Around the turn of the twentieth century, imperialism invoked positive meanings for many nationalists when referring to Canada's role in the British Empire. Such feelings often had anti-American implications, though Canada and the United States alike unquestionably practised settler and extractive colonialism within their own borders.

But when applied to the Canada–United States relationship, imperialism referred to the extension of American power over Canadian politics, economy, culture, and natural resources. The forms that such imperialism took evolved over time, as did critiques of it. What many Canadians saw as welcome continental integration, others saw as imperialism. The latter was particularly pronounced by the 1970s, when the slogan "Continentalism is Treason" began appearing on university campuses and car bumper stickers, books featured titles such as *Close the 49th Parallel* and *Silent Surrender*, and the NDP's Waffle Movement decried the "American Empire."[12]

It is worth noting that while the Canadian left wing was critical of Canada-US integration from the 1960s onward, during the interwar years the centre-left had been more receptive. Continentalist interpretations were prominent in the Carnegie Endowment for International Peace series on Canadian-American relations, edited by James Shotwell and capped by John Bartlet Brebner's 1958 book *North Atlantic Triangle: The Interplay of Canada, the United States, and Great Britain*.[13] That interwar continentalism was "[a]bove all, an environmental creed that focused on the ways in which the continent had transformed Canada's European settlers into North Americans."[14]

NATURAL SECURITY

This book expands on the idea that shared environments have strong explanatory value. The title, *Natural Allies*, reflects the importance of natural resources in the bilateral relationship as well as the thesis that resources, landscapes, and geography help account for the relatively harmonious nature of this relationship. At the same time, I walk a fine line between stressing the importance of the natural world and avoiding environmental determinism – the more extreme version of which holds that the character or trajectories of societies and countries are inevitably directed in certain ways by their environmental setting. Unlike Canada and the United States, many countries that share rivers, mountains, and other natural features have not exhibited a long history of congenial relations or integration. Many, in fact, have entered into armed conflict over those natural resources. I contend that the Canadian and American systems co-evolved with, were enhanced and constrained by, the ecologies in which they were embedded. Generally speaking, these were ecologies of abundance, rich in caloric, electric, and carboniferous energy, which gave rise to societies, economies, and modes of governance based on expectations of material abundance.

There are many ways that Canada has benefited materially from allying and trading with the United States.[15] But I also believe Canada's modern history of hitching itself to the US wagon is a sort of Faustian bargain in the long term, a privileging of prosperity over autonomy. Measured by each country's capitalist propensity to exploit natural resources and by the dedication of both governments and economies to liberating energy in its various forms, they appear almost identical. From the perspective of the rest of humanity as well as the non-human world, the differences many Canadians like to boast about, such as the social welfare state, will ultimately be inconsequential compared to the shared tendency to voraciously consume natural environments for the sake of profits. In the grand scheme of things, Canada's purported dissimilarities from the United States will be of little help or significance if ecosystems are collapsing.

What I offer in the pages that follow is, in some respects, a selective history. My approach intentionally emphasizes elements of certain subjects, or entire subjects, which are often ignored. Many of the common themes and tropes of the standard histories of Canadian-American relations will not be engaged in much detail. That said, many of those have direct or indirect natural resource dimensions, even if they are not usually highlighted. For example, the 1923 Halibut Treaty is generally mentioned in any survey history on Canadian-American relations since it involved Canada signing a treaty solo for the first time; as far as this book is concerned, however, this agreement is equally significant because it is about fish stocks.

Natural Allies is informed by new approaches to Canadian international history that emphasize subjects such as race, gender, and culture.[16] This book also draws on the many North American transnational and borderlands studies penned in the last few decades.[17] Such studies demonstrate that the many types of crossborder contacts and migrations, affiliations formed by border communities, unions, cultural associations, ethnic groups, economic ties, and other types of transborder networks are an integral part of the Canadian-American relationship. Not only did ideas and organizations frequently cross the border, but so did scientists, conservationists, and environmental activists. These types of informal diplomats played a key role in spreading environmental attitudes and knowledge. But since I am focusing on the state and official diplomatic relations in this book, unless those contacts involve the governments or governmental negotiations about the environment, I will not go into them in much detail. This book is therefore not intended as a history of environmental transnationalism since that approach involves a greater emphasis on non-state organizations and actors than is provided in these pages. Nor is this an environmental history of the border, as valuable as that would be, though I would certainly like to think it contributes to such a history.

The same goes for business histories and commodity chain studies, particularly US multinational firms and their Canadian subsidiaries that harvest and export staples – unprocessed or semi-processed resources – such as paper, minerals, and oil. I will mostly leave the finer details of corporate activities aside. This study does not intend to be an economic or trade history of Canada-US relations. Of course, government policies create and determine the parameters of the "free" market in which business and financial interests operate: the National Policy tariffs or NAFTA changed how American companies operated in Canada, for example, and the type and quantity of goods Canada sent to the United States and vice versa. I will consider the broad strokes of bilateral economic diplomacy by examining trade or financial agreements and policies that clearly altered the activities and patterns of capital and business across the border insofar as they pertain to natural resources. Similarly, American agricultural policies, both domestic and international, often had deep ramifications for Canadian farmers and agricultural production. Nonetheless, except for those cases where agriculture was the subject of direct US-Canada relations, I will not go into much detail on that topic.

Having outlined some of what this book is not, I want to conclude by saying more about what it is. As I have already suggested, this book will show that energy and environment have always been central to Canada-US relations, and that this diplomatic relationship has had far-reaching consequences for environments and landscapes in upper North America (especially in Canada). We cannot understand our contemporary ecological predicaments without understanding past patterns, priorities, irritations, and compromises, all of which I hope *Natural Allies* identifies and elucidates. Moreover, the northern North American history of environmental diplomacy might be the most consequential in the world. No other bilateral relationship has produced as many noteworthy agreements or precedents nor, arguably, had environmental and energy consequences on the same scale. Few other nation dyads have contributed so heavily to carbon emissions, both on a total and per capita basis. If climate change and biodiversity loss are the biggest existential challenges facing human society today, which I believe is the case, then excavating the history of environmental and energy relations is of vital importance. Contemporary attempts to make sustainable decisions and policies require cognizance of how we have affected, harmed, and manipulated ecosystems in the past.

Most American international historians ignore Canada and, like most American presidents and policymakers, take their northern neighbour for granted. Canadians, perhaps responding to such slights, tend to exaggerate how big of a player Canada was, or is, on the international scene. But Canada actually is a premier power in the realms of natural resources and energy. Perhaps scholars of American foreign relations will begin to pay more attention to Canada if the northern North American relationship is framed as one heavily constituted by energy and environmental factors. And perhaps the claims about Canada's international importance that Ottawa politicians frequently make will have some truth when viewed through that frame (of course, given contemporary Canada's status as a climate villain, this may be more of a negative importance quite at odds with the peacekeeper and helpful fixer mythologies).

Designating Canada as this type of international power suggests that a reevaluation of its past and present international activities is in order. Historians of Canadian-American relations, often concerned with national security, have mostly ignored *natural security*.[18] This concept, as I employ it, has several facets. First, even within conventional conceptions of national security, countries that do not have access to sufficient energy supplies are insecure strategically and economically. Secondly, this concept connects to another orthodox preoccupation of diplomacy: sovereignty. Throughout this book, sovereignty and nationalism are reoccurring themes. These two countries have an uncommonly cordial relationship in part because the more powerful state has rarely tried to impose its will using force (at least not in the past two centuries), realizing that to do so was not usually in its self-interest. For its part, Canada has fairly consistently chosen to prosper by integrating with the United States (and sacrificing some sovereignty) rather than going it alone or branching out (which presumably would result in greater sovereignty but less prosperity). As a way of safeguarding sovereignty to an extent, Canada and the United States have historically entered into many nonbinding diplomatic agreements. Though there are no hard legal obligations to carry out the terms in these agreements, in contrast to a formal treaty, it does not mean they are inconsequential or will not be adhered to.

Finally, natural security can refer to the relative public and national safety from environmental harms, particularly those caused by human actions like climate change, poisoned water, species extinctions, and habitat loss. It equally refers to the safety and health of the natural world itself, which along with human populations, is threatened by anthropogenic forces. In a sense, traditional conceptions of national security, and the type of natural security I am forwarding here, are at odds. After all, the production of the fossil fuels, steel, and minerals necessary for the types of armaments and military capabilities associated with national security simultaneously causes environmental harms that threaten human and non-human well-being. The US military alone is one of the world's biggest polluters. The natural world deserves protection for its own sake, and thriving human societies are not possible in the long term without thriving ecosystems. Natural security, therefore, offers a way of reconceptualizing traditional diplomacy and prioritizing justice for people and nature.

This book's organization is a mix of chronological and thematic. That is, *Natural Allies* proceeds in roughly chronological order from the late-nineteenth century to the present, but the chapters are also organized according to certain environmental and energy themes, meaning that there is some temporal overlap. For the first part of the book, I intersperse chapters addressing water with chapters covering other issues. The first chapter brings readers through Canadian Confederation to the start of the First World War, followed by a chapter focused on water during most of the same timeframe. Chapter 3 looks at other issues between the two world wars, with chapter 4 addressing water in that era. The transition from hot war to cold war is the central theme of chapter 5, with subsequent chapters looking at the Great Lakes, water in other regions, and fossil fuels during the early and late Cold War periods. The last four chapters delve into the different things that crossed borders in some way from the later twentieth century through today, with chapter 12 looking at the trade of resources, including free trade agreements, from the 1980s up to the early twenty-first century. The penultimate chapter returns to energy and brings climate change diplomacy into the mix, and a concluding chapter considers the contemporary state of affairs, offering final thoughts about the history of Canada-US environmental and energy relations.

1

Beginnings

Natural Allies focuses on the period from Canadian Confederation to the present. However, most of the environmental diplomacy issues that faced the two nations immediately after implementing the British North America Act began before 1867. Some background history is therefore in order. I will first outline the relevant points of the evolving Canadian-American relationship in the lead-up to Confederation, particularly as it concerns natural resources, so that we can understand the post-1860s international relationship in its proper context. Then I will turn to the geopolitics of fish, birds, borders, and seals up to the First World War.

A central point of this chapter is establishing that early Canadian-American relations were generally environmental diplomacy. Many of Canada's initial diplomatic forays involved natural resources, which deeply shaped the young country's evolving conception of itself as a sovereign international actor and as one of the three sides of a North Atlantic Triangle.[1] Fish were central to the 1871 Treaty of Washington, the first significant treaty a Canadian representative signed. Canada learned valuable lessons about navigating its interests amongst American and British pressures through that treaty, as well as the subsequent Alaskan Boundary Dispute and bilateral conservation agreements to protect fish and other species.

THE PRE-CONFEDERATION PERIOD

Channelling Harold Innis, the exploitation of cod, furs, and other staples was arguably the major preoccupation of the nascent, and then fledgling, political unit that became Canada. This involved environmental diplomacy with Indigenous Peoples, which was nation-to-nation diplomacy, to be sure, though it also took the form of settler and resource colonialism. Indeed, the subsequent history of modern Canadian-American environmental relations is only possible because of this sordid legacy of resource and land appropriation.

The Revolutionary War (1775–83) resulted in the creation of the United States of America. It also involved American invasions of British Canada. Some of those in the Thirteen Colonies that remained loyal to the Crown, as well as First Nations allies, fled north as refugees. The 1783 Treaty of Paris ending the war established part of the Canada-US border along the centre of Great Lakes, and between Maine and New Brunswick. The location of the international border is relevant for our purposes here since it helped determine what environments would be borderlands and thus the subject of future international negotiations.[2]

The Treaty of Paris ensured that American anglers would have the liberty to fish within three miles of British territory on the east coast. Europeans had been coming to fish for hundreds of years in the Grand Banks off Newfoundland and Nova Scotia. Nation-to-nation diplomacy concerning fisheries access in the territory that would become Canada long predated that country's existence as a sovereign state. In the eighteenth century, this fishery was still a fairly small-scale affair. But the number of fish caught, consumed, and exported increased significantly during the nineteenth century, at least until the last few decades when fish stocks started to decrease. There would be struggles over the fisheries for much of this period, even coming close to war.

The Treaty of Paris was often imprecise when it came to the border's exact location, for much of the new frontier line had never been surveyed. The 1794 Jay's Treaty between Britain and the US dealt with some of these unresolved issues, as well as new problems that had arisen. Jay's Treaty set up two joint boundary commissions to establish the boundary line in the northeast at the Saint Croix River, and for the Northwest (though this one never met, and the boundary was not settled until later). A conflict between Maine and New Brunswick was the most serious of the disputes that arose over the international boundary. Though there were understandable reasons for using waterways as dividing lines between political territories, the practice of bisecting rivers and lakes with borders would come to have significant ecological repercussions later on.

US-British tensions continued to simmer until they boiled over in the War of 1812. The Treaty of Ghent ended this conflict, which was in many ways a carryover of the American Revolutionary War. But the treaty did not reopen the Grand Banks fisheries, which had been closed during the war, to the Americans. The Anglo-American Convention of 1818 excluded Americans from the fisheries within three miles of British North America's territory, though they could call on harbours for supplies, shelter, and repairs.[3] The 1818 convention recognized the 49th parallel as the boundary from Lake of the Woods to the Rockies – the disputed Oregon territory west of that would be jointly occupied until a settlement was reached.[4]

The War of 1812 proved to be the last direct military conflict between Britain and the United States. But suspicions remained and both sides made some efforts to fortify their North American border, which would remain a rather nebulous and uneven demarcation even after Canadian Confederation. Euro-Americans new to the British part of the continent primarily settled along the Great Lakes–St Lawrence system at first, where they began reshaping environments. In addition to fishing and hunting and other resource activities, settlers cleared forests for agriculture and timber. The fur trade was still going though it had largely moved west; the ramifications of introduced disease and buffalo extirpation would be disastrous for both First Nations and ecosystems. By the middle of the nineteenth century, railways began snaking around the Great Lakes region. Some rail lines crossed the border, promoting interdependence in these regions. Before long, iron horses chugged from the Atlantic to the Pacific.

Logging was at the centre of the so-called Aroostook War. This unofficial 1838–39 conflict between the US and UK concerned the disputed border between New Brunswick and Maine and access to timber. Both sides marched troops to the border, but diplomats created a neutral area and pursued negotiations. Maine received the better part of the disputed area in the 1842 Webster-Ashburton Treaty. This accord resolved several outstanding boundary disputes along the whole of the frontier from the Atlantic coast to the vicinity of the present-day border between Ontario and Manitoba. The border was eventually extended along the 49th parallel to the Pacific Ocean, though Britain would retain Vancouver Island. The only casualty of the so-called Pig War of 1859, over possession of the nearby San Juan Islands, was in fact a pig.

Back on the east coast, the Americans claimed that they had rights to the nearshore fisheries dating to the colonial period. The encroachment of New England fleets on the Grand Banks fisheries off Newfoundland sometimes resulted in the seizure of their boats; the British sent out armed vessels to enforce the 1818 regulations. This was an attempt to use the fisheries issue as a bargaining chip in free trade negotiations, a strategy the Americans resented. In 1854 a reciprocity, or free trade, agreement was struck between the United States and British Canada. In 1865, the Americans gave notice that they wished to abrogate the reciprocity treaty, and it ended the following year.

While the reciprocity treaty was in effect the Americans had access to the Grand Banks, one of the richest fisheries in the world.[5] That agreement also allowed for the free movement of mostly raw materials: grain, coal, livestock, timber, and fish. Coal was the first primary energy source traded between the two countries in significant volumes, chiefly American coal sent to Canada West (which became the Province of Ontario in 1867). Electricity followed several decades later, flowing mainly from Canada to the United States, as did some oil and natural gas (which was predominantly exported by the United States until the latter half of the twentieth century when Canada began exporting fossil fuels in large quantities). Contemporary scholars argue that transboundary energy governance in the twenty-first century is defined by several features: siloed by energy type; a lack of harmonization at federal and state levels; a lack of coherent national policies; and a lack of sufficient regulatory processes, particularly for the siting of energy extraction and transportation infrastructure.[6] Many of these features hold up if we read North American energy history backward into the nineteenth century.

In the second half of the 1800s, industrialization spread across upper North America. As a consequence of reciprocity, American capital and expertise moved north. Much of it was directed at lumber. Historian Arthur Lower called this process a "North American assault on the Canadian forest."[7] Earlier, the New Brunswick and St Lawrence forests had been cut because the British Navy required wood for the Napoleonic Wars. Now Canadian timber would be used to construct the houses of the US Midwest. Though there are debates amongst historians about the extent to which colonial and then provincial governments encouraged the exportation of wood products to the United States, it was clear that this was happening on an increasingly larger scale.[8]

In addition to obliterating habitat for many species, removing the forest precipitated hydrological and microclimatic changes. Streams and rivers were dammed for lumber and grist mills, which had adverse ecological consequences, such as undercutting aquatic resiliency and assimilative capacity. Dams and mills changed water speeds and temperatures, while the byproducts and waste of sawmills smothered the bottoms of waterways, robbing them of oxygen and burying spawning grounds.

The height of the BC gold rush in the Fraser River region coincided with reciprocity. Up to that point, it appeared likely that the territory that is now southern BC might become part of the United States. But the British quickly established this region as the colony of British Columbia to deal with the massive influx of foreign miners that started in 1858. Most of the miners were Americans, often with experience from the earlier California gold rush. Tens of thousands of miners concentrated in riverine areas caused erosion, impacted fish spawning and habitat, and interfered with traditional Indigenous uses.

FISH AND THE TREATY OF WASHINGTON

American territorial ambitions to the north and Washington's protectionist economic policies were prime motivations for implementing the British North America Act that created the Dominion of Canada. The continent's foremost political event of this period, the American Civil War, was not only significant for the country it rent asunder: fear of US invasion or absorption helped drive Canadian Confederation. At first, the new country only included the territory that is now Quebec, Ontario, Nova Scotia, and New Brunswick. Prince Edward Island, Manitoba, Rupert's Land, and British Columbia joined within a decade, then Saskatchewan and Alberta in 1905 and Newfoundland in 1949.

In the first two decades after Canadian Confederation, fish remained a perennial concern of government officials. A number of other conservation issues also came to the fore. These included various forms of wildlife conservation as well as boundary waters developments. Many of these issues would find their resolution in progressive-era agreements. But we should not get too far ahead of ourselves yet. Canadians had opted not to join the Americans politically, but wanted to join with them, at least in a fashion, economically – by winning them back to free trade. They tried to sweeten the deal by allowing

Americans to access the inshore East Coast fisheries via licences. When that did not prove a sufficient inducement, the new country outlawed foreign fishing and sent out a small fleet to enforce the new regulations. Americans kept encroaching on Canadian waters, and offending vessels were seized. Matters were complicated by the fact that the local baitfish industry welcomed the American business and many Canadians served on the American fleets. Furthermore, Prince Edward Island and Newfoundland were not yet part of Canada, and thus could set different regulations for their waters.

Fisheries were a key part of the 1871 Treaty of Washington between the US and Great Britain. This accord's primary purpose was to settle the outstanding issues between the US and Great Britain. New Canadian prime minister John A. Macdonald was part of the British delegation. He hoped to obtain a return to reciprocity, but that was a non-starter for a protectionist Republican administration. From the British perspective, Canadian concerns could not be allowed to stand in the way of a modus vivendi between the two global powers. Gordon Stewart argues that whether American policymakers believed in protection or continental free trade, the goal in either case was pulling Canada away from the British sphere of influence, or even outright annexation.[9] That Canada was destined to fall into their lap, sooner or later, was a widespread belief in the United States.

The result of the treaty was, in many respects, a free trade deal for fish – it did not apply to shellfish – cod in particular since that was the prime east coast catch. Washington received access to the fisheries off the coast of Quebec, Prince Edward Island, Nova Scotia, and New Brunswick; an arbitration commission would later establish the level of cash compensation. Canadians received the right to sell fish in the United States and to fish in American waters down to the 39th parallel. Canadians also received navigation rights in Lake Michigan and three Alaskan rivers, and the Americans received navigation rights on the St Lawrence River.[10]

In Canadian historiography, the Treaty of Washington is often portrayed as Britain sacrificing Canadian interests to appease the United States.[11] But this 1871 agreement had positive ramifications for Canada in the long run. Given the benefit of hindsight, the Treaty of Washington essentially marked the end of the on-and-off tensions that had characterized British-US relations going back to the previous century, with upper North America often the locale where they directly butted heads. Though the "undefended border" is largely a myth, with British

North America no longer a dependent colony and United States and Britain on a harmonious trajectory, the peaceful coexistence of Canada and the United States solidified after 1871.

East coast fisheries remained a point of contention. Macdonald's Conservative government instituted the National Policy in 1879. Though this high-tariff strategy was protectionist, at first Macdonald hoped it would induce the Americans to restore reciprocity. When that failed, he made a virtue of necessity. The National Policy brought more US foreign investment and branch plants into Canada, first and foremost Ontario and Quebec; however, as a result more Canadian exports, predominantly natural products, started going to Britain rather than the United States.[12] In 1885, the arbitration commission created by the Treaty of Washington finally awarded Canada $5.5 million as compensation for US access to the fisheries. American officials thought this ludicrously high and cancelled the fisheries articles of the Treaty of Washington. This meant that regulations concerning the inshore fisheries reverted to those of the 1818 convention. It also meant that Canadian fish again faced tariffs in the US market.

In the hopes of luring the Americans back to free trade, Prime Minister Macdonald did not initially enforce the 1818 regulations. When that failed to work, he tried the opposite tack. By September 1886, the American Minister in London was complaining that "interference with American vessels by Canadian authorities is becoming more and more frequent and more and more flagrant in its disregard of treaty obligations and of the principles of comity and friendly intercourse." According to US Secretary of State Thomas Bayard, Canadian actions were creating "exasperation and unneighborly feeling [leading] to collision between the inhabitants of the two countries."[13]

A high commission convened in 1887–88 focused on fisheries. The resulting treaty did contain definite repudiation of the American right to trawl the Canadian inshore fisheries, but was ultimately rejected by the US Senate. Canada, therefore, established a licensing system that gave Americans access to fisheries, a system that would last for several decades. The United States still needled for unfettered access: it fought the interpretation of the 1818 regulations and then tried inking a separate understanding with the British colony of Newfoundland. But Canadian objections put paid to that notion. Repeated Canadian reciprocity overtures were again spurned, as the Americans rightly remained suspicious that Canada was using the fisheries to gain tariff concessions. Meanwhile, changing technologies, such as improved nets and vessels, meant fishing moved further offshore and out of Canadian waters; thus, shifting fish populations and technologies affected the practices of fishers which in turn affected diplomacy. An agreement early in the twentieth century would finally bring some closure to this particular fisheries question.

ALASKAN BOUNDARY DISPUTE

In 1867, the same year as Canadian Confederation, the United States purchased Alaska from Russia. The boundary zone between Alaska and Canada was mostly unsettled, aside from the Indigenous inhabitants and a smattering of missionaries. But the discovery of gold in Canada's Yukon territory meant that the Alaska boundary question could be deferred no longer.[14] Up to 100,000 prospectors flooded in as part of this Klondike gold rush. Since most were American, Canada dispatched a force to maintain order and protect its sovereignty. However, the most realistic way of getting there was through Skagway – occupied by Americans – which brought the location of the Alaskan border to a head.

At issue was interpreting the Anglo-Russian Convention of 1825, which had laid out vague parameters for establishing the boundary in the future. The United States and Canada submitted competing claims about the size of the Alaskan panhandle. Recognizing the implications for future resource development in the area, they disagreed about how the border would be set where inlets penetrated deep into the coastline.

As far as the gold rush was concerned, whether the Lynn Canal was in Canada or the United States became a principal point of contention. Both countries put forth separate claims for this canal in southeast Alaska, which runs about ninety miles from an ocean inlet. A Joint High Commission formed in 1898 to resolve boundary questions could not agree about the Alaska-BC boundary and dissolved. In the meantime, the gold rush ended. But the Alaskan border problem remained. The US granted Canada temporary use of the head of the Lynn Canal in 1899, which the Liberal government of Wilfrid Laurier accepted. A settlement was almost reached, but the deal and commission blew up when American public opinion reacted quite strongly to the impending compromise.

The United States had become decidedly more expansionist and powerful – militarily and commercially – by the close of the Gilded

Age. Foreign imperialism in Cuba, the Philippines, Puerto Rico, and Hawaii in the late 1890s serve to illustrate the point. Theodore Roosevelt assumed the presidency in 1901. Known for an aphorism – "walk softly and carry a big stick" – that exemplified this American imperialism, Teddy often eschewed the first part about walking softly, at least within the western hemisphere. He was determined to ram through an Alaskan settlement favourable to the United States, which included sending troops to the area. The British, hoping to improve relations with the US, seemed willing to go along with that – at Canada's expense.

The British desire not to alienate the US contributed to an agreement: the Hay-Herbert treaty. The British agreed in 1903 to submit the Alaskan boundary dispute to a mixed commission of six jurists, three from each party. The US side was composed of three American partisans appointed by the president; the other side consisted of two Canadians and a British representative. Roosevelt warned that he would use force if the ruling did not favour the US. The commission's decision gave the Americans the majority of the land, the heads of all the contested inlets, control of the head of Lynn Canal, and half of the islands in dispute.

This was all high drama in Canada. The decision came as a shock to many Canadians even if, in retrospect, the end result was rather predictable and, legally and politically speaking, probably the right one. But Prime Minister Laurier, and many Canadians, had misplaced confidence in Canada's case and Britain's willingness to back it if doing so hurt their own relations with the Americans. The two Canadians representatives on the commission refused to sign the decision. Lord Alverstone specifically – and the British government generally – was painted as the betrayer of Canada.

The Alaskan boundary dispute proved to be an important sea change for the North Atlantic Triangle. It did hurt Canada-US relations for a time, but removing one of the major remaining irritants on the continent between the British and the Americans improved the diplomatic climate for Canada. It also inspired the Canadians to deal more directly with the Americans rather than through British intermediaries. The British, for their part, were eager to reduce their responsibilities in North America. Norman Hillmer and J.L. Granatstein conclude that "The Alaska settlement may have been hard for the Canadians to take, but it laid the groundwork for rapprochement by sweeping away the last of the great boundary disputes."[15]

Another less consequential border dispute, and one on the other side of the continent, was wrapped up in the Alaskan issue. Passamaquoddy Bay is an estuary between the St Croix River and the Bay of Fundy. The complications from the Treaty of Paris about which river was actually the St Croix had left the New Brunswick-Maine border in Passamaquoddy Bay in dispute. During the Jay's Treaty process, a commission was created to address this issue, but it did not provide a definitive solution. Another commission, with the same result, was formed as part of the Treaty of Ghent. Then another commission established in 1892 failed to determine the precise location of the boundary. The late-1890s Joint High Commission was set to address the Passamaquoddy issue, but the Alaskan boundary dispute wrecked that.

The stumbling blocks at Passamaquoddy remained an island and access to fishing grounds; in a 1910 treaty, Canada got the former and gave up the latter. This treaty grew out of the work of the International Boundary Commission (IBC), founded in 1908. This commission went to work accurately locating and clearing up a host of other border line placements. Though it would take decades for some of these lines to be definitively resolved, the IBC effectively depoliticized the process. The IBC's model of institutionalizing technocratic expertise would eventually be applied to many other aspects of bilateral relations.

PROGRESSIVE-ERA CONSERVATION TREATIES

US-Canada relations in the first decade of the twentieth century were predominantly occupied by issues which had obvious environmental aspects. To illustrate, consider a 1906 meeting between Prime Minister Wilfrid Laurier and US secretary of state Elihu Root. Of the top five items on Root's list of subjects needing attention, all but one concerned natural resources: 1) pelagic sealing, 2) the North Atlantic fisheries, 3) the inland fisheries, 4) United States pecuniary claims, and 5) boundary waters.[16] Those issues, and others, would soon be addressed in treaties or agreements: many of the long-festering problems in US-Canada environmental relations were resolved in the 1908–11 period.[17] This was a uniquely fruitful stretch in Canada-US and US-UK relations, since Canada could not independently handle all aspects of its foreign relations even with a skeleton Canadian Department of External Affairs created in 1909.[18]

Within a short period, Canada and the United States inked agreements about border-crossing wildlife, along with the 1909 Boundary

Waters Treaty, in what can be characterized as an era of cleaning the slate: Inland Fisheries Treaty (1908), North Atlantic Cod Fisheries Agreement (1910), North Pacific Fur Seal Convention (1911), Migratory Bird Treaty (1916). These were part of the wider Progressive era, a period of optimistic social activism from the 1890s to the 1920s informed by the social gospel movement. In response to urbanization and industrialization, many reformers saw activist governments and technocrats as the ideal vehicles for using expertise and scientific methods to bring about efficient changes that would raise living standards and the moral order.

To put that movement in its proper context, we need to back up a little. Prior to the Progressive era, both American and Canadian leaders generally believed that continental natural resources were inexhaustible. Both nations had seemingly untapped western frontiers, and the federal governments of both countries created policies to maximize resource development. First, however, they had to actively remove or outright eliminate those Indigenous Peoples who stood in the way of state-sponsored expansions. Some of this was accomplished by formal treaties, though these were often achieved under coercion or deception, or the terms as understood by Indigenous Peoples were not honoured by governments.

The US federal government came to control huge swaths of land and the accompanying timber, land, wildlife, fish, and minerals. The Canadian federal government did too, at least until the western territories became formal provinces and achieved control over their resources.[19] The first of the famous national parks in both countries – Yellowstone and Banff – were created in the 1870s and 1880s to turn what were deemed unproductive areas into revenue generators that would attract tourists and promote the new transcontinental railroads. Moreover, though there were certainly egalitarian impulses at play, many of the parks and newly protected areas were also intended for white elites who wanted to get away for hunting and fishing – thus excluding those people groups that had historically used these areas. By the First World War, the United States had created sixteen national parks and a National Park Service. Canada followed suit.

Some of the earliest conservation scientists in the United States endorsed the efficient use of natural resources through the application of scientific principles. Exhibiting utilitarian or instrumentalist approaches in which nature's value lay only in what it could provide for human society, natural resources were to be shepherded so they could be repeatedly harvested for maximum sustainable yield. But out of this milieu came preservationists, such as John Muir. Perhaps the continent's most famous naturalist, Muir was raised in Wisconsin. A conscientious objector to the US Civil War, he spent the internecine conflict working at a sawmill in Ontario; returning from Canada, he roamed across the United States and abroad, spending a great deal of time in the California mountain ranges with which he became so identified. To Muir, and others like him, wilderness gave aesthetic and spiritual benefits, but it also had intrinsic value aside from how it could benefit society. That is, the non-human world should be protected for its own sake, not just conserved for human use.

In Teddy Roosevelt, the conservationists had an avid outdoorsman in the Oval Office. They also had another distinguished voice in his righthand man, Gifford Pinchot. Both believed in wise-use policies that maximized the benefit of resources. Head of the fledgling US Forest Service, Pinchot's famous dictum was "the greatest good for the greatest number of people for the longest time." The Newlands Reclamation Act of 1902, later to birth the Bureau of Reclamation, set forth a policy of conservation and best-use practices for the western United States.

At first, Canada generally followed the US model when it came to conservation and park creation.[20] The Canadian Commission of Conservation was formed in the first decade of the twentieth century, drawing from similar American practices. The preservationist ethos did not seem to gain as much traction north of the border. Perhaps this was because Canada was not experiencing the same level of urbanization, industrialization, and loss of wilderness, or because the Canadian economy relied more heavily on staples extraction and export.[21]

Environmental historians have rightly critiqued the traditional usage of terms such as wilderness and nature. The latter is problematic since it suggests a false divide between humans and the natural world, a conceptual outlook underpinning many of our unsustainable practices. The result is that highly populated and urbanized areas, for example, are seen as bereft of nature and thus as undeserving of protection. The flip side of this is the way North American societies have framed "wilderness" as areas completely free of human impact. However, going back several centuries, there are very few, if any, substantial tracts in North America completely untouched by humans. Furthermore, in the twenty-first century, anthropogenic climate change means that there are no parts of the globe that have not been affected by human activities in some way.

Fisheries remained a perennial political issue. Problems spread from the east coast to other geographic areas, such as the Great Lakes and the Pacific. This was partly because, after seemingly centuries of negotiations, the North Atlantic fishery disputes had come to at least some type of resolution. In 1909, the two countries submitted their outstanding claims over the east coast fisheries to an arbitration tribunal at The Hague. A North Atlantic Coast Fisheries Agreement was made the next year: Americans received the same rights as British subjects to fish and utilize the coastline of a specified part of Newfoundland and Labrador and renounced those rights outside of the specific areas. Canada also changed some of its fisheries regulations in response to US complaints, and the two nations agreed to submit any further points of contention to The Hague.[22]

The Canadian federal government has more jurisdiction over fisheries than the American federal government (though in both countries, provinces and states have a higher degree of jurisdiction over inland fisheries than coastal fisheries). As a result, there were generally more uniform fisheries regulations on the Canadian side of shared waters. In places like the Great Lakes, the international border created an inadequate mishmash of laws. The lack of across-the-border rules only increased the taking of fish – and by the early twentieth century, it was becoming obvious that fish stocks were crashing.[23] Whereas past fisheries agreements were negotiated to maximize each country's share of the abundance, now it was as much about preventing the extirpation of the catch.

When it comes to the Great Lakes, Margaret Beattie Bogue contends that the commercial fisheries, dominated by Americans, had reached their peak by the early 1890s.[24] In 1888 alone, twenty-six million pounds of fish were taken from the Great Lakes, the majority by the Americans. Atlantic salmon had been the first fish species commercially harvested in the Great Lakes – by the 1890s it had more or less disappeared, while other commercial fisheries, such as trout, whitefish, and sturgeon, had been decimated. From then until the Depression, when commercial fishing in the largest freshwater basin in the world was essentially finished as a leading enterprise, the story was one of decline. First Nations caught fish long before Europeans arrived, but they had harvested them at a sustainable pace. Settlers around the Great Lakes–St Lawrence basin overfished and engaged in other activities that harmed the ability of fish to reproduce and thrive. Mills, dams, and deforestation all changed the water quality and temperatures of the tributaries in which many fish species lived or spawned. With the Great Lakes divided between different political jurisdictions – not only two countries but also one province and eight states – transbasin or interstate conservation regulations were unwieldy and unsuccessful.

Canada's federal Fisheries Act of 1868 was more progressive than the laws prevailing on the US side. Both countries did engage in conservation measures such as stocking and artificial reproduction. In 1892, the two countries instituted the Joint Commission Relative to the Preservation of the Fisheries in Waters Contiguous to Canada and the United States. This commission was tasked with collecting information and making recommendations, though the findings would be purely advisory. After several years of study, the prime culprits were identified as overfishing, the use of certain net types, pollution, and habitat destruction. But the commercial fishing industry was opposed to limits on its actions, and this joint commission's solutions were not deemed politically and economically palatable – and were subsequently ignored.[25]

It was clear the fisheries had been decimated, and nothing much was being done. Discussions reopened in 1906. Picking up where the Joint High Commission had left off, the United States and Great Britain (acting for Canada) arrived at the 1908 Inland Fisheries Treaty. The accord called for an Inland Fisheries Commission, composed of one expert apiece from Canada and the US, which would recommend regulations. If implemented, the treaty would apply to various boundary waters across the continent and address key areas such as open seasons, net types, and stocking fish. The Canadian Parliament adopted the treaty, but the United States never ratified it because of lack of support from the public and certain constituencies.[26]

Nevertheless, this failed Inland Fisheries Treaty did help set the stage for subsequent agreements informed by scientific expertise. Granted, one of these, the 1909 Salmon Treaty, met the same fate. This 1909 pact created a fisheries commission for Pacific salmon that recommended immediately adopting a bevy of regulations concerning closed seasons, fishing gear and techniques, and licensing systems. Canada adopted the new rules, but they could not get through the US Senate, bedevilled by the American fishing and canning industry and states' rights advocates. The fisheries commission was dissolved in 1914.

Another conservation treaty at this time, the 1911 North Pacific Fur Seal Convention, met a better fate.[27] The Pribilof Islands were a rookery for Pacific fur seals that Inuit had hunted for generations. Intensive hunting by Euro-Americans in the early nineteenth century set the seal population back, and these islands came under American jurisdiction when they acquired Alaska. The US government leased the area to a private company to harvest seal skins. But hunters from British Columbia and other US ports captured the seals on the high seas, where they spent most of their lives. Since the seal herds originated on the Pribilofs, Washington claimed they were American property even far out in open waters.

As seal populations plummeted, an open spat developed between the United States and Canada involving vessel seizures. In the early 1890s, they appointed a four-member scientific committee to study the problem and agreed to arbitration. The arbitrators created a buffer zone and a closed season to protect the seals from pelagic hunting (which meant hunting them at sea). The US claim that the Bering Sea was its proprietary territory was not upheld, and it had to pay compensation for vessels seized there. This settled the matter temporarily. But as Canadians looked elsewhere for seals, Japanese vessels not bound by the agreement replaced them. By the turn of the twentieth century, the seal population that had once been estimated at 2.5 million was less than 10 percent of that number.

In early 1909, US secretary of state Elihu Root proposed a seal conference to Britain, Russia, and Japan. It was obvious to US scientists that overhunting was the problem and that a ban was necessary. But the four nations squabbled about compensation for giving up the hunt. After two years, an agreement was reached that banned pelagic sealing in the northern Pacific for fifteen years and left all sides reasonably satisfied. Essentially, it bought out the rights of the others to catch seals. Canada would receive 15 percent of the American's Pribilof catch, 15 percent of the Russian take on the Commander Islands, and 10 percent of the Japanese harvest on Robben Island.[28] Overall, Canada was guaranteed 20 percent of the seal harvest. In addition, the United States paid a $200,000 advance on the future catch, which Canada could use to indemnify its sealers.

Another success story from this era is the Migratory Birds Treaty of 1916. Economic arguments were the primary reasons for protecting seals and fish. When it came to migratory birds – which generally spend the summers in northern Canada and then winter in the southern US and Mexico – there was growing evidence that, as insectivores, they benefitted agriculture. There was also an aesthetic and moral motivation: people tend to like birds.[29] American conservationists had pushed through several bird protection laws in the US: the 1900 Lacey Act and the 1913 Migratory Bird Act (Weeks-McLean law). But for these to be effective, given the transboundary flyways, Canada had to protect them too. The same year as the First World War started, the two countries began diplomatic discussions and soon had a draft treaty. The roles of the states and provinces still needed to be accounted for – British Columbia, for example, had qualms. This took another two years to smooth out, partly because the war slowed things down, though the treaty language did not change much.

The Migratory Birds Treaty outlaws the "taking" of a range of wild birds on either side of the border – which meant killing or possessing parts of a bird, including feathers, nests, and eggs. Of course, the treaty still had to make its way through Congress as well as a court challenge. Opponents took different tacks, including constitutional arguments about the federal government's powers under the proposed accord. Proponents, including the Audubon Society, sold it as a food conservation measure and assistance to a wartime ally. The US Supreme Court ultimately upheld the treaty in 1920.[30]

According to Kurkpatrick Dorsey, the ability of scientists and conservationists to shape the various conservation treaties and influence public opinion determined the success or failure of these agreements. Unlike fish, birds and seals gained some purchase with the public as charismatic species. Finalizing these treaties was possible because of the intersection of science, sentiment, and economics.[31] In the long run, the implementation of the 1908 Inland Fisheries Treaty turned out to be a failure. On the other hand, the North Pacific Fur Seal Convention can be considered an early success in environmental diplomacy, preventing the looming extinction of the herds. The seal population rebounded rapidly, and the convention lasted until 1941, when the Japanese withdrew. But sealing regulations were renewed after the Second World War, and the hunting of seal fur ended in 1984. The Migratory Bird Treaty was a clearer success – the "first broadly effective wildlife conservation treaty"[32] – and remains in effect.

Taken together, this grouping of treaties constituted a notable advance in international wildlife conservation. They represented a shift from the type of environmental diplomacy that had characterized the decades following Canadian Confederation. Granted, protecting fish had been important before Canada was a country – but protection occurred so that stocks could be exploited for the longest period of time, maximizing each jurisdiction's total catch. Fixing the border and disputed areas was another concern in this era; in a number of cases, it was gold and timber rushes that precipitated the need to establish the edges of each country. That urgency sometimes created political conflicts that threatened to spill over into bigger conflicts. The Alaskan Boundary Dispute is the most significant of these. However, along with other Canada-British-US rapprochements, this dispute's resolution helped ease tensions and make the northern North American relationship less adversarial and more attuned to mutually beneficial resource exploitation. The process of negotiating over all these resources helped Canada find its diplomatic feet, so to speak, and begin carving out an independent approach to its southern neighbour outside of the British intermediary, which had shown a willingness to sacrifice Canadian interests in the name of better British-US relations.

Along with the 1909 Boundary Waters Treaty, which is addressed in the next chapter, the early twentieth-century wildlife protection agreements positioned Canada and the United States at the global vanguard of environmental diplomacy and international environmental law. However, this trend of North American wildlife conservation agreements did not continue; the continent would not see a similar surge in environmental protection treaties until the Cold War.

2

Early Water Relations

Freshwater has always been a prominent aspect of Canada-US relations. That is not only because the two countries share such a fluid border, with the Great Lakes–St Lawrence system bisected by the international boundary for over one thousand miles while many other waterways cross or form the border, but because water is tied to both environmental and energy concerns. Hydro power profoundly conditioned the political economy of Canada and its relations with the United States. Contemporary scholars have applied the label of "petro state" to countries that are deeply dependent on the rents from fossil fuels. In the same vein, fin-de-siècle Canada was a "hydro state." Hydroelectricity played an outsized role in shaping the politics, economics, and political imaginary of the largest provinces and the nation as a whole, fostering an expectation of growth and abundance. And since so many of the earliest hydroelectric developments were along border waters, a distinctive form of North American energy diplomacy emerged.

This chapter will focus on transborder water issues, particularly in the Great Lakes–St Lawrence basin, from the late nineteenth century up to the Boundary Waters Treaty of 1909. In the decades after 1867, various forms of border water infrastructure that altered flows and levels across the international boundary – such as canals and hydro power projects – became subjects of bilateral contention. So too did water pollution that crossed the border begin to attract attention. Diplomatic negotiations about border waters culminated in the signing of the Boundary Waters Treaty, which created the International Joint Commission. That treaty was a major step, not just for crossborder waters, but for the Canadian-American relationship in general. The

Boundary Waters Treaty proved to be one of the most important agreements the two countries ever signed, and the International Joint Commission became the primary vehicle for mediating a host of water projects involving the international border.

EARLY CANALS AND HYDROELECTRICITY

Many canals were constructed in the nineteenth century either on, or connecting to, border waters. In the wake of the War of 1812, security concerns led to placing canals further away from the border. New York State's Erie Canal, an enormous undertaking, was completed in 1825. This route allowed vessels to move from Lake Erie to Albany and down to New York City via the Hudson River. The Oswego Canal connected the Erie Canal to Lake Ontario. The response in British North America was the Welland Canal running north-south across the Niagara Peninsula. The Welland, Erie, and Oswego canals were all subsequently improved. The Rideau Canal, completed in 1832, was etched out from the future site of Ottawa to Kingston. During the 1830s, work started on a series of canals on the north shore of the international stretch of the St Lawrence River. The Cornwall Canal was finished in 1842. A little upriver, the Williamsburg canals (Farran's Point, Rapide Plat, Iroquois-Galop) opened in the 1850s. By the middle of the nineteenth century, a navigable channel with a depth of nine feet was available from the Atlantic to Lake Erie. Without this water-borne transportation system, linking various colonies into the new Dominion of Canada may not have been conceptually or physically possible.

Even these early canals had a range of ecological impacts. They generally needed to either utilize existing rivers or tap nearby waterbodies. Many wetlands, swamps, creeks, ponds, rivers, and lakes were fully or partially sacrificed to create an artificial river. Canals hurt fisheries, especially in cases where existing rivers and streams were reworked. These artificial waterways also opened the door for the introduction of non-native species. Another impact of canals was that they could change water levels in the surrounding areas. Moreover, canals attracted industry. In the nineteenth century this included mills, which had numerous ecological impacts; by the twentieth century, industrial factories along these canals were much bigger and included steel, cars, paper, etc. The knock-on land use changes and water pollution began to "unravel nature's assimilative capacity."[1]

The 1871 Treaty of Washington definitively established that the St Lawrence west of Cornwall would serve as the international boundary between Canada and the United States. However, it also stipulated that American access to the Canadian canals could be terminated on two years' notice. A royal commission had been struck to study the canal situation in the new Dominion of Canada. For defence and economic reasons, the canal commission recommended that the Canadian canals be dug to a depth of fourteen feet and that the river channels be dredged to an equal depth. Ottawa embarked on this expansion program. The Cornwall Canal was enlarged to the recommended depth, although this was not completed until 1904, along with the Williamsburg canals. By 1905 there was a navigable channel with a minimum depth of fourteen feet from the Atlantic to Lake Superior.

Expansion work on the Welland Canal was also underway. In the 1840s the second Welland Canal was installed. This newer version followed virtually the same course but had fewer locks and a greater depth. Then a third Welland Canal was built in the 1880s with all locks deepened to fourteen feet. Early in the twentieth century, ground was broken on the fourth Welland Canal – though it was not fully finished for several decades. About the same time, work began on joining the Erie and several other upstate canals into the New York State Barge Canal. A Georgian Bay Ship Canal, connecting Lake Huron to the upper Ottawa River via the French River, seemed like it might become a reality in the lead-up to the First World War. But that dream died with the 1911 defeat of Wilfrid Laurier's government. Instead, the Trent-Severn waterway linked Georgian Bay and Lake Ontario when it was finally finished in the early twentieth century.

Moving further west in the Great Lakes basin, the first lock around the St Mary's Rapids had been put in place at the very end of the eighteenth century by the North West Company. (The St Marys River flows from Lake Superior to Lake Huron, bisecting the sister cities of Sault Ste Marie in Michigan and Ontario.) The locks were destroyed during the War of 1812 and not replaced until the United States put in navigation works on the Michigan side in the 1850s. By the latter half of the nineteenth century, the Soo had become an essential transportation corridor, fuelled by the many natural resources in the surrounding areas, such as the copper and iron ore deposits discovered in Michigan's Upper Peninsula and later in the Mesabi range.

The need to utilize the American locks combined with the east-west transportation goals of John A. Macdonald's National Policy led

Canada to complete its own works at Sault Ste Marie in the 1890s.[2] The Canadian lock was the largest in North America and boasted a small hydro plant to power the locks and provide electric lighting. The US would then construct additional locks here with progressively larger dimensions that would dwarf those of their northern neighbour. Several private hydro stations had been built on the American side of the river by the early twentieth century. These stations and plans to expand their electric production would impact transborder water levels. Consequently, hydroelectric production at the Soo was a factor in the push for the Boundary Waters Treaty, and subsequent structures to control water flows here would fall under the aegis of the International Joint Commission.

Both Canada and the United States were global pioneers in the field of hydro power. Hydroelectricity uses falling water to spin turbines, transforming water's embedded kinetic energy into electricity. Usually, dams are required to create a sufficient fall of water, the head, and this process robs water environments of some of their biotic energy and gives it to humans in a different form. In doing so, hydroelectric dams turn rapids and rivers into reservoirs, stopping the movement of many fish, eels, and other species, preventing their migration and spawning, changing their habitat, and altering the energy and nutrient flows within aquatic food webs.

BORDER WATERS

Amidst the flurry of canal proposals and developments in the 1890s, various voices articulated the first serious conceptions of a deep St Lawrence waterway. This, and other water control schemes such as navigation improvements in the Detroit River, motivated bilateral discussions about some sort of international agreement to govern shared waters.[3] The United States and Canada both became embroiled in protracted and intertwined internal debates concerning private versus public power, state/provincial versus federal control of power, and unbridled economic expansion versus conservation or preservation of resources.

In 1892 motions were put forward in both the Canadian Parliament and the US House of Representatives calling for improved navigation on the Great Lakes–St Lawrence route. Then, at the 1894 International Deep Waterways Convention in Toronto, Canadian and American delegates called for the cooperative improvement of the St

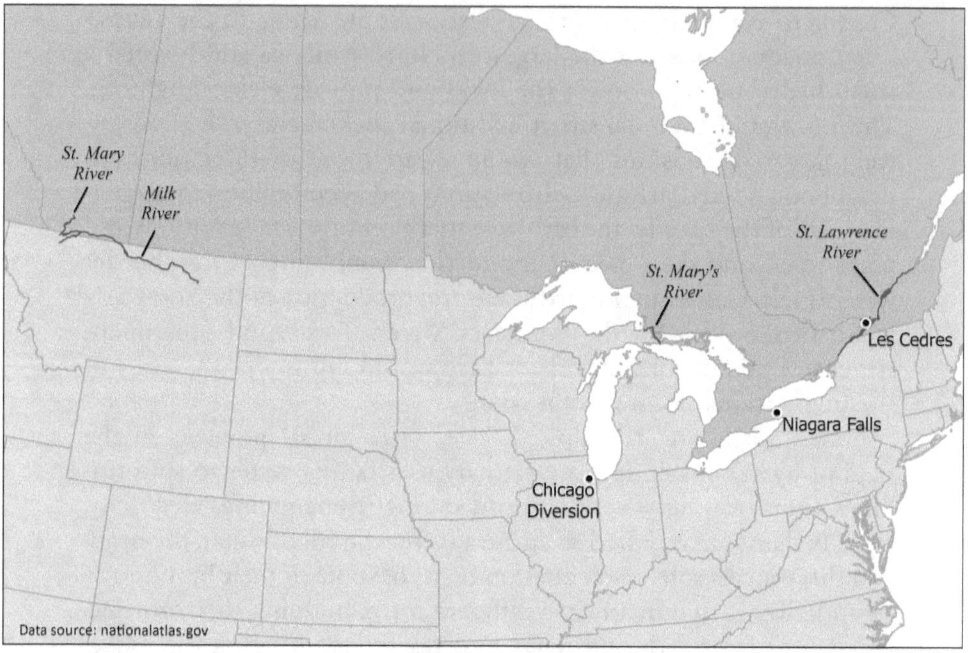

Figure 2.1 Border waters issues that were controversial in the lead-up to the Boundary Waters Treaty.

Lawrence canals. They formed the International Deep Waterways Commission, which was charged with studying the feasibility of constructing waterways to allow ocean-going vessels to pass between the Great Lakes and the Atlantic Ocean. Each national group released a report in 1897. The American contingent saw the utility of the St Lawrence but highlighted several different routes which were partially or wholly in American territory, while the Canadian report favoured the St Lawrence.[4] Although it would be another half-century before a St Lawrence deep waterway was built, these proposals helped spur on a general crossborder water pact.

Several other considerations created momentum for such an accord. One of the most prominent was power development at Niagara Falls. Niagara of course had long been an iconic natural landmark. It became a symbol of the North American natural sublime in the nineteenth century and was well on its way to becoming a symbol of the technological sublime. In the mid-nineteenth century, hydraulic canals were built on the American side of Niagara Falls to bring water to mills and return it below the waterfall, turning the riverbank into a mishmash of factories and industrial buildings. A burgeoning preservationist movement meanwhile agitated for various park developments to replace the visual blight created by these developments.

The first hydroelectricity generation at Niagara took place in 1881. The world's first crossborder electricity connection reputedly took place here too. In the 1890s, the Adams station at Niagara enabled the first large-scale hydro power production and long-distance distribution from a central station. The station was placed just upriver from the Falls on the New York side. In short order, this station began sending electricity to Buffalo and then expanded its generating capacity. By 1905, several powerhouses modelled on the Adams central station design had been constructed on the Canadian side to harness the waters of the Niagara River. Granted, most of these were owned by American concerns and exported the power to that country. Like the Adams station, these involved long tunnels or canals that diverted water from above the Falls and returned the water below the waterfall.

Various schemes for damming or turning off Niagara Falls kept surfacing, and preservationists kept decrying the impact on the scenic beauty of Niagara. Some officials pushed for a crossborder agreement to monitor and regulate the diversions. In his 1905 message to Congress, President Roosevelt called for the preservation of the Falls and promoted a crossborder accord. The US government and influential segments of the public did appear to be more concerned than Canadians about protecting the appearance of Niagara Falls. But congressional talks about Niagara were complicated by debates about federal versus state jurisdiction over water power. The Burton Act, passed by Congress in 1906, put federal limits on how much water could be diverted in New York State, and how much hydro power could be imported from the Ontario side of Niagara. The latter was an indirect way of limiting how much the Canadian powerhouses could abstract. But when the US and Canada signed a border waters treaty in 1909, its Niagara measures were more lenient. Consequently, Congress passed several joint resolutions to extend the Burton Act.

Much of the electricity produced on the Canadian side of Niagara was exported because there was little market for it in Ontario at that time. Several other crossborder interconnections soon followed, each involving the firm export of electricity (i.e., long-term and uninterruptible) from Canada to the US.[5] Hydro power would henceforth play an outsized role in Canada's politics and political economy, particularly in provinces such as Ontario, Quebec, and British Columbia. Because so many of the earliest and large hydro developments were on border waters, this *hydro democracy* also shaped Canada-US relations.[6] Canadian electrical utilities tended to be government-owned, while American ones have historically been more likely to be privately owned (with some exceptions). This dichotomy may stem from Canada's early reliance on hydro power, which, for a variety of reasons, occasioned heavier government involvement. For our purposes here, those reasons include the ways that Canadian hydroelectricity quickly became politicized, especially because of the transborder Niagara Falls situation, plus hydro power as an energy form requires large upfront investments that the state was well suited to provide. This also meant that, aside from the first Niagara stations, the hydro power industry in Canada did not become dominated by American capital, unlike later forms of exportable energy.

A provincial movement for cheap public power led to the Government of Ontario's creation in 1906 of a publicly owned power utility, the Hydro-Electric Power Commission of Ontario (HEPCO, or Ontario Hydro). The New York counterpart to Ontario Hydro, the Power Authority of the State of New York (PASNY), would be established in 1931, modelled on Ontario Hydro. That no equivalent to Ontario Hydro was created in New York State for a quarter-century had as much to do with pragmatic factors – such as the state's existing spatial distribution of and access to electricity, differing riparian rights, and Ontario's lack of coal supplies – as it did with ideology concerning public versus private ownership. Ontario Hydro would begin with the distribution of electricity, but over the following decades, it acquired the private Niagara generating stations, built several of its own massive hydroelectric facilities along the Niagara River, and expanded the hydroelectric transmission network throughout Ontario (while continuing its contractual exports to the United States).

Some of the same concerns that spurred the formation of Ontario Hydro were linked to the Canadian formation of the National Commission of Conservation as well as the passage of the federal Fluid and Electricity Export Act of 1907. Though the federal government, led by Wilfrid Laurier's Liberals, had promoted a laissez-faire approach to electricity exports, this act was a partial rejoinder to the export discrimination under the Burton Act. Moreover, it represented the national Liberal Party's attempt to curb the growing public power movement in Ontario and reassert some federal jurisdiction over utilities and water rights in response to recent Niagara developments.[7]

The 1907 act required Canadian power exports to secure an annual licence, gave Parliament the authority to levy an export duty on hydroelectricity, disallowed hydro power from being sold at a lower price in the United States, and featured a recall clause that allowed exports to be quickly revoked if the power was required in Canada. Granted, the act was ambiguous about how to determine much of this, and some of these powers were never really exercised or enforced.[8] Therefore, the federal government's authority to regulate power exports remained unsettled, and as of 1910 about one-third of the total electricity generated in Canada was sent across the border.[9] It is worth pointing out that neither country ever created a licensing system for electricity imports – just for exports. Nevertheless, there were cases where the US moved to indirectly restrict electricity imports, with the Burton Act an obvious example.

In addition to Niagara stations, hydroelectricity was exported from Quebec. In 1912, Montreal Heat, Power and Light signed an eighty-year contract to send 60,000 hp from the Les Cèdres power station on the St Lawrence to the Alcoa aluminum plant at Massena, New York. Quebec soon accounted for one-third of Canada's electricity exports.[10]

Numerous other small and localized electricity exports, not always generated by water, took place in both directions in the borderlands. For example, industry-related exchanges obtained between New Brunswick and Maine (e.g., St Croix, Aroostook, and St John Rivers), as well as western Ontario and Minnesota. Minor electricity exchanges also developed between the prairie provinces and the adjacent American states. There were few exchanges in the Pacific Northwest prior to the Second World War, besides British Columbia providing power to the Point Roberts enclave and Puget Sound Power & Light connecting across the border with the BC Electric system. After 1945, interconnected grids would blossom here.[11] Many small exchanges involved short transmission lines to isolated communities, Indigenous reserves, islands, or companies with subsidiaries on the other side of the border. In most of these cases, it was simply more economical or practical to get power from the other country. However, utilities began to build larger transmission lines to export surplus electricity.

Around the time of Niagara's large-scale hydroelectricity debut, the Chicago Sanitary and Ship Canal also became an international problem. That canal facilitated the withdrawal of water, which is referred to as the Chicago, or Illinois, diversion, the first large-scale diversion out of the Great Lakes basin. This artificial watercourse, built between 1892 and 1900, reversed the flow of the Chicago River *away* from Lake Michigan to provide sewage disposal for the city of Chicago as well as navigation and small-scale hydro production.[12] This diverted water eventually ended up in the Mississippi River system. The system-wide impacts of the Chicago diversion were unclear at the time, but Canada and Great Lakes states feared it could lower water levels in the Great Lakes–St Lawrence system as far away as Montreal (studies would show a drop of up to half a foot).[13] It received opposition from Canada and other American states bordering Lake Michigan and other waterbodies downstream. The diversion would prove to be a thorn in the side of later US-Canadian diplomacy.

Much further west, the St Mary–Milk controversy was heating up.[14] The Milk River, a tributary to the Missouri River, begins in Glacier National Park in Montana, flows northeast and then crosses back and forth over the border between Canada and the US several times. The St Mary River originates near the Milk River, but eventually becomes part of the South Saskatchewan River, part of the Hudson Bay watershed. Both Montana and Alberta began diverting water from these rivers for irrigation in the late nineteenth and early twentieth centuries. As a result, water was overappropriated there. In a competition for scarce water, proposals for various water diversion canals were bandied about, and some were built on each side of the border, including diversions from the St Mary into the Milk. This would persist as a diplomatic problem far out of proportion to its actual significance, as we will see in future chapters.

Many of the water and energy issues broached above set the course for the future of continental environmental and energy diplomacy. The St Mary–Milk, Chicago, Niagara, and St Lawrence developments, as well as the 1909 treaty on boundary waters that I will address below, remained important issues over a century later. That these continued to be controversial speaks to the importance of water – navigation, power, irrigation – for economic development in the border regions, and the importance of water for determining the nature of the bilateral relationship. Negotiations over water, and other natural resources, required types of local or national knowledge that the British government, far across the ocean, was scarcely equipped to provide. Since Canadian officials did have this expertise, water and hydro power allowed Canada to carve out a more independent diplomatic role in relation to the United States. Homegrown expertise also enabled the fledgling Canadian diplomatic corps to hold their own in negotiations with the United States, giving Ottawa more room to maneuver. Furthermore, the water agreements, structures, and mechanisms put in place around the turn of the twentieth century demonstrated to the two countries that transborder cooperation was generally more beneficial and profitable than conflict.

BOUNDARY WATERS TREATY

Those many border water issues helped launch discussions for the International Waterways Commission.[15] Formed in 1905, it focused chiefly on the Great Lakes–St Lawrence basin, with Niagara diversions a top priority.[16] The two sides batted back and forth various proposals for diversion limitations at Niagara, eventually issuing a joint report that promoted partial Niagara preservation. The Americans convinced the Canadians to set Niagara diversion limits, while the latter convinced the former, using Niagara Falls as a bargaining chip, to enshrine such measures in a comprehensive accord setting joint rules for *all* border waters. The International Waterways Commission called on the two countries to adopt principles of law governing the various uses of all border waters and create an international body with the authority to study and regulate the use of these waters.

Several years of further discussions eventually led to the signing and ratification of the 1909 Boundary Waters Treaty (BWT). The BWT notably granted equal navigation access to the many shared waters and adopted regulations concerning water diversions and changes to water levels. As such, any changes in the level of a border water needed agreement through the International Joint Commission (IJC), or a special agreement between the federal governments outside of the IJC (though the subsequent construction or maintenance of any infrastructure that affected water levels at the border needed IJC approval). The International Joint Commission is a six-member body with an equal number of Canadian and US appointees who are technically independent from the government that appointed them. Canada wanted a powerful commission; the US wanted a weaker one – the result was a compromise.[17] The fact that the United States agreed to a commission within which the two countries were equal was a noteworthy achievement for Canada. So too was the fact that Canadian representatives did most of the negotiating for the BWT, even though Britain signed for Canada since it still technically had the final say on the dominion's foreign affairs.

The BWT gave the IJC four categories of function that the new commission was expected to discharge: administrative (article VI); quasi-judicial (articles III, IV, and VIII); arbitral (article X); and investigative (article IX). The majority of the IJC's activities have proven to be in the judicial and investigative realms. Article VIII sets forth the order of precedence for approving different types of uses of boundary waters: (1) domestic and sanitary purposes, (2) navigation, and (3) power. Notably, this made no reference to industrial or recreational uses. Nevertheless, those uses were adopted into the IJC's considerations over the following decades, as were ecological benefits in the second half of the century.

In addition to setting out general rules, the Boundary Waters Treaty specifically addressed some of the festering border water disputes. Article V of the treaty dealt only with Niagara Falls. Canada could divert no more than 36,000 cubic feet per second (cfs) from the river (which had an average flow of about 200,000 cfs) above Niagara Falls, and the United States 20,000 cfs, which was slightly more than the 18,500 cfs in the IWC's recommendations. These volume caps were meant to avoid disturbing the existing vested power rights at Niagara and to avoid hurting Lake Erie and Niagara River levels. Another article in the treaty dealt specifically with the St Mary–Milk dispute.

The Boundary Waters Treaty is often characterized as a pioneering form of international environmental governance, while the IJC has been portrayed as a model for bilateral cooperation. (Canada would sanctimoniously lecture other countries – such as Germany and France after the First World War – with the advice that they should emulate the BWT and IJC.) According to a former commissioner, the philosophy of dispute-settlement and conflict avoidance built into the BWT and IJC was far more sophisticated than any comparable piece of bilateral machinery then existing in Western society.[18] Moreover, the treaty addresses "pollution," using that specific word for what appears to be the first time in the history of transborder environmental governance. The IJC provided mechanisms, such as public hearing sessions in the concerned watershed, so locals could have their voices heard. "If the oft-proclaimed 'special relationship' has any substance," proclaimed the authors of *Canada and the United States: Ambivalent Allies*, "the IJC is its essence."[19]

At the same time, it is easy to exaggerate the role and importance of the IJC for the bilateral relationship. Though it was explicitly set up so that commissioners are technically independent of the government that appointed them, the IJC's influence can be limited since the two federal governments must refer an issue to the commission (and the two federal governments have made water agreements outside of the IJC). The two national governments do not need to, and often do not, heed the recommendations of the IJC. Moreover, made up of appointees, the IJC can become politicized and partisan, and sometimes has made poor recommendations or rulings.

The BWT itself had some weaknesses. On American insistence, the treaty did not include Lake Michigan, as it is wholly in the United States (though, hydrologically, it is essentially one waterbody with Lake Huron). But lowering the levels, or polluting the waters, of Lake Michigan has effects downstream in Canada, as the Chicago diversion made all too clear; even back then, most who studied the hydrology realized all the Great Lakes should be treated as an interconnected system. In fact, part of the reason for omitting Lake Michigan seems to have been to satisfy Illinois and Chicago political interests, which did not want the Chicago diversion subject to the BWT. The treaty only applied to boundary waters that formed the border, not tributaries. This represented a partial incorporation of the Harmon Doctrine – which gives the upstream riparian the sole authority to do what it desired with water – also on American insistence. Granted, if the treaty had been more ambitious, it may not have been able to get through either Parliament or Congress. Additionally, over time the US did back away from the Harmon Doctrine since there were many cases where its strict application would benefit Canada more.

Furthermore, though this treaty contained the seeds of environmental protection and crossborder cooperation, it was an agreement that at its core was as much about mutual exploitation. The two nations were now free to aggressively pursue their desire to develop border waters. An extended analysis of the IJC's first century of operation shows that its behavior, role, and function changed significantly over time. In some respects, it has been an elite form of water apportionment that favours industrial and government interests at the expense of environments, recreational activities, local interests, and Indigenous communities. The IJC for many decades was a chief proponent of what we now know to be ecologically destructive megaprojects. Moreover, the claim that this commission is globally seen as a model for transborder environmental governance is a myth.

The history of the IJC is, as we shall see in subsequent chapters, characterized by an initial half-century of mixed results, followed by a mid-century period of partisan politics resulting in large-scale endeavours with dubious environmental impacts, followed by a period of more noticeable success up to about the 1990s. In the last few decades, it has occupied a somewhat marginalized position.[20] Nevertheless, the BWT and IJC succeeded in providing a framework and ground rules that have, for the most part, prevented, contained, or resolved bilateral disputes over boundary waters. In the limited areas in which it has power, it tends to do a good job. In doing so, the BWT and IJC have together proven to be a foundation stone for modern Canada-US ecopolitics and natural security, particularly in the realms of border waters and crossborder pollution.[21]

3

Interwar Years

Fish remained a prominent part of US-Canada diplomacy between the two world wars. The first attempts at fish statecraft in this period aimed to create comprehensive agreements on a suite of related subjects. A 1918 fisheries commission tried to encompass salmon, halibut, and sturgeon. When that proved impossible, given the competing interests involved, separate agreements for different species and different regions followed: 1919 Halibut convention; 1923 Halibut treaty; 1930 Halibut convention; salmon conventions in 1929 and 1930; and more salmon and halibut conventions in 1937.

As the repeating names in that list suggest, during the interwar period, a common refrain in Canada-US relations was deferred agreements. Some crossborder accords were only delayed by a decade or two, while others were stalled until after the Second World War. Free trade was rejected right before the First World War, but then embraced two decades later. The Trail Smelter case, which is also a focus of this chapter, was equally a protracted affair. Those deferrals sometimes had weighty repercussions since politics, economics, and technologies changed noticeably during the intervening years, leading to important alterations to the agreements that eventually resulted.

Covering this wide topical range of negotiations, it should be apparent that Canada-US relations during the interwar years cannot be fully understood without placing environment at the centre. The particular nature of natural resources, whether it is fish or smelter smoke, requires close attention. They exhibit their own types of agency when it comes to political affairs and are often unpredictable. Fish disregard borders, some spawning in one country's freshwater while spending other life stages in the ocean. Smelter emissions are at the mercy of prevailing winds, their negative impacts potentially accruing to a political jurisdiction that does not receive the economic benefits.

CONSIDERING FREE TRADE

Leading up to the First World War, the US moved towards an "open door" trade policy, and its manufacturers hoped to sell more in the Canadian market. American newspaper interests acquired much of their pulp and paper from Canada. By this time, Canadian imports from the US, which mostly involved natural resources in some way, almost equalled those from Great Britain; the same was generally true for Canadian exports, which became dominated by wheat and wheat products. The Wilfrid Laurier Liberals had long been believers in free trade, even if domestic political reasons had motivated them to hide this inclination. After President Taft approached the Canadians, a free trade agreement was signed in early 1911. It included complete free trade in natural products, encompassing almost all Canadian exports to the south. At the same time, there were only limited reductions in tariffs on Canadian imports of manufactured goods from the US, thus extending the National Policy's protection of Canadian industry. Since it was an agreement, rather than a treaty, Canada did not need British consent.

But Canadians narrowly rejected Laurier's party, and free trade by extension, in the 1911 election. After decades of relative American inattention towards Canada, what one historian called "[t]he first constructive American policy initiative toward her northern neighbor" had been rebuffed.[1] In truth, there was widespread support for free trade in the eastern and western parts of the country, and Laurier's defeat likely had as much to do with the opposition of central Canadian manufacturers and other issues.

Yet continental economic and cultural integration only increased, even without free trade. Duty alterations in both countries made exporting newsprint more attractive. Since Canadian policies discouraged the export of raw pulpwood, American companies like the Chicago *Tribune* and Kimberly-Clark had already created Canadian subsidiaries to manufacture paper. After the tariff removal, these companies expanded their operations in Canada. By the mid-1920s, more newsprint used in the United States came from Canada than domestic sources. American newspapers became dependent on an integrated continental newsprint network. By the midpoint of the twentieth century, the US imported almost five million tons of newsprint.[2] The ensuing environmental repercussions of flattening the Canadian forest, especially in northern Ontario and Quebec, were thus a direct result of the American appetite for consuming the news.

For most of the first half of the twentieth century, coal was Canada's major energy source: as of 1913, coal accounted for 77 percent of total energy consumed, though that dropped to roughly 50 percent by the midpoint of the century and less than 10 percent by 1975.[3] Until the Second World War, about half of the coal used in Canada was imported from the United States, primarily by Toronto, Hamilton, and Montreal. Western and eastern Canada developed their own coal resources but only exported a small amount to the United States (though the exports would pick up in the 1970s – see table below). Though tariffs, subsidies, and other trade mechanisms were applied to coal, exports of this fossil fuel were not subject to the same level of crossborder regulatory oversight as electricity (or later oil and gas), nor did they require much in the way of direct Canada-US relations or agreements. That the coal trade never occasioned much diplomatic discussion or controversy, compared to other energy forms, may have chiefly stemmed from the fact that Canada needed to import this fossil fuel because it lacked adequate domestic supplies.

Canada had entered the First World War right at the beginning; the US held out until 1917. "America counted her profits," observed Canadian diplomat Hugh Keenleyside, "while Canada counted her dead." This engendered resentment north of the border, but many also realized that Canada's economic fortunes were tied to the United States. Canada emerged from the great global conflict as a more sovereign nation, both on paper and in the country's collective imagination. This process proceeded gradually after the war. Canada signed the Treaty of Versailles and joined the League of Nations, which the US did not. In the Balfour Declaration of 1926, Canada and the other dominions were recognized as "autonomous communities within the British Empire, in no way subordinate to Great Britain … But united by a common allegiance to the crown." In line with Prime Minister Mackenzie King's desire to decentralize the Commonwealth, Vincent Massey was appointed the first Canadian envoy, or minister, to the United States. Technically, the future governor general's title was "Envoy Extraordinary and Minister Plenipotentiary." In 1927 Canada opened its first diplomatic post (a legation) in Washington; the Amer-

Table 3.1
Canadian utilization of coal, 1935–1975 (quantities in thousands of tons)

Year	*Production*	*Imports*	*Exports*	*Consumption*
1935	13,888	12,079	418	25,548
1940	17,567	17,437	505	34,489
1945	16,507	25,062	841	40,728
1950	18,529	26,955	395	45,089
1955	14,411	19,743	593	33,561
1960	10,776	13,565	853	23,488
1965	11,500	16, 595	1,226	26,869
1970	16,604	18,864	4,392	31,076
1975	27,843	16,833	12,891	31,785

Source: Statistics Canada.

icans returned the favour the next year. The Statute of Westminster in 1931 gave Canada and the other dominions legislative equality with Great Britain, more or less finishing the process of Canada's independence in the realm of foreign affairs.

Both countries entered into a more internationally withdrawn and self-absorbed, though not isolationist, phase in the 1920s – Stephen Azzi rightly suggests that "independent internationalism" would be an appropriate term for Canada in this period.[4] Nevertheless, the 1920s and 1930s were a dynamic era in the Canada-US relationship. Of course, the latter part of this era was defined by the Great Depression and the Dust Bowl, which highlight the ways that nature can be a decisive player in human drama. At the start of the Depression, US investment in Canada almost doubled that of England's investment, despite high tariffs. The US was also the primary recipient of Canadian exports and the primary source of Canadian imports.[5] Canada still fancied itself as the linchpin in the North Atlantic Triangle. By the start of the Second World War, the United States had equalled, if not surpassed, Great Britain as Canada's most important ally.

The roster of Canada-US matters handled in the interwar period remained full. American investment, branch plants, and culture continued to move north, while many people and resources moved south. The Aluminum Company of America (Alcoa) had started producing its eponymous product in Quebec at the start of the twentieth century and continued to expand its operations in that province. American firms financed the extraction of zinc, copper, gold, and lead in Canadian shield country. Prohibition created frictions and opportunities. Both countries were protectionist throughout the 1920s, exemplified by the Smoot-Hawley tariffs in the United States. The 1929 Stock Market Crash and Great Depression at first precipitated a decline in trade and a rise in autarky. But by the second half of the 1930s, Canada and the United States had arrived at two free trade agreements.

Mackenzie King dangled the possibility of trading action on a St Lawrence Seaway for Canadian exemptions from the Smoot-Hawley tariff. However, the Canadian prime minister abruptly reversed course when he sensed opposition to the St Lawrence project, especially in Quebec. After years of high tariff diplomacy, by the mid-1930s, free trade seemed possible. Returning to power after the Bennett years, King moved to quickly secure a limited free trade agreement in 1935 with the United States. At lower rates, hundreds of goods, mostly manufactured items, could now move to Canada, and hundreds of items, mostly raw or semi-finished resources, could move to the United States. Another trade agreement, in 1938, built on and extended its predecessor. Deals on tariff rates were secured for hundreds of other products. The majority of items leaving Canada were still natural resources: wood, paper, fish, grains, and metals.[6]

King has been accused of taking Canada down a continentalist road, selling out Canada to the United States. But his approach to both the US and Britain was that Canada should not become too dependent on either country. This reflected the position of O.D. Skelton, whom King recruited from Queen's University in the mid-1920s for the position of External Affairs under-secretary. Skelton had considerable latitude in terms of moulding the expanding Canadian diplomatic service. He hired several mandarins who would go on to play leading roles in the formulation of Canadian foreign policy during the ensuing decades, such as Norman Robertson and Lester Pearson. As biographer Norman Hillmer writes about the chain of command and decision-making in External Affairs, until his death in 1941 "[t]he department *was* Skelton."[7]

During the 1930s and 1940s, US federal politics were dominated by one figure and party: Franklin Roosevelt and his Democrats. The president and prime minister would forge a good, if not personally close, relationship. FDR's 1938 speech at Ivy Lea on the St Lawrence, in the context of German and Japanese aggression, promised that "the United States would not stand idly by if domination of Canadian soil is threatened by any other empire." Of course, when it came to Canadian sovereignty, this was as much a threat as a promise. American policy toward Canada after the First World War – not that the State Department had a coherent policy towards Canada – was to encourage Canada to become more North American and less imperial in its outlook. At least with Roosevelt, the holder of the Oval Office actually had knowledge of, and some affection for, Canada.[8]

FISHERIES

While we have already discussed Pacific sealing as well as fish stocks off the east coast and in the Great Lakes, I have said little about fishing in the Pacific Northwest. Salmon and halibut, the two most lucrative catches in that region, were sources of contention. The halibut stocks here were the greatest in the world; they were usually harvested on the high seas, outside the jurisdiction of the individual states and provinces. Salmon, by contrast, were generally taken from inshore and freshwater areas. Salmon are an anadromous fish, which means that the various species (five main types) return to their natal streams to spawn. BC's Fraser River is well known for its sockeye, the most valuable of the Pacific salmon. In order to return to their spawning grounds, they often pass through both BC and Washington State waters in the Strait of Juan de Fuca. Each country had developed lucrative salmon canneries in the nineteenth century. But by the First World War, the salmon fisheries – indeed, fisheries of all kinds all over North America – were under great stress, and catches dwindling, because of overfishing.

In the decade before the First World War, the US and Canada had negotiated an Inland Fisheries Treaty (1908), Salmon Treaty (1909), North Atlantic Cod Fisheries Agreement (1910), and North Pacific Fur Seal Convention (1911). The Canadian government suggested a conference on Great Lakes and Pacific fisheries in early 1917, and the Woodrow Wilson administration agreed. Each country designated three commissioners. Following a series of public hearings and investigations, they presented a joint report. This 1918 report recommended the following: (1) the enactment of reciprocal legislation on a closed season on halibut fishing in the North Pacific; (2) the negotiation of a treaty and regulations for the protection of sockeye salmon of the Fraser River system; and (3) the adoption by US states of legislation similar to the existing Canadian four-year prohibition of sturgeon fishing in Lake Erie.[9]

The inland fisheries accord, however, did not stick, caught as it was between too many geographic areas, fish types, and conflicting interests. Officials decided to deal with the various species separately. To keep things clear, I will first address salmon and then turn to halibut. For the sockeye salmon, an international fisheries commission was created to craft appropriate policy recommendations. It proposed bridged seasons, net regulations, and licence limits for the commercial fishing industry. An agreement based on these terms was signed in September 1919 and soon received parliamentary approval in Canada. But certain industrial fishing and canning interests objected, and Washington State had reservations about federal intrusion; the US Senate did not give its consent, and the agreement was withdrawn. An amended treaty was sent to the Senate the following year but met the same fate. In the wake of this failure, the subfederal jurisdictions tried to enact matching regulations, but this too was a non-starter. An ongoing problem was that the federal government had primary jurisdiction in Canada, while Washington State mainly controlled the policy reins in US waters.

By the late 1920s, there was greater bilateral trust and scientific consensus on the status of the fisheries in both nations.[10] Diplomatic negotiations resumed, and a new salmon convention was signed in 1929. The Americans agreed to share equally with Canadians the Fraser River runs. But now Canada's Parliament refused to ratify an agreement, the first time it had rejected a bilateral treaty.[11] The 1929 agreement was then used as the basis for another kick at the can. A new pact was signed in 1930, called the Sockeye Convention. It instituted a joint commission to study the science of salmon, recommend appropriate commercial fishing seasons and gear restrictions, and extend the treaty area to the high seas.

Now the Canadian Parliament approved. However, there was again resistance in the US Senate. Changes of opinions and governors in Washington State brought some around over time, provided certain changes were made to the 1930 agreement. Canada was reluctant but assented, realizing that accepting these alterations would allow progress. The new convention came into force in July 1937. The International Pacific Salmon Fisheries Commission it created immediately started up, although the convention's regulations would not come into force until 1946.

Turning now to halibut, as I previously mentioned the 1918 commission recommended the enactment of reciprocal legislation for a "closed time" on halibut fishing in the North Pacific. The halibut stocks had clearly been decimated by overfishing, the annual catch dropping by about one-third during the First World War. In 1919, the US and Canada signed a convention agreeing to establish a closed halibut season and study the fish and the fishing industry. But other clauses in the agreement, such as those concerning free trade in lobster and fish, meant that this had little chance of success in the United States.

After further whittling it down to focus on just the Pacific halibut, a treaty was signed and ratified in 1923. This Halibut Convention often makes it into the general literature on Canada-US relations because it represented an important nation-building step: it was the first time that Canada was able to append its signature solo to an international treaty. Not only was this treaty the first by a dominion that did not require Britain to co-sign, but it was reputedly the "first one concluded anywhere for the conservation of a threatened deep sea fishery."[12] The 1923 Halibut Convention outlined a closed season from mid-November to mid-February. It created an International Fisheries Commission to study the halibut and make conservation recommendations accordingly.

But the annual three-month cessation of halibut fishing failed to make much of a difference. The commission concluded that a more extensive and selective regulation of the fishery was needed. The new Halibut Convention signed in 1930 converted the commission from an investigatory body into a true regulatory agency. More precisely, the commission was now authorized to alter or suspend, rather than just make recommendations, about closed seasons and areas, gear, harvest limits, and licences. The appropriate governments would enforce these provisions. The International Fisheries Commission divided the coastal area into four zones and set catch limits for each. Another convention signed in 1937 replaced that of 1930, slightly broadening the commission's power. For example, it now applied to the bycatch of halibut fishing. A new convention in 1953 made further changes. It changed the name to the International Pacific Halibut Commission and increased its size, added further powers applicable to halibut bycatch, and gave the commission more authority to alter open seasons.[13]

In the Great Lakes, the collapse of the commercial fisheries – from overfishing and other anthropogenic factors such as pollution, deforestation, and habitat loss – somewhat reduced the urgency for formal crossborder measures such as those for sturgeon in the 1918 fisheries commission. Given that these sweetwater seas had arguably once been the greatest freshwater fisheries in the world, even the diminished catch volumes were still noteworthy, and recreational fishing would soon begin its rise to prominence. Despite its status as the smallest of the Great Lakes by volume, Lake Erie is the most productive from a fish biomass perspective. In the 1930s, representatives from the US federal government, four US states, and Ontario signed a voluntary pact to conserve Lake Erie fish stocks, known as the Toronto Agreement. But it had no teeth, and enforcement proved impossible. Other efforts were made to come to some sort of fisheries arrangements that involved the Great Lakes states. No progress, however, would be made until after the Second World War.[14]

TRAIL SMELTER

The Trail Smelter dispute, from 1927 to 1941, is a well-known diplomatic spat between the United States and Canada. It was also a precedent-setting ruling for international law on transboundary air pollution.[15] In the early twentieth century, Consolidated Mining and Smelting Company (Cominco) developed an enormous smelter complex in southeastern British Columbia. This complex is near the community of Trail, along the Columbia River, and close to the border with northeastern Washington State. Zinc and lead were processed at this complex, releasing sulphur dioxide emissions. The Columbia River valley effectively acted as a funnel that directed emissions southward into Washington State.

By the First World War, there were already localized complaints about the impacts of this air pollution on agriculture. Cominco offered compensation, bought out farmland, and raised its smokestacks higher in the mid-1920s. The latter action better dispersed the fumes, but in doing so, they wafted further across the international border. The company offered compensation for crop damages south of the 49th parallel, but most claimants rejected it as insufficient. It also found that, as a foreign entity, buying out properties in the United States was not legally an option.

These steps did not assuage agricultural growers around the vicinity of Northport, Washington. The two countries took the matter to the IJC in 1928 – the first air pollution reference for this commission. Its ambit was to determine what fumigation damage had been done, the appropriate level of compensation, and the likely impact of future operations. Several years and millions of dollars were spent on field investigations and studies. In the meantime, Cominco continued to admit it had some liability and undertook a range of remediation measures. By 1932, its sulphur dioxide emissions had been reduced by two-thirds. In fact, it found that it could profitably convert harnessed byproducts into fertilizer.[16] The company was able to convince researchers that its technical solutions had largely eliminated the problem.

The IJC produced its findings in 1931. It found the Trail Smelter at fault and estimated damages at $350,000. Though the scientific studies were impressive, this figure represented more of a political compromise reflecting the conflicting national interests within the IJC. But this figure was only about half the amount claimed by the aggrieved farmers – granted, their claims may have been inflated or unfounded, at least in some cases – and the ruling did not require Cominco to stop emissions completely.

President Herbert Hoover planned to accept the IJC's proposed settlement. However, pressure from Washington State led the federal government to remain noncommittal, essentially amounting to a rejection.[17] The matter remained at a diplomatic deadlock for some time. Given the smelter's economic importance, Canada was reluctant to give in. But the Roosevelt administration was motivated to settle the Trail Smelter case because of other linked factors: the 1932 Great Lakes–St Lawrence Treaty, and the realization that precedents in the Trail case might come back to bite the US in regard to transboundary air pollution in other places, such as the Detroit-St Clair region.[18] Moreover, the smelter industry in the United States, hoping to avoid tighter regulations on its domestic practices, supplied information to Cominco to help the Canadian company strengthen its case.[19]

In 1935, the two governments agreed to a convention that established an arbitral tribunal apart from the IJC.[20] They charged the tribunal with determining how much pollution had occurred since the start of 1932 and asked it to recommend any necessary compensation and remedial measures. The convention also stated that the United States would accept the $350,000 payment from Canada for damages before 1932. The tribunal was not to consider the matter prior to 1932 or reexamine the commission's studies. Thus, they implicitly accepted the IJC's ruling and accepted it as the basis for arbitration.[21]

The arbitration tribunal met for several years starting in 1935, releasing a preliminary report in 1938 and a final judgment in 1941. It found many of the Washington State claims unfounded. Though the tribunal stuck to legal issues and avoided ruling on some of the trickier scientific questions, it rejected the American "invisible injury" thesis. This thesis was based on the idea that sulphur dioxide exposure could lead to long-term chronic damage that was not immediately apparent (this was actually quite prescient and anticipated later scientific findings about the way that toxic substances and persistent organic pollutants cause harm). In the preliminary report, the tribunal assessed a $78,000 damages indemnity covering the period from 1932 to October 1937. The tribunal also directed Cominco to follow strict emissions guidelines and undertake technical changes to reduce fumes and acids. Emissions were capped during growing seasons at one hundred tons daily.

Furthermore, the 1941 decision declared a principle that has taken Trail from a localized dispute between two North American entities to a staple of international environmental law. Namely, it enshrined the "polluter pays" principle. Nevertheless, in his book on the Trail Smelter dispute, John Wirth argues that it was a missed opportunity to set broader standards against pollution: "Trail, and by extension the North American smelter industry as a whole, won too big a victory, while society received too little compensation in terms of a deeper awareness of the dangers of air pollution to health and the environment."[22]

That assessment of the Trail case could be applied to most other aspects of Canada-US environmental diplomacy during the interwar years. When it came to crossborder conservation, such as fish, the emphasis was on protecting species to some extent, but chiefly so that their harvest could be maximized into the future. Development ultimately won out over protection. When bilateral accords stalled, it was frequently special and domestic interests protecting their own position, often using the US Senate as a backstop. The history of environmental diplomacy between the two world wars therefore underscores a perennial problem common to all forms of Canada-US relations: getting treaties through Parliament and Congress, especially the latter.

4

Border Flows

Rivers can be reconfigured by humans, but they also shape human history. Water and hydroelectricity have historically been among the most important aspects of the Canada-US relationship. Border water projects such as canals and dams normally require transnational coordination because of water's physical properties and behaviour. That is, intentionally altering levels on a waterbody that forms the border or flows across it will impact the other country, as will pollution or floods. This reality has the potential to result in cooperation or conflict. However, the fluid abundance of the northern North American border and the concomitant potential for shared hydroelectricity usually resulted in Canada-US collaboration.

A prime example of water cooperation is the Boundary Waters Treaty. It created the International Joint Commission, which began meeting in 1912. As the designers of this commission expected, its quasi-judicial role was more pronounced at first. Of the fifty cases handled by the commission prior to 1944, thirty-nine were applications for approval of specific works under the judicial power of article VIII, and only eleven were references under article IX. Thereafter the story was reversed, and the investigative role – in which the national governments ask the IJC to study and recommend solutions for specific problems – became more prominent. Over its first half-century, the International Joint Commission favoured pragmatic solutions and was reluctant to establish legal precedents.

The IJC frequently became involved with hydroelectric developments in the Great Lakes–St Lawrence basin. But three different regional groupings of border hydro stations can also be identified: Pacific Northwest, Rainy River/Lake of the Woods, and Maine-New

Brunswick. The largest stations are within the Great Lakes–St Lawrence and Pacific Northwest systems, with relatively small stations in the two other regions. On the prairies, IJC activities have been more concerned with water apportionment, flood control, and pollution. In the Great Lakes basin, navigation and water pollution joined hydro power as pre-eminent issues. This chapter will cover water diplomacy in these various regions roughly from the First World War until the start of the Second World War.

IJC CASES

After its inception, the first few dockets the IJC dealt with involved hydro power and waterbodies to the west of Lake Superior that ultimately flowed to Hudson Bay: the Rainy River and Lake of the Woods watersheds. The result was a 1925 Lake of the Woods Treaty establishing a range of stable and acceptable elevations for the lake. Nearby, at Sault Ste Marie, in 1914 the commission approved the building of the binational Lake Superior Compensating Works (a sixteen-gated structure with eight gates on each side of the international boundary). This directed water from the St Marys River to the hydro power stations. At the same time, the IJC established the first of its joint boards, the Lake Superior Board of Control, to partially regulate the water level and outflow of Lake Superior.[1]

Border hydroelectric developments on the east coast primarily involved waters that form or cross the Maine–New Brunswick boundary. Several early dockets dealt with projects on the St Croix, Aroostook, and Saint John Rivers. In the Richelieu and Champlain basins, shared by Quebec and several northeastern US states, the IJC considered various applications for navigation and remedial works during the 1930s, and created boards of control. By the Second World War, the IJC had appraised various water matters out west: Shoal Lake, Souris River, and Milk-St Mary Rivers in the prairies/plains region, and the Kootenay, Creston, Skagit, Poplar, Okanagan, and Columbia Rivers in the Pacific Northwest. The American impact on Canadian waters was not just restricted to border waters either. American companies and capital played the leading role in developing certain waterbodies in Quebec, building dams in the Outardes, Manicouagan, and Saguenay basins.[2]

While we will not review all of these in detail, I should say more about several of the most consequential. The St Mary–Milk debate, which revolved around irrigation water, is worth considering since it received its own article in the Boundary Waters Treaty, and it has remained a problem up to the present day. Under the treaty, these two rivers are treated as one and apportioned equally. Soon after the 1909 BWT, conflicts about sharing the water flared up. The IJC issued an order in 1921, but this failed to resolve matters. The United States brought the matter back to the commission on several occasions in the 1920s and 1930s and requested that it reconsider the apportionment ratio. Canada, happy with the status quo, declined. A 1932 vote in the IJC about reopening the order split along national lines. The two governments then set up an engineering board to oversee further modifications for storage and distribution. But the Milk–St Mary dispute would never entirely go away.

On the Kootenay River, the IJC approved a scheme to build a dam and create a Kootenay Lake Board of Control. The Corra Linn dam was erected in the early 1930s as a multi-purpose structure, which included supplying Cominco with electricity for its new fertilizer plant in Trail. However, there were complaints from groups affected by the reservoir. Other dams were built on this river and elsewhere in the Pacific Northwest. For example, construction of the Grand Coulee, the most powerful dam in the US, started in the 1930s; the IJC approved this and formed an International Columbia River Board of Control. Other proposals for the Columbia and Skagit Rivers were also put before the IJC.

Returning to the Great Lakes–St Lawrence basin, the IJC considered several issues that did not proceed very far during the first half of the century but came to fruition in the second half of the century: water pollution, Niagara power and remedial works, and St Lawrence navigation and power. Pollution across the water border, particularly from Detroit, had been one of the main reasons for including a clause about pollution in the BWT. The IJC's fourth docket addressed transboundary water pollution in the Niagara, Detroit, and St Clair Rivers, finding those waters polluted to the detriment of public health. This study "contributed significantly to greater awareness of bacterial contamination and potential responses" and promoted the importance of treating the public water supply.[3] Canada and the US inked a treaty in 1920 about pollution, but it was not implemented. A further reference on the pollution of boundary waters would not be submitted until after the end of the Second World War.

Meanwhile, the IJC considered private applications to develop power in the upper St Lawrence at Waddington and Massena, both in New York State. In 1912, the Aluminum Company of America (Alcoa) built a canal taking water from the St Lawrence to a power plant near Massena, and its subsidiaries soon began surveying power dam possibilities in the river at Barnhart Island. Alcoa applied for permission to build a St Lawrence dam, but that was unsuccessful in part because of Canadian opposition. Nevertheless, the concept of combining navigation works with a power development had been broached and would feature in future discussions to modify the international stretch of the St Lawrence.

In early 1914 the American government approached Canada with a diplomatic note suggesting that the IJC be allowed to investigate the possibility of a jointly developed St Lawrence deep waterway. Diplomatic notes are an exchange of information between an embassy and a foreign ministry that do not require the formal steps involved in other documents such as a treaty; these notes are common in Canada-US relations and have different functions ranging from a statement of position to a formal agreement. However, Prime Minister Borden was concerned about railway expenses and the political consequences of funding a project perceived as primarily benefitting Ontario. At any rate, the First World War soon intruded, and the Canadians never replied to the note. However, the Canadian cabinet did authorize two of its members to travel to Washington to propose a joint project. But the timing was not propitious. The US Army Corps of Engineers had recently advised against any improvement in the International Rapids section (IRS) of the St Lawrence until Canada had sufficiently deepened the connecting links in the St Lawrence. The Canadian proposal did not elicit a response from the American government.

The Boundary Waters Treaty had put limits on Niagara River diversions for power: water could be abstracted from above the Falls at a rate of 36,000 cfs by Ontario and 20,000 cfs by New York. During the First World War, the diversion limits imposed by the US via the Burton Act were lifted, and all water that could be utilized was made available for power diversions. Even before the United States formally entered the war, the War Department requisitioned all Niagara hydro power and directed it toward war-related uses.[4] Many New York establishments in Niagara Falls and Buffalo depended on the electricity imported from Canada to make vital wartime products such as chlorine, phosphorus, carborundum, aluminum, silicon, chromium, and magnesium. In January 1917, the War Department was authorized to license the use of Niagara River waters, and the secretary of war issued revocable permits totalling up to the 20,000 cfs limit of the Boundary Waters Treaty.[5] With the addition of new generating stations, total capacity now stood at 100,000 horsepower, and they soon took water up to the 20,000 cfs ceiling.[6]

There was strong domestic resistance in Canada to electricity exports to the United States, particularly in Ontario. The Canadian federal government grew concerned about Niagara electricity exports across the border. Such sentiments reached a fever pitch during the war, resulting in the so-called Repatriation Crisis and various studies into the nature of Canadian electrical development and exports, such as the Drayton Report.[7] Adam Beck, the chairman of Ontario Hydro, pressured the federal government to stop all power exports from Niagara to the United States.[8] Canadian authorities resisted such a step, but cut electricity exports to the United States by almost 20 percent. This became a point of friction in Canada-US relations. The United States threatened to cut off coal exports to Canada in retaliation. But Canadian and American officials came to an understanding about the Niagara electricity situation that kept export restrictions to a minimum.

One of the First World War's lessons was the importance of hydroelectricity and the need to obtain even more. Between 1917 and 1920, electrical generation in the United States went up by 42 percent, with a total installed hydroelectric capacity of nine million horsepower.[9] There was no drop-off in demand after the war. Canada's electrical generating capacity had gone up only 3 percent during the war, but the country made up for its lack of wartime expansion by almost tripling its kilowatt output in the postwar decade. As of 1920, hydro represented 97 percent of the electricity produced in Canada and 20 percent in the United States. This postwar era marked the start of a gradual shift in which the American and Canadian grids became more interconnected and "electricity trade between the two countries changed from unidirectional firm power sales from Canada to the United States to interruptible power sales in both directions."[10]

In 1925, the Canadian government enacted a minor duty on electricity sold to the United States (0.3 mills per kwh) by modifying the Fluid and Electricity Export Act of 1907. This duty remained in place until 1963. A provincial act in 1926 meanwhile aimed to reduce Quebec's electricity exports to the United States. Some power projects on the Quebec side of the Ottawa River went ahead, but others were cancelled because they were predicated on exporting power south of the border. In the later 1920s, the Canadian Parliament also came close to passing legislation that would have put further limits on hydro power exports.[11]

The Federal Water Power Act, which created the Federal Power Commission (FPC), came into effect in the United States in 1920.[12] The FPC was made up of the heads of the War, Interior, and Agriculture departments. Its purpose was to replace the previous piecemeal way of approving hydro power projects – the new commission could grant fifty-year licences – and systematically preserve and strategically develop the nation's water power resources. Hydro power projects in the US, including those at the border, henceforth needed to be licensed by the FPC. In 1930, the Federal Water Power Act made the FPC an independent agency, and the Federal Power Act of 1935 gave the FPC responsibility for regulating interstate whole power rates.[13]

ST LAWRENCE AND NIAGARA

During the interwar years, Canada and the United States arrived at a number of diplomatic agreements concerning the water resources of the Great Lakes. These were headlined by the St Lawrence and Niagara agreements, both of which took place outside the IJC (though based on the IJC's technical recommendations), reflecting the politicization of technical goals and the extent to which engineers and technocrats frequently became quasi-diplomats. Neither of these agreements would be implemented, however, because of domestic opposition from different sectors and debates about which level of government should develop hydro power, or whether governments should develop hydro power at all. Still, the diplomacy surrounding these agreements is worth considering in some detail. Not only did these failed accords prove influential in the long run, but they serve as case studies elucidating how Canada-US relations developed and matured during this era, as well as the ways that the physical properties of water and hydroelectricity both enabled and constrained technical, economic, and political choices.

After the end of the First World War, Washington and Ottawa had created a joint two-person engineering board to study the St

Lawrence question, and the IJC began holding an extensive series of hearings. The joint engineering board produced the Wooten-Bowden report, named after the two presiding engineers, which was in favour of deepening the river from Lake Ontario to Montreal.[14] At the end of 1921, the IJC concluded that the St Lawrence offered the best possible route, and recommended that the two national governments enter into a treaty to authorize the project and include the Welland Canal as part of a wider waterway system. Some American interests continued to push for an alternative all-American route from the Great Lakes, such as a new waterway connecting to the Hudson River.

In response to the Wooten-Bowden report and the IJC recommendation, the United States, after some initial delays, sent Canada a formal note recommending the conclusion of a treaty pledging the two governments to undertake the project. But Prime Minister Mackenzie King was hesitant to embark on such an endeavour because of constitutional questions about whether the federal or provincial governments had the right to create a St Lawrence power, plus potential opposition in Quebec gave him pause. South of the border, hostility came from Atlantic port cities, New England, and downstate New York. In 1922 the IJC approved the construction of a submerged weir in the St Lawrence River for diverting up to 25,000 cfs into the Massena Power Canal.[15]

Further reports recommending a large navigation project continued throughout the 1920s, with President Hoover a strong advocate of a St Lawrence waterway. Indeed, a St Lawrence development was the top concern for the newly opened American embassy in Ottawa. As debates about federal-provincial jurisdiction over power development continued, so too did American pressure for a St Lawrence treaty, including threats to delay the ratification of two accords concerning Canada: Pacific salmon fisheries and cooperative action to divert water from Niagara Falls for hydro power while simultaneously preserving its beauty. But these linkage attempts did not achieve the desired results.

R.B. Bennett, who was Canadian prime minister from 1930 to 1935, was more willing than King to take up Hoover's offers to discuss a treaty. Talks commenced in November 1931 and continued at intervals over the next eight months, culminating with a treaty in July 1932. Ontario and the federal governments reached a division of costs agreement right before the signing of the treaty under which Ontario would receive the rights to the Canadian share of St Lawrence power. Ontario would pay for power development and 70 percent of the cost of joint power-navigation facilities while Ottawa picked up the tab for the navigation elements. This Great Lakes Waterway Treaty provided for a twenty-seven-foot canal system from the head of the Great Lakes to Montreal. The United States was responsible for any improvements above Lake Erie, while Canada agreed to furnish the appropriate navigation works in the Quebec part of the St Lawrence. Both countries would cooperatively build in the International Rapids Section, with each providing a lock and canal on its side, and perform other channel improvements. There would be a St Lawrence power dam at the border, with Canadian and American powerhouses forming the dam, which would produce an estimated 2,200,000 horsepower. Each country would get half of this power. Canada received credit for the Welland Canal and work in the Thousand Islands. The treaty also addressed other transborder water issues in the basin, such as Niagara Falls power and various Great Lakes diversions.

But the Great Lakes Waterway Treaty, hampered by a range of domestic interests and disputes about who should control hydro power, could not make it through Congress. Washington's subsequent inquiries about the Bennett government's willingness to introduce the treaty into Parliament or approve of changes to the American St Lawrence bill met with either empty promises or outright refusal. Canadian officials had apparently lost interest because of the Depression and potential opposition to a Seaway in Quebec. Ultimately no action was taken by Canada.[16] Franklin Roosevelt was elected president in the interim, and he preferred a new St Lawrence agreement, especially once Mackenzie King returned to power. The new Ontario premier, Mitchell Hepburn, was opposed to the St Lawrence development. He did seek some of the provisions from the 1932 treaty: namely, to generate power through additional diversions at Niagara Falls, which would be aided by diverting water from northern Ontario into Lake Superior. However, these diversions required the consent of the United States, as they were boundary waters.

We need to fill in some gaps about the Chicago diversion since it is intertwined with the St Lawrence story. Between 1912 and 1924, Canada had filed six objections to this diversion. In 1925, the Secretary of War issued a new permit that allowed Chicago to divert an average of no more than 8,500 cfs. Since Canada, and other Great Lakes states, kept complaining that the Sanitary and Ship Canal lowered water levels throughout the basin, hurting navigation and hydro power, the US Supreme Court appointed a "special master" to adjudicate the situation. This master ruled in 1930 that Chicago needed to complete sewage treatment plants and whittle down its diversion until it was at 1,500 cfs by 1939, unless Congress set different parameters. But after a few years, Chicago had made little progress. In the meantime, the diversion impacted the bilateral St Lawrence talks. Treaty negotiators for the Great Lakes Waterway Treaty of 1932 included limitations on the Chicago diversion. The US Congress had in fact voted down the treaty because of these limitations, among other reasons.[17]

Also wrapped up in these St Lawrence negotiations was the matter of Niagara Falls. There were worries that the huge quantities of water diverted for power purposes were harming the scenic beauty of the Falls, as was natural erosion (the lip of the Horseshoe Falls was receding up to seven feet per year) and low levels throughout the Great Lakes. As more and more water was abstracted for industrial and hydro power purposes, the flanks of the falls were left dry; with a thinner flow, rock broke through the solid curtain of water projecting over the lip, hurting its appearance. Canada and the United States had formed the International Niagara Board of Control in 1923 to monitor power diversions. Representatives of the power industry disingenuously argued that, since the Falls were eroding themselves, the best way to preserve them was to reduce the amount of water flowing over the precipice. This, not coincidently, would open the door to further water diversions.

After Canada had suggested an increase in the amount of water that could be diverted from the river, in 1925 the US proposed further joint governmental consideration. The following year the two countries established a Special International Niagara Board to focus on how best to maintain the scenic beauty of the Falls. In its interim report, the board proposed the use of weirs – they were also termed "artificial cascades"[18] – to strategically divert water from the middle part of the Falls to the edges. This would improve the appearance of the crestline, both in quantity and colour. The report also suggested that, outside of tourist season, power companies be permitted to divert 10,000 cfs from each side.[19] Ontario Hydro asked the Canadian federal government to open negotiations with the Americans on increased diversions at Niagara. Based on the Special International Niagara Board's interim report, the Niagara Convention and Protocol

Table 4.1
Canadian annual exports of electricity to the United States, 1920–40 (volume in millions of kilowatt hours)

Year	*From Ontario*	*From Quebec*	*From other provinces*	*Total Canada*	*Exports as % of Canadian production*
1920	643	282	25	950	16
1921	619	365	36	1,020	18
1922	501	324	37	862	13
1923	653	357	44	1,054	13
1924	723	425	52	1,200	13
1925	809	379	51	1,239	12
1926	814	376	63	1,253	10
1927	1,202	390	17	1,609	11
1928	1,250	413	12	1,675	10
1929	1,144	444	16	1,604	9
1930	1,028	449	20	1,497	8
1931	1,206	522	22	1,750	11
1932	660	327	21	1,008	6
1933	444	188	20	652	4
1934	789	391	19	1,199	6
1935	959	337	21	1,317	6
1936	1,080	477	21	1,578	6
1937	1,253	571	23	1,847	7
1938	1,232	571	24	1,827	7
1939	1,290	597	26	1,913	7
1940	1,471	637	28	2,136	7

Source: A.E.D Grauer, "The Export of Electricity from Canada," in R.M. Clark, ed., *Canadian Issues: Essays in Honour of Henry F. Angus* (Toronto: University of Toronto Press, 1961), 267.

was signed in 1929 by the two countries. It called for remedial works that would disperse water to ensure an unbroken crestline in all seasons and permitted experimental diversions of 10,000 cfs by each country between 1 October and 31 March for a period of seven years.

But the 1929 convention was not able to make it through the US Senate because of concerns that it granted too much to private power interests. In 1931 the Special Niagara Board released "Preservation and Improvement of the Scenic Beauty of the Niagara Falls and Rapids," which was the final version of its interim report. The report analyzed every aspect of the Niagara Falls aesthetic appearance. Considering that the visual appeal of the Falls stemmed from diverse factors and perspectives, the report gave consideration to what exactly constituted "scenic grandeur." Was it the height, width, volume, colour, or lines that made Niagara such a spectacle? The report concluded that a sufficiently distributed volume of flow, or at least the "impression of volume," which would create an unbroken crestline, was most important. It recommended that the riverbed above the Falls be manipulated in order to apportion the necessary volume of water to achieve the desired effect.[20] Remedial works, in the form of submerged weirs and excavations, would achieve that while allowing for increased power diversions. This report, along with the 1929 treaty, would serve as the conceptual basis for the subsequent attempts in the following decades to deal with the tension between creating both beauty and power at Niagara.

Niagara provisions had been included in the failed 1932 Great Lakes Waterway Treaty. In the wake of the treaty's failure, Premier Hepburn advocated for the Niagara measures, as well as Long Lac–Ogoki diversions into Lake Superior which would allow Ontario to take extra power diversions at Niagara. At Ontario's urging, the Bennett government inquired about pursuing the Niagara power issue, but President Roosevelt worried that further Niagara diversions could diminish the grandeur of the Falls. After all, there had been a spate of rock falls at the famous cataract during the 1930s.[21] Ontario Hydro had also recently finished its new power plant at Queenston-Chippawa (later redubbed Sir Adam Beck Generating Station No. 1, this was the world's largest hydroelectric plant when it was completed), which diverted water via a canal that took water around the Falls.[22]

In 1935, the US president approached Canada with a draft treaty on Niagara remedial works for the purpose of beautification only. However, Ottawa did not wish to separate the scenic and power components out of concern that doing so could jeopardize enhancing the power production capabilities.[23] Concerned about maintaining the scenic quality of Niagara, Roosevelt did not want to deal with Niagara separately from a wider agreement to take care of all transborder issues in the Great Lakes–St Lawrence. Mackenzie King was sympathetic to Roosevelt's concerns, and the prime minister's relationship with Hepburn became openly hostile.

The Roosevelt administration decided, with Canadian concurrence, to withdraw the still-unratified 1929 Niagara treaty from Senate consideration and fold the Niagara issue into an agreement to replace the 1932 treaty that would comprehensively deal with all Great Lakes–St Lawrence navigation, power, and diversion issues.[24] The Americans produced a draft treaty in 1938 that did just that. It stipulated remedial work at Niagara to preserve the visual appeal of the Falls while allowing for the increased power diversions. But with Hepburn resolutely opposed to a larger agreement, King claimed his hands were tied, and the situation appeared intractable. It would take the Second World War to dislodge this log jam.

Though little tangible was achieved between the two world wars in terms of moving the Niagara and St Lawrence projects forward, the technical plans articulated in these accords would shape the final results after the Second World War. Despite the lack of ratification, the water developments covered in this chapter, along with the Trail Smelter and other interwar international issues, demonstrated that environmental and energy issues occupied a prominent place in bilateral diplomacy. The desire for energy was so strong that top diplomats, and prime ministers and presidents, were directly involved in the negotiations.

This high-level summit diplomacy speaks to the extent to which Canada was able to hold its own politically and technically in direct discussions with the United States. During these years, Canadian officials and diplomats gained the respect of their American counterparts and solidified Canada's international transition from colony to nation. We also see the roots of other aspects that came to define Canada-US relations in the putative "golden age" of external affairs during the early Cold War: assertions of their respective national interests balanced by a willingness to compromise for mutual gain; increased technological capacity to exploit environments on a massive scale; the increasing role of subfederal jurisdictions in foreign affairs; and the ability of sectional interests to stop international agreements and projects, but also collaboration between Ottawa and Washington to circumvent domestic opposition within both countries.

5

World War to Cold War

The Second World War wreaked havoc on the global biosphere. In many ways, the greatest ally of the United States and Canada in the fight against fascism was nature; natural resources brought the two countries together, literally and symbolically. In fact, it is only a bit of an oversimplification and exaggeration to suggest that geography and the wealth of North American natural resources primarily explain their side's triumph in both the Second World War and the Cold War.

Since the fighting during the Second World War predominantly took place far from North American shores, Canada and the United States were spared most of the direct physical destruction visited on the other participants. Even so, the two countries' war efforts had an enormous impact on their natural environments. Hydroelectric production expanded enormously, along with the attendant consequences of damming riverine ecosystems. So too did the mining, extraction, and smelting of minerals and metals, which had a tremendous environmental cost. Canada and the United States coordinated the production of scores of other war industries and armaments. This included Canadian plutonium at Chalk River and uranium from Saskatchewan and northern Ontario, both of which contributed to the American nuclear bomb program and set Canada up for a post-war nuclear industry.[1]

The intensified integration of the Canada-US relationship that occurred during the war had many environmental dimensions, as this chapter will demonstrate. Diplomatic and political decisions made by a coterie of officials had enormous repercussions for landscapes across the continent. The Second World War unleashed or amplified patterns of technology, industry, and consumption that allowed the exploitation and extraction of resources on an unprecedented scale. The war further militarily and economically integrated the Canadian and American states – exemplified by the Permanent Joint Board on Defence and the Hyde Park declaration – a process that continued after the war. Out of necessity, Canada turned from Britain to the United States as its main ally. The Commonwealth connection undoubtedly remained important for Canadians, but henceforth the United States clearly had more influence on Canada than did Great Britain. The breadth and depth of the Canada-US natural alliance were set to expand enormously.

WAR INFRASTRUCTURE

Even before Pearl Harbor, American forces had built bases and military installations in Alaska and the Aleutian Islands. With the entry of the US into the war and the potential threat of Japanese invasion, those needed to be upgraded. But there was no land connection to the lower forty-eight states. In 1942 Canada agreed to let the US construct the Alcan (Alaska-Canada) Military Highway from Dawson Creek, BC to Alaska, mostly running through Canadian territory. Canada granted a right of way and the right to use resources, but the US funded construction. Half a year after the war ended, the portion of the highway that ran through Canadian territory would revert to Canada. Some 40,000 American troops – dubbed the "army of occupation" – arrived to build the 1,420 mile road. The highway connected with airfields along the Northwest Staging Route, jointly built by Canada and the United States to move materiel, and a Northeast Staging Route was also created. The Canadians retained control of those airfields they had already built, while the Americans were responsible for building new ones.[2]

The Canol (Canada Oil) project was a primarily American-built and -financed oil production and distribution system on Canadian territory intended to provide fuel from Norman Wells along the Alaska highway and the Northwest Staging Route. Under a binational agreement, a refinery and pipeline would be the property of the US, but at the end of the war Canada would be given the first right of purchase. Imperial Oil already produced oil at Norman Wells in the Northwest Territory's Mackenzie Valley, which was far enough inland to be theoretically protected from the Japanese. In 1942, the Americans enlarged the existing Norman Wells facility and built a pipeline to Whitehorse, where they established a refinery. From there, pipelines could distribute oil to several points in Alaska. The project – built by the US Army Corps of Engineers, a consortium of American contractors, and Imperial Oil – also required an array of storage facilities, buildings, roads, and airfields.[3]

It took until April 1944 for the oil to start flowing, but the Americans halted this after only about a year. In total, they drilled eighty-five wells, though some estimate that the number of barrels of oil delivered by the $140 million project (far over budget) was well under one million.[4] It was an expensive failure for the Americans. Canada declined to purchase the Canol facilities after the war; within a few years of the end of hostilities, the refinery was dismantled and shipped to Alberta. Much of the infrastructure was left behind, polluting in perpetuity the surrounding area.

All these northern projects were controversial in Canada because of perceived threats to sovereignty: Canadians worried that they had too easily given "the Americans the keys to the national attic."[5] Wary that the Americans were making important decisions about Canadian territory by themselves, the Mackenzie King government even created a special commissioner to keep Ottawa in the loop. Though the Canadian government did not purchase the wasting assets mentioned above, it did later pay over $100 million for airfields, weather stations, and other facilities so that there could be no question about American ownership and Canadian sovereignty.[6]

The environmental impacts of building, operating, and abandoning the Canol undertaking, staging routes, and Alaskan highway may well be the most significant legacies of these projects. The social and environmental effects were enormous.[7] For all these projects, the builders had little to no experience dealing with the sensitive subarctic conditions such as muskeg and permafrost, and they lacked basic information about local ecosystems. Fish and wildlife near construction zones were extirpated, and oil spills befouled waterways. According to historians William Morrison and Kenneth Coates, "Some of the most dramatic damage involved the regions where the permafrost was found. Here, as elsewhere, the overburden was ripped off with bulldozers; when the warm season arrived, the permafrost melted, and the roadway turned to thick mud. Land wounded in this fashion took decades to heal, and building pipelines across it was a massive challenge."[8] Perhaps the greatest damage came from the many forest fires started by construction. Trees not burned by fires were cut down and the sawdust dumped into the water where it smothered aquatic life. The influx of soldiers brought new diseases to the First Nations and Inuit of the region, who were already suffering under the army of occupation.

WARTIME HYDRO

Hydro power was the source of about 90 percent of the electricity generated in Canada in the 1930s, led by Ontario and Quebec. Industry and manufacturing consumed most of the electricity, while household consumption (especially outside of urban areas) remained low, relative to the United States, until about the midpoint of the twentieth century. Indeed, the average Canadian household relied on wood and coal much longer than did Americans.[9] By 1941, oil represented 17 percent, coal 53 percent, and electricity 6 percent of total energy consumed in Canada.[10]

In the lead-up to the Second World War, Ontario accounted for about two-thirds of exported electricity stateside, with Quebec providing most of the remainder. Of course, Quebec, which had already become the major hydro power–producing province in terms of total wattage, was also selling electricity to Ontario, contributing to that province's ability to export to the United States. During the 1950s, Ontario's proportion of the power produced throughout the country would increase, while Quebec's decreased. Later in the Cold War, after completing various generating stations on northern rivers leading to James Bay, Quebec's proportion would rise, as would Manitoba's when it completed projects in the northern part of the province. British Columbia also became a bigger exporter after the signing of the Columbia River treaty.

Both the United States and Canada led the globe in expanding hydroelectric capacity during the Second World War.[11] That was without the benefit of the largest border hydro power projects they had been discussing for some time. As the previous chapter demonstrated, various power schemes in the Great Lakes basin had been at loggerheads throughout the 1930s. The election of a new government in Quebec, and the need for hydro power in light of the war, led Ontario premier Mitch Hepburn to do a volte-face. All sides involved sought ways to make a St Lawrence treaty happen, accelerating studies and negotiations.

The result was a 1941 executive agreement that echoed the 1932 Great Lakes Waterway Treaty. In March 1941, Canada and the United

States entered into the Great Lakes–St Lawrence Basin Agreement. This accord created the Great Lakes–St Lawrence Basin Commission to oversee construction of a twenty-seven-foot deep St Lawrence waterway from the Great Lakes to the Atlantic in conjunction with a hydro dam. There were also stipulations applying to water diversions and scenic quality at Niagara, limits on the Chicago diversion, and parameters for the other diversions – such as Ogoki and Long Lac – into the Great Lakes–St Lawrence watershed.

As an executive agreement, this only needed one-half of the US Senate's approval, rather than the two-thirds required for a treaty. But even this was asking too much. American entry into the Second World War changed priorities, and a number of powerful regional and economic interests in the United States continued to oppose such an undertaking. The executive agreement was introduced into the House of Representatives' Public Works Committee in June. Before a vote could take place, however, the attack on Pearl Harbor in December 1941 brought the United States into the war. The omnibus bill to which the agreement had been attached was indefinitely deferred, and it had virtually no hope of passage while the war persisted.

Nevertheless, several aspects of this Great Lakes–St Lawrence Basin Agreement did proceed under the aegis of the war emergency. Ontario built the Ogoki and Long Lac diversions into Lake Superior. These separate diversions are often grouped together because they both draw from the Albany River watershed. They both use various regulating works and dams, featuring hydroelectric stations, to divert water into Lake Superior water that would otherwise drain north to Hudson Bay. Though the United States had been reluctant to approve these in the past – which was necessary since they raised Lake Superior's water level and were therefore subject to US approval under the Boundary Waters Treaty – it now consented.

The Long Lac diversion was completed in 1941, the Ogoki diversion in 1943. The former diversion used an extensive network of dams and canals to reverse the flow of the Kenogami River south via Long Lac into the Aguasabon River. The enormous Ogoki diversion also employed large dams and canals to reverse the flow of a river, in this case the Ogoki River southward through Lake Nipigon. Long Lac diverted an average of 1,5000 cfs with Ogoki averaging 4,000 cfs. Together they are the largest diversion *into* the Great Lakes basin, putting in about as much water as the Chicago diversion takes out. While hydro power stations were built into these reversals, the main attraction of the Ogoki-Long Lac diversions was that the same amount of water they put into the Great Lakes system could be legally diverted by Ontario Hydro at their Niagara Falls power facilities.[12]

Article IX of the Great Lakes–St Lawrence Basin Agreement also provided for the construction of remedial works in the Niagara River and immediate diversions of 5,000 cfs per side. Even beyond this 1941 agreement, the two countries agreed to temporarily increase the limits on the amount of water diverted at Niagara Falls for wartime needs: 5,000 cfs more for the US (to be followed by another 7,500 cfs) and 3,000 cfs for Canada.[13] Further withdrawals were allowed during the war, rising to a total diversion of 54,000 cfs for Canada and 32,500 cfs for the United States. Canada and the US agreed to split the cost of constructing remedial works above the Falls, which Ontario Hydro and the US Army Corps of Engineers would build. This primarily involved a stone-filled weir – a submerged dam – about a mile above the Falls, which would raise the water level to facilitate greater diversions without an apparent loss of scenic beauty.[14] It cost just a little less than $800,000 and reportedly raised the water level right before the waterfall about one foot and doubled the flow over the American Falls.[15]

The United States considered authorizing the St Lawrence project as a war measure in conjunction with a simple exchange of notes with Canada. However, this ran afoul of a War Department policy that eschewed any Army Engineers projects that could not be completed before the end of 1943. Funds for the St Lawrence project were thus unavailable stateside. Several bills to approve the St Lawrence agreement were unsuccessfully introduced into Congress. The St Lawrence project seemed no closer to fruition than during the First World War. But many other bilateral projects, large and small, had been completed in the intervening years, and many would be completed in the early Cold War period.

COLD WAR INTEGRATION

The United States exited the Second World War as unquestionably the dominant world power. Canada was briefly a major power in the geopolitical vacuum created by the war, then moved into the self-designated role of a middle power based on the principle of functionalism (which held that Canada should have influence and a role in certain areas dictated by its special interests and capabilities). As much as Canadians may have psychologically retained ties to the British Empire, it was decimated and continued to decline, no longer able to be an effective counterweight to the expanding American empire nor the guarantor of Canadian security.[16] "Being next door to a superpower," historian Robert Bothwell writes, "inevitably muted Canada's pretensions to being a linchpin between the United States and Great Britain."[17]

By virtue of its geographic position and long border with the United States, Canada was very important to Washington from a security perspective. After all, an undefended Canada was an open door through which the Soviets could access the US heartland. Washington was going to defend its exposed flank, with or without cooperation. Cooperation sounded better to most Canadians and their leaders. The Liberal governments of King and St Laurent realized that Canadian economic and physical security required closer alignment with the United States. This generally occurred with public support, or at least not outright opposition, from most domestic quarters. Louis St Laurent, who replaced King as leader of the Liberal Party and prime minister in 1948, represented a continuation of many aspects of the King regime. But in the realm of foreign affairs, and Canada-US relations, the St Laurent era brought a much more internationalist and multilateralist stance.[18]

Canada was securely ensconced within the western alliance, opposite the Soviet Union and Communism. The United States, with firm Canadian support, was the unquestioned leader of the self-titled free world. This era has been called the "golden age" of Canadian external relations and the high point of the "special relationship" between Canada and the United States. Both adages involve hyperbole, even myth. Nevertheless, they do speak to Canada's relative importance on the world scene in this period and the level of integration and cooperation the two countries manifested. But it was not all smooth sailing: Canadian secretary of state Lester Pearson suggested in 1951 that "easy and automatic relations" between the two countries were a thing of the past.[19] Nevertheless, both countries were committed to liberal international markets and organizations, such as the new General Agreement on Tariffs and Trade (GATT), as well as western security through multilateral organizations such as the United Nations and then NATO, backed by the American nuclear arsenal (which in turn was partly backed by Canadian uranium and plutonium).

Multilateralism made sense for a country like Canada. But it is easy to exaggerate how much of this came from a penchant for cooperation – it was in Canada's self-interest to support these types of international organizations and systems since what benefitted the United States economically and in terms of collective security would likely redound to Canada. Multi-party forums and alliances were a way to ensure, from the Canadian perspective, that the Americans did not retreat into isolationism. At the same time, multilateral forums also provided counterweights and checks on American unilateralism.

The Canadian-American economic and natural resource integration that accelerated during the war generally continued and increased in the first few decades of the Cold War. The two nations were each other's largest trading partners and coordinated in many respects the defence of North America (often through the new Permanent Joint Board on Defence). The United States sought to acquire secure sources of the natural resources needed for national security and its global commitments. As the leader of the western alliance, the United States was spending massive amounts on armed forces, defence, foreign relations, and international aid. Canada was, too, relative to its size.

Integration of the northern North American economy would have been even greater had Mackenzie King not balked at full free trade as the Cold War heated up in the late 1940s. Nevertheless, the volume of trade between the two nations would grow to become the largest in the world, even as myriad tariffs, antidumping duties, and other barriers remained in effect.[20] Since Canada was integral to American natural security, both geographically and as a source of resources, the latter at times granted preferential economic treatment to the former.[21] Leaders in the two countries generally believed that helping private capital was in the public interest. In other words, what was good for a firm like INCO was good for Sudbury, or what benefitted Imperial Oil benefitted Alberta.

In these years, the US sought important natural resources, many of which Canada could supply in abundance. Canada was its largest supplier of nickel, aluminum, and wood products. The western Canadian discovery of large fossil fuel reserves in the late 1940s began a trajectory of energy integration – namely pipelines – that differed in some respects from electricity exports and imports, which also continued to expand. All these resources had both defence and domestic market uses. Given the roles of provinces and states in constitutionally controlling energy resources, subnational governance and subnational diplomacy throttled up after 1945. So too did frictions between the federal and subfederal governments.

Resources were developed at an accelerated pace and scale in the first few decades of the Cold War, motivated by the exigencies of the capitalist-communist conflict. In Canada, those resources were often exploited by American-owned branch plants; no other advanced industrial nation was subject to such high levels of foreign ownership. Canada did not necessarily have the expertise, capability, or capital to defend itself or successfully develop all its natural resources. American-owned investment in Canada reached $6.4 billion (Canadian dollars) by 1953; this figure had almost doubled by 1960. Teasing out all the various forms of direct and indirect American investment is well beyond my scope here. I will mostly restrict myself to describing broad patterns and government actions that intersect with the focus of this book, such as policies that directly affected or targeted foreign investment as well as some specific resource industries where foreign capital had a considerable stake. Regardless of whose capital financed the exploitation of these natural resources, the results were rarely ever ecologically sustainable.[22]

The 1952 Paley Commission Report, ordered by President Harry Truman in response to the Korean War, predicted that future US security and strategic needs would require access to many natural resources. A number of these could best be obtained from Canada. This was music to the ears of Canadian industrialists. The prospect of harvesting resources and sending them south, along with concomitant higher levels of economic activity and standards of living, was attractive for most Canadians. To others in the country, however, it was the tune of imperialism or extractive colonialism; the domestic development of those resources dangled the means to make Canada more fully self-sufficient and distant from economic reliance on the United States.

Still, we should not let the Paley report fool us into thinking that American policy towards Canadian resources during the early Cold War was consistent and coherent. It was generally reactive and ad hoc, often subject to circumstances and personalities. Officials in Washington, and politicians in Congress, held many different opinions about the degree to which the border should be erased when it came to stockpiling resources: some wanted to treat Canada almost as just another American state, and others believed Canada was just like any other foreign country.[23] Most did not think much about Canada at all or assumed Canadian compliance.

To the extent that there was resource colonialism or imperialism, it was more often American financial interests and capital taking advantage of free markets rather than the direct decisions of American policymakers. Granted, those free markets were ensured and directed by the postwar economic systems set up at the behest of the US government and American multinational corporations. At the very least, the US engaged in a version of "dollar diplomacy" whereby Washington encouraged and facilitated the investment of US capital in Canada. Moreover, as Lawrence Aronsen points out, it was frequently the case that Canadian authorities or industrialists pushed the US to buy their nation's resources rather than the US pressuring Canada to sell them.[24]

Buying into the American system was labelled by some critics as selling Canada out. Scholars who have applied the staples theory of Canadian development to the Cold War legitimately question the extent to which the interests of the state reflected those of the dominant economic groups that stood to benefit the most – and convinced average Canadians that integration was also in their best interests.[25] The answer was often in the affirmative. But Canada also did not have much choice, at least not if it wanted to find markets for its raw products, manufactured goods to import, and capital to invest. After two decades of depression and war, growth and prosperity were the top priorities across all levels of society. Furthermore, Canada generally made out quite well when it came to direct Canada-US economic relations.[26] Canada sometimes received special treatment relative to other countries. However, that was as much a result of pragmatic and strategic considerations as it was a special cultural or political affinity between the two countries.

Because of uranium's perceived scarcity in the 1940s, and the strategic nature of nuclear matters, this was one area where, for a time, the US did give Canada unique treatment. Between 1942 and 1952, the US received about 2,500 tons of uranium ore through Eldorado Canada, a crown corporation.[27] That uranium went towards the American nuclear program, as did the plutonium Canada provided.[28] The United States Atomic Energy Commission also assisted with Canada's construction of a uranium ore refinery at Port Hope on the north shore of Lake Ontario. Canadian titanium went into American jet engines – thus a refinery built at Sorel, Quebec, was backed by American financing. In 1950, about 90 percent of US supplies of nickel and asbestos, half its platinum, and 15 percent of its aluminum came from Canada.[29] For nickel, the US continued to be supplied primarily by Canada but sought to reduce its dependence on INCO by encouraging competition from other Canadian firms and sources.[30] In the 1960s, Saskatchewan emerged as the main supplier of potash. Semi-processed lumber and paper products continued to be important Canadian exports to the United States in the first decades of the Cold War, with mill expansion in places like Thorold, Ontario, and Baie-Comeau, Quebec. Most of this was harvested by Canadian subsidiaries of a handful of US firms regularly subject to anti-trust investigations.[31]

At the midpoint of the twentieth century, the United States produced about half the world's aluminum. Its voracious appetite for this lightweight metal meant that it also needed aluminum from Canada, which was responsible by 1953 for roughly 20 percent of global production – led by Alcan, the Canadian subsidiary of Alcoa. Alcan's new Kitimat operation in British Columbia was then the world's largest aluminum facility. Until the Second World War, when mines opened in northern Ontario, Canada had obtained most of its iron ore from the US (and bauxite, a necessary part of smelting aluminum), as well as coal, food, and agricultural products. Predictions that the Mesabi range in Minnesota was dwindling turned attention to the Ungava iron ores of northern Quebec and Labrador. Bringing these ores to the Great Lake steel mills would be a prime motivation for finally building the St Lawrence Seaway.

The Canadian government formed, in conjunction with private American capital, the Iron Ore Company of Canada. With the expansion of the industry, Canadian exports of iron ore to the US skyrocketed. So did steel. Canada became one of the world's major steel manufacturers, and half of its exports would regularly go to the United States. In 1948 Canada sent over three million gross tons south of the border; by 1976, that figure was above fifty million tons.[32] The extraction, smelting, and processing of all these minerals and resources had a tremendous environmental impact: surface and groundwater pollution from mining and refining, air pollution from smelting, and many toxic by-products. The past and present ecological health of Hamilton Harbour, the centre of Canadian steelmaking, is a case in point.

Much of that steel went towards defending the continent. The quickest route for Soviet bombers and missiles to reach North American cities was over the Canadian north. That reality led to joint efforts to install three different radar lines in northern Canada during the 1950s (and then through North American Air Defence Command, or NORAD, an extension of continental security arrangements). Radar stations could provide early warning of an incoming Soviet attack. The Pinetree Line included thirty-three stations arrayed across the country from Vancouver Island to the coast of Labrador, complemented by a similar line of radar monitoring facilities along the American border. The costs were shared by the United States and Canada, including American labour.[33]

Before the Pinetree Line was even finished, work was underway further north on the Mid-Canada Line (McGill Fence): almost a hundred, mostly unstaffed, radar stations around the mid-north along the fifty-fifth parallel. Concerned about sovereignty, Canada completed this line on its own. Before the Mid-Canada line was operational, Canada and the US agreed to establish the Distant Early Warning (DEW) line of radar stations along the Arctic Coast. Over three years, twenty-two radar stations were built between Alaska and Baffin Island. All costs (approximately $400 million) were underwritten by the United States, with the Canadians responsible for some of the sites. The two countries also set up a system of Joint Arctic Weather Stations.

Inherent in these projects was a mindset that the north was a hostile enemy that needed to be defeated. Though this desire to conquer nature led to many negative outcomes, implicit in it was a recognition that northern environments could be powerful actors that materially and conceptually shaped, constrained, and resisted human endeavours. The reality of cold weather and frozen ground circumscribed what was physically possible. The DEW line "likely did more to alter the lives of northern inhabitants than any other Cold War initiative."[34] The environmental impact lived on after these radar lines were obsolete. Decommissioning and clean-up started in the 1990s. But many components and parts were left to decay or be salvaged by local Inuit for building materials. Those included asbestos, PCB lubricants, and lead-based paint.

Nevertheless, those various radar lines exemplify the extent to which Canada-US integration, on many levels, had accelerated during the war – as well as the extent to which this integration had ramifications for North American environments. Under the spectre of war, first from Nazi Germany and Japan, then the Soviet Union, Canada had aligned itself politically, economically, and militarily with the United States. When it actually looked at Canada, the United States saw its northern neighbour as a storehouse of resources but also a potentially wide-open flank. The new national security realities meant mobilizing familiar resources for armaments, such as hydro power and aluminum, as well as developing previously ignored environments and resources, such as the north or uranium.

After the depredations of the Great Depression and Second World War, many Canadians were willing to ride American coattails, shelter under their nuclear umbrella, and send resources south if it meant prosperity. That affluence and protection then helped underwrite the expansion of the Canadian welfare state – meaning we can draw a direct line between that and resource diplomacy. The question was balancing prosperity with potential losses of sovereignty. Or, if not outright reductions of sovereignty, then further Americanization. By the mid-1950s, with many Canadians now able to take a high standard of living for granted, concern about American investment in Canada expressed itself in different ways. Was it better to be a prosperous and safe quasi-dependency, or vulnerable and poorer but more independent? Or somewhere in between? That seemed to be the perennial paradox. Granted, in the words of John Holmes, author of a classic book on Canadian foreign policy in this period, living with paradox when it came to the binational relationship was something that "Canadians do rather well."[35]

6

Water Megaprojects

In 1945, hydro power was still responsible for about 90 percent of the electricity generated in Canada. That country has historically been among the top, or at the top, of global per capita users of energy in general and electricity specifically. Today, Canada is one of the three largest producers of hydroelectricity in the world. The United States has remained a top-tier global hydro power player, though hydroelectricity has progressively become a smaller and smaller fraction of the total American energy portfolio.

The centrality of energy to Canadian development, and Canada-US relations, meant that it, and the landscapes and waterscapes from which energy was derived, became intertwined with national identity in ways that impacted geopolitics. The Canadian and the American states are deeply structured by the energy forms they rely upon. Hydroelectric, nuclear, and fossil fuel developments have been central to North American democracy, federalism, and nation-building. Canada's historical and contemporary reliance on hydro power enhanced democracy in certain ways, both tangible and symbolic, while undermining or negating it in other respects. Cheap power allowed for a growth-oriented society and an ideology of abundance in the two countries.

Most water resources that involved both countries were at least partly funnelled through the International Joint Commission. Between 1944 and 1979 this commission handled thirty-five references and twenty applications; a reversal compared to the first half of the century. Moreover, most of the twenty applications dealt with issues of relatively minor diplomatic importance compared to several references for large undertakings: namely, the St Lawrence, Niagara, and Columbia projects. As we have seen in previous chapters, the two countries had been trying to develop these water megaprojects in the decades before the war. In the first decades of the Cold War, all three would finally reach a diplomatic denouement and be built.

This chapter will focus primarily on those three water control projects. I do so not only because they were so important to Canada-US relations in the early Cold War, but also because they offer fine-grained opportunities to show how environmental and energy diplomacy worked in practice in this period. These were not just side issues shunted off to a few technocrats and low-level diplomats. Manipulating those large waterbodies across a border had wider security and political implications – consequently, high-level officials, including prime ministers and presidents, were involved, along with many technical experts. Moreover, since planning for all three of these megaprojects stretched back to at least the early twentieth century, engaging them in some detail offers an opportunity to compare not only the evolution of the technical schemes and aspirations but also the evolution of bilateral diplomacy over many decades.

NIAGARA FALLS

When we last left the Niagara Falls and St Lawrence deliberations during the Second World War, they were stalled by congressional inaction. Canada and the United States had authorized additional wartime diversions of water away from the Niagara River for power production. These diversions continued on a "temporary" basis after the war.[1] Officials began considering whether they should deal with the Niagara matter separately from the St Lawrence, as had been attempted in 1929.

Inter- and intragovernmental negotiations heated up. Details had to be worked out at various levels, including federal and provincial/state, as well as with the private companies and public utilities involved. Ontario Hydro, the US Federal Power Commission (FPC), the Power Authority of the State of New York (PASNY), and the Niagara Hudson Company had been working on a plan for the Niagara River that would preserve the Falls while providing maximum power production. It was clear that both Ontario Hydro and PASNY planned to build massive new hydroelectric generating facilities to absorb the enlarged diversions they anticipated.

This paradiplomacy, referring to the involvement of provinces and states in foreign affairs, helped produce the 1950 Niagara River

Diversion Treaty. That agreement called for remedial works and virtually equalized water diversions between the two countries while restricting the flow of water over Niagara Falls to no less than 100,000 cfs during daylight hours (of what they deemed the tourist season: 8 a.m. to 10 p.m. from April to mid-September, and from 8 a.m. to 8 p.m. during the fall), and no less than 50,000 cfs during the remainder of the year. This worked out to Canada and the United States together taking about half of the average flow (around 200,000 cfs) during tourist hours and three-quarters the rest of the time.[2]

The treaty managed to get through the US Senate, the usual stumbling block. But the Senate did attach a reservation that would come back to be a problem later on. Though this was a direct US-Canada treaty, per the Boundary Waters Treaty the IJC would still need to approve any engineering works. It therefore created boards to oversee the Niagara renovations. Studies showed that, without remedial works, the diversions authorized in the treaty would have a very negative impact on the scenic beauty of the area: the level of the Chippawa-Grass Island Pool above the Falls would drop by as much as four feet, exposing areas of the river bed, turning the American Falls into an unsightly spectacle and greatly reducing the appearance of the Horseshoe Falls, especially at the flanks.

The IJC's 1953 "Report to the Governments of the United States of America and Canada on Remedial Works Necessary to Preserve and Enhance the Scenic Beauty of the Niagara Falls and River" was based on model readings and the recommendations of the International Niagara Falls Engineering Board. The objectives remained basically the same as they had been in the 1920s: to ensure the appearance of an unbroken and satisfactory "curtain of water" over the precipice that had a pleasing consistency and colour, while allowing for maximum power diversions. The remedial works were also intended to reduce the spray and mist that visitors complained about.[3]

The report recommended a control structure, a gated dam, above the Falls, and excavations and crest fills on the flanks of the Horseshoe. It also called for the establishment of a new binational board to supervise the construction and operation of the proposed control structure, ensuring that the levels of the Niagara River and Lake Erie were not adversely affected. The two governments concurred with the report, and transborder construction started before the end of 1953, with most of the remedial works completed by 1958.

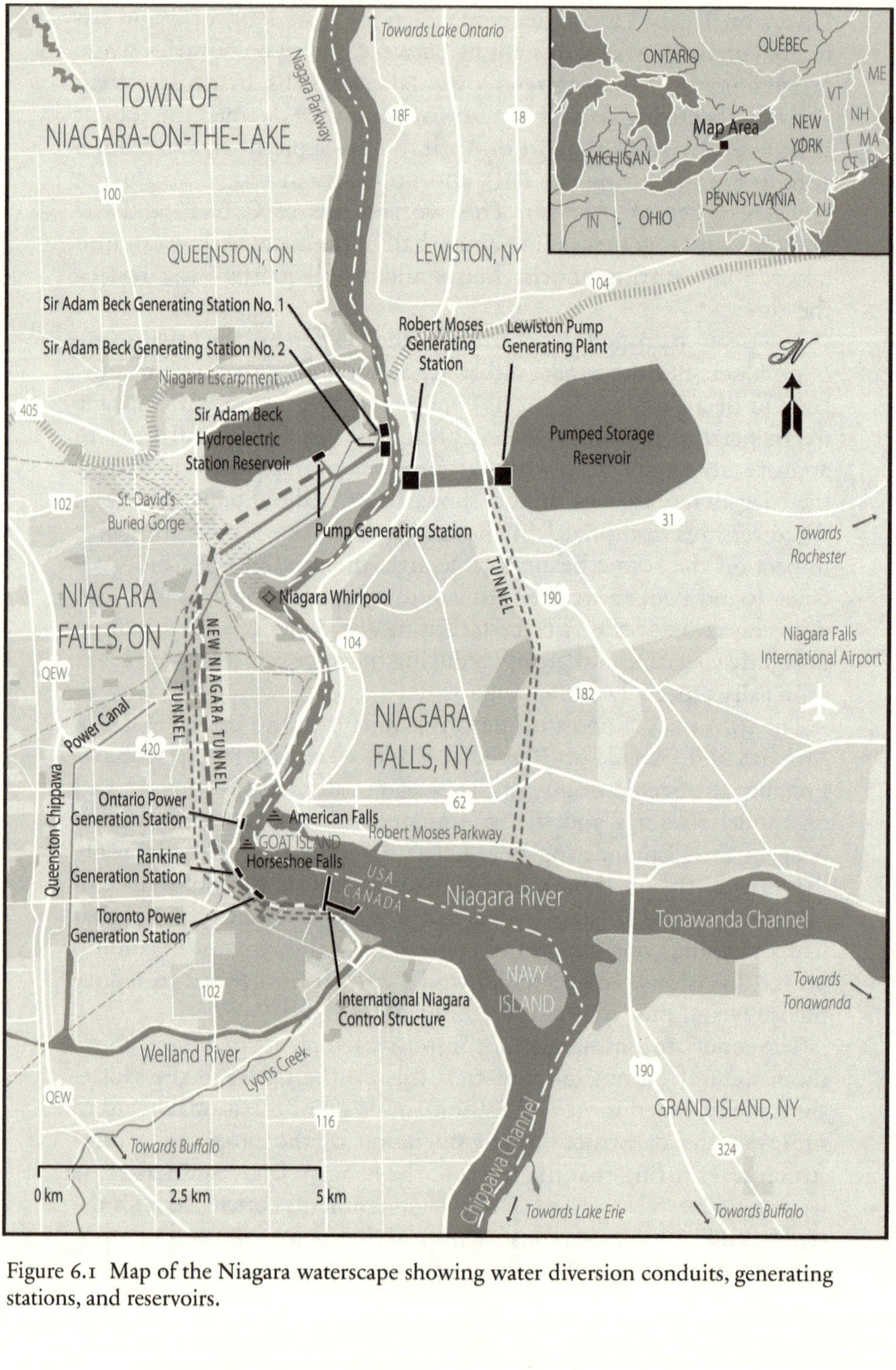

Figure 6.1 Map of the Niagara waterscape showing water diversion conduits, generating stations, and reservoirs.

The 1,550-foot control structure extended in a straight line from the Canadian shore, parallel to and about 225 feet downstream from the weir built in the 1940s, featuring sluices equipped with control gates. The purpose of this structure was to control water levels in the Chippawa-Grass Island Pool in order to adequately supply the water intakes for both countries and spread out the water to maintain the aesthetic appearance and prevent flows from concentrating in certain places where they caused more erosion damage. From the intakes, water went under the sister cities of Niagara Falls in huge tunnels and canals to the new hydro power stations that were built downstream. In 1954, Ontario Hydro opened Beck #2, beside its Queenston-Chippawa station (which was renamed Beck #1). In the early 1960s, the Power Authority of the State of New York unveiled its Robert Moses Generating Station across the gorge. This station generated 2.4 megawatts (MW), making it the largest hydro power station at the time in the western world.

The flanks of the Horseshoe Falls were designated for significant modification. About 100,000 cubic yards of rock were excavated to create a better flow distribution and an unbroken crestline at all times. To compensate for erosion, crest fills were undertaken, parts of which would be fenced and landscaped to provide prime public vantage points. All this meant that the transborder team of engineers and contractors had noticeably reshaped the Horseshoe Falls – the lip was shrunk by some 355 feet – to disguise the fact that most of the water was diverted for power production.

As detailed in the book *Fixing Niagara Falls*, the treaty and rhetoric surrounding it reveal how these North American governments conceptualized the natural environment and their ability to master it through technology.[4] Both governments – and their respective bureaucracies and experts – exhibited an infallible sense of their ability to manipulate and control riverine environments. Planners relied on high-precision scale models, which reputedly saved costs by avoiding mistakes. Government officials spoke of the cataract as if it were a water faucet to be turned on and off according to aesthetic whim. The majestic waterfall was reduced to cubic feet per second, a schematic or blueprint where the beauty for the engineers lay in their precision and control. The Horseshoe Falls was regulated and fine-tuned to produce maximum beauty and maximum power. While many technocratic assumptions and knowledge systems seamlessly crossed the border, the models and technical plans produced by each country's experts sometimes differed; expertise thus became a subject of diplomatic debate with the final results a compromise between competing political and engineering considerations.

However, if the power entities diverted all the allowable water from the Niagara River, which was expected with the completion of New York's Robert Moses generating station, the river above the Falls could not be maintained at the authorized levels during non-tourist times.[5] As a result, in 1961, Ontario Hydro and PASNY requested further remedial works in order to make greater use of their allotted water. They also asked to increase their diversions beyond those specified in the 1950 treaty. While the additional diversions were eventually nixed, in large part because of public opposition, some aspects of the proposed remedial works, such as an extension to the control structure, went ahead.

A campaign began in the mid-1960s to remove the "unsightly" rock talus that had formed at the base of the American Falls (with the result that the American Falls were half waterfall, half cascade) and led to calls for remedial action to prevent further erosion and rock slides, such as those that had occurred in 1931 and 1954.[6] Canada and the US asked the IJC to investigate and report on measures necessary to preserve or enhance the beauty of the American Falls, specifically in regard to the talus.[7] The US Army Corps of Engineers undertook a range of studies, and the American Falls were de-watered – actually turned off via a cofferdam – in 1969 so that the Corps of Engineers could perform tests and stabilize the rock face.

The Corps of Engineers concluded that the talus was a "dynamic part of the natural condition of the Falls and the process of erosion should not be interrupted."[8] Moreover, it found that removing the 280,000 cubic yards of talus might actually weaken the rock face. As a result of this recommendation, and likely in large part because of the estimated cost of approximately $26 million, the IJC decided in 1974 against further artificial measures to prevent rock erosion at the American Falls. To the experts, it seemed "wrong to make the Falls static and unnatural, like an artificial waterfall in a garden or a park," and the fundamental conclusion of the report was that "man should not interfere with the natural process."[9] This attitude represented a remarkable shift, compared to the high modernist remaking of the Horseshoe Falls in the 1950s. Nevertheless, they undertook a range of remedial works, essentially stapling together the face of the waterfall with anchors and cables while installing sensors and implementing other measures to guard public safety against rock slides (which included blasting off unstable parts of Terrapin Point in the early 1980s).

ST LAWRENCE SEAWAY AND POWER PROJECT

As I previously mentioned, the 1941 St Lawrence–Great Lakes agreement remained stalled in the US Congress after the Second World War. Both Canada and the United States had previously looked at constructing their own purely national waterways. Faced with Congress's continued resistance to a bilateral seaway, the government of Louis St Laurent began to seriously consider an all-Canadian seaway. Further study showed a unilateral waterway to be technically and financially feasible for Canada, although to be deep enough, it would have to be done in conjunction with a hydro power project, which legally needed to be a shared crossborder undertaking.[10]

In January 1952, Canada and the United States exchanged diplomatic notes in which the latter promised cooperation in moving the Canadian waterway and Ontario–New York power project forward. Washington had determined that the power developer on the American side, which would eventually prove to be the Power Authority of the State of New York, would need to be approved by the US Federal Power Commission. Both countries would also need to submit applications to the International Joint Commission. The IJC granted its approval for the joint power aspect of the St Lawrence project later that year. By this time, the St Laurent government had firmly decided to pursue an all-Canadian seaway. This idea struck a strong nationalist chord with the public for numerous reasons. For instance, St Lawrence nationalism cast it as a *Canadian* river and a fundamental part of the nation's historical development and identity. There was also environmental and technological nationalism: developing the hydro power and seaway was a means of demonstrating that Canada had arrived as a mature and independent nation capable of such grandiose undertakings and meeting its own energy needs.[11]

Nevertheless, before the power works could be constructed – keeping in mind that the deeper water created by a hydro dam was considered necessary to make a seaway cost-effective – the Federal Power Commission still needed to authorize the hydro development in the United States. Despite repeated promises, the Truman administration, along with parts of the US Congress, adopted different means of delaying. This included stalling the requisite power licence from the FPC despite the fact that the IJC had already sanctioned the development. This interference and linkage stemmed primarily from American resistance to sole Canadian control of a seaway because of national security concerns as well as economic and trade considerations. However, American interference was also partially the result of Washington's misreading of Canada's intentions to go it alone with the waterway. Ottawa had contributed to this situation by initially sending mixed messages about its commitment to proceed unilaterally, tentatively leaving the door open to American participation in the hopes that such a prospect would allow the hydro aspect to commence quickly.

The new president, General Dwight D. Eisenhower, remained undecided about the St Lawrence issue before and during his first months in office. However, in May 1953, the Eisenhower administration decided to seek American participation in a joint seaway, primarily for national security reasons. It continued to delay Canada's attempt to proceed alone. Even though Canada had declared the 1941 seaway agreement as having been superseded, it was technically possible for the US to pass legislation for a new agreement; Canada, however, was under no obligation to consider it. Even with the Korean War ongoing, the seaway had become the paramount issue in Canadian-American relations. An American official stated, with only a bit of hyperbole, that the St Lawrence issue could "probably injure our relations with Canada more than any other single incident which has occurred during this century."[12]

The US stalling continued until Congress finally sanctioned American participation in the seaway project by passing the Wiley-Dondero Act in January 1954. Despite strong Canadian dissatisfaction with the terms that this bill set for American involvement in the proposed development, Canada had kept silent and avoided informing Washington of these objections because of the apprehension that doing so would imply Canadian acceptance of the principle of a joint project. Additionally, as mentioned earlier, Canada had continued to leave the door open to the possibility of American involvement. Fearing the bilateral repercussions of ignoring the Eisenhower administration's request, the St Laurent cabinet allowed the American bill to be used as a basis for negotiations when the two sides met for high-level negotiations in the summer of 1954.

During the Canadian-American meetings in July and August, it became evident that there were several outstanding points of contention between the two countries: compensation or continuation of the Canadian fourteen-foot canals near Cornwall (which the power dam would flood out), the $15 million cost for works common to both the power and navigation aspects of the project, and the US refusal to guarantee Canada their desired navigation rights in American seaway facilities. Canada insisted on building the canal and lock in the International Rapids section at Iroquois Point on the Canadian side, which meant the Americans would only control the Barnhart locks (and thus only two of the seven locks in the St Lawrence River and two out of fifteen in the entire seaway when the Welland Canal is taken into account). This stemmed from a desire to appease Canadian public opinion since an all-Canadian plan was being abandoned. The St Laurent government further insisted that it be allowed to build the infrastructure near Cornwall for the remaining connecting links for a future all-Canadian seaway.

In the end, although several cabinet members and the Canadian government preferred a unilateral seaway, and even though the financial terms were far less attractive than the previous agreement (which gave Canada credit for the Welland Canal), Canada reluctantly agreed to a joint project. The agreement was formalized in an August 1954 exchange of notes, with the IJC given an oversight role for construction. The Chicago diversion again reared its head during final treaty negotiations, and again thereafter. The US Supreme Court had lowered the allowable volume of this diversion to 1,500 cfs, though Congress temporarily upped the volume on several occasions and twice legislated a permanent increase. Canada formally objected to the legislation, asserting treaty violations and the impact of hydro power production, navigation, and pollution dilution; President Eisenhower consequently vetoed the congressional legislation.

The Seaway and Power Project was cooperatively built between 1954 and 1959.[13] As a complex and highly integrated navigation, power, and water-control project, it had an enormous visual and sensory impact on the St Lawrence. It required a massive manipulation of the river. More than 210 million cubic yards of earth and rock were moved. Approximately 110 kilometres of channels and locks were built, and others rerouted, and even more kilometres of cofferdams and dykes were required. Three new dams were built in the international section of the upper St Lawrence: Moses-Saunders power dam, Long Sault control dam, and Iroquois control dam. These joined the already existing power dam at Beauharnois, though Quebec turned

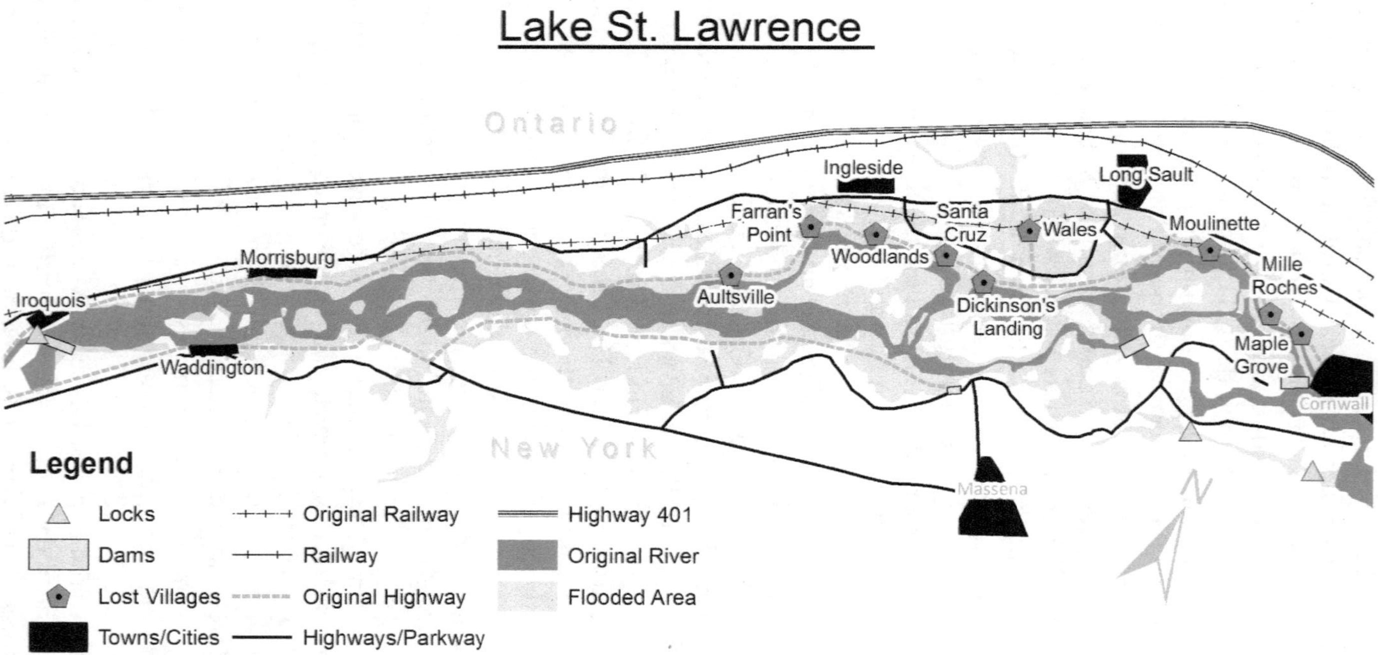

Figure 6.2 Map of Lake St Lawrence created by the St Lawrence Seaway and Power Project showing land, communities, and infrastructure flooded.

down a power dam across the Lachine Rapids at Montreal. The centrepiece is the Moses-Saunders powerhouse, a gravity power dam with thirty-two turbine/generator units capable of generating 1.8 megawatts, which is bisected by the border with the Canadian and American halves meeting in the middle.

As a result of the dams, Lake St Lawrence inundated some 40,000 acres of land. On each side of the border, numerous roads, bridges, railroad tracks, and power lines needed to be relocated because of the flooding, while traffic tunnels were constructed under the Beauharnois and Eisenhower locks, and bridge modifications were necessary in the Montreal area. New international bridges went up at two places over the St Lawrence between Ontario and New York, and another across the Niagara River in conjunction with the power developments there. These joined the already existing international transportation connections that had been established upstream in the 1920s and 1930s: the Peace Bridge at Buffalo, the Thousand Islands Bridge over the St Lawrence, the Detroit Tunnel under the eponymous river and the Ambassador Bridge over top of it, and the Blue Water Bridge joining Sarnia and Port Huron.

All this dislocation along the St Lawrence required what is perhaps the largest rehabilitation project in Canadian history – moving the towns, people, and infrastructure that would be under water. On the Canadian side, 225 farms, seven villages and three hamlets (referred to as the Lost Villages), part of an eighth village, eighteen cemeteries, around 1,000 cottages, and over one hundred kilometres of the main east-west highway and mainline railway were relocated. The project hit the Mohawk First Nations at Akwesasne and Kahnawake particularly hard. So as not to create navigation and other difficulties in the new lake, *everything* had to be moved, razed, or flattened, including trees and cemeteries. Ontario Hydro was primarily responsible for the Canadian share of this work and compensating relocated people, which required an enormous logistical and public relations effort. Many people chose to transport their houses via special vehicles to the new communities created west of Cornwall to house the displaced residents. Flooding out thousands of people was justified in the name of progress, as defined by the state, and for the benefit of the nation. The reorganization and resettlement of those affected by the power development would be for their own good as they would be placed in consolidated new towns – instead of scattered about in inefficient villages, hamlets, and farms – with modern living standards and services.

Implicit in the engineering and governmental planning was a high modernist hubris regarding their ability to control and remake the St Lawrence, one of the world's largest rivers based upon volume of flow, through various dams and other works. Like in the Niagara project, Canadian and American engineers collaborated to build a range of scale models of the river environment that they used for planning.[14]

The St Lawrence Seaway and Power Project was an impressive achievement from an engineering perspective, and there are undoubtedly many economic and energy benefits. Yet, the project has a decidedly mixed legacy. The hydroelectric generation aspect of the project generally fulfilled expectations and aided Ontario and New York's industrial expansion. But it also required the creation of Lake St Lawrence and the flooding of land and relocations, which dramatically impacted the adjacent communities. Much of the local anticipated long-term prosperity did not materialize. The cargo carried on the Seaway never came close to raising enough tolls to be self-amortizing.

The reconfiguration of the local ecosystem by the St Lawrence project disrupted aquatic life, which included circumscribing the mobility of certain species. Eels, which once constituted an appreciable percentage of the fish biomass of the Lake Ontario-St Lawrence watershed, could barely traverse the dam-blocked river. Movement was not the only negative impact on fish, for the extensive dredging and digging changed spawning and feeding grounds. Natural habitats were radically altered, and the water was certainly more polluted from construction. Beyond the initial enormous ecological impact of the construction phase, other long-term environmental concerns have arisen. There were concerns about the attempts to control ice formation and extend the shipping season.[15] The unnatural peaking and ponding – the controlled increase and decrease of the water levels via the dams – are environmentally problematic. All the submerged organic and plant matter slowly leached methane, a potent greenhouse gas. Some averred that the new lake changed the local climate. Invasive species were another long-term result of the Seaway, for it offered a water freeway for foreign intruders to infiltrate the Great Lakes basin (new non-natives enabled by the Seaway's opening will be addressed in chapter 8).

COLUMBIA BASIN

The headwaters of the Columbia River, the fourth largest on the continent, are in British Columbia. It flows north from its source before turning south to the United States, where its volume increases as it runs through Washington State, serving as the border with Oregon until it debouches into the Pacific Ocean. Unlike the St Lawrence and Niagara Rivers, the Columbia is mountain-fed and fluctuates enormously with the seasons – the flow at the flood stage has been one hundred times greater than the minimum flow. Bilateral discussions to modify the Columbia River basin also preceded the Second World War. Like the St Lawrence and the Niagara, it took decades of diplomatic negotiations before a Columbia treaty came to pass. And once it was achieved, like those other two water megaprojects, it produced a great deal of electricity and ecological damage.[16]

While inland navigation was not nearly as significant in the Columbia basin as on the St Lawrence, the total hydro power potential was even greater because of the elevation changes. Plus, flood control and irrigation were important considerations. The various tributaries – Snake, Kootenay, Pend d'Oreille – are noteworthy rivers in their own right. The United States had begun damming its stretch of the Columbia between the world wars: two of the largest dams in the world, the Bonneville and the Grand Coulee, were put astride the main stem. The Canadian side, by contrast, was relatively undeveloped.

US officials realized that dams and reservoirs to store floodwaters and release them seasonally would average out the annual flow. The US Army Corps of Engineers undertook studies to determine how to make this happen. Near the end of the Second World War, the Canadian government concurred with an American proposal to ask the IJC to determine how greater use could be made of the Columbia River. The IJC subsequently established the International Columbia River Engineering Board. Little was known about the hydrology of the Canadian portion of the basin and ascertaining baseline information took up a good deal of time. By 1949, the Army Corps of Engineers had finished its comprehensive report on the American Columbia basin. The previous year, catastrophic flooding in the lower Columbia underlined the benefits of flood control.

The populist, right-wing Social Credit premier of British Columbia, W.A.C. Bennett, had other ideas. He seized on a proposal made by the Kaiser Aluminum and Chemical Corporation, an American company, to develop a large storage dam in the Arrow Lakes. In return for a fifty-year water licence, Kaiser would build the dam, pay provincial taxes and water licence fees, and return to British Columbia 20 percent of the electricity generated downstream. But, as we have seen, largely because of its Niagara experience the federal government had long prohibited the firm export of bulk electricity. Plus, the Kaiser plan would also preclude the types of development under study by the federal governments and the IJC. Ottawa also suspected that the deal was too favorable to the American company. The St Laurent government therefore passed the International Rivers Improvement Act in 1955. This stipulated that any dam on an international river, such as the Columbia, required a federal licence.

With Bennett's scheme seemingly thwarted, in spring 1956 the Canadian and American governments began direct negotiations on the Columbia issue. Soon afterward, the United States agreed on a method of proceeding. This included US acceptance of the principle of downstream benefits. But there were competing ideas about how to best use the waters of the Columbia and how to calculate downstream benefits. For example, General A.G.L. McNaughton, the chairman of the Canadian section of the IJC, favoured an all-Canadian plan in which the Kootenay River would be diverted into the Columbia in Canadian territory for the purpose of power production in British Columbia. This would involve extensive flooding in the Kootenay Valley, where several small hydro power dams had already been built.[17] McNaughton also had a plan for diverting water from the Columbia into the Fraser River for power development on that waterway – which would derail American hydroelectric plans for the lower Columbia. This Canada-first Columbia plan seemed to be inspired by McNaughton's experiences pushing for an all-Canadian St Lawrence Seaway. Canadian nationalists lined up behind McNaughton's proposals, and matters seemed at an impasse.[18]

After the Diefenbaker Progressive Conservatives replaced the Louis St Laurent Liberals, they continued negotiations with the United States. The International Joint Commission adopted the principle that Canada could claim half the power and flood control benefits conferred on downstream American interests by storage in Canada. In January 1959, both national governments asked the IJC for recommendations, and the International Columbia River Engineering Board put forward three plans to control flooding and harness the hydro potential. Two of these proposed diverting the headwaters of the Kootenay River north into the Columbia (the Copper Creek diversion and the Dorr diversion), and a third instead proposed constructing the Libby dam further south on the Kootenay River with no diversion of its waters into the Columbia. All three schemes envisioned a dam below the southern tip of the Arrow Lakes. However, the engineering board suggested that two very different dams were possible, a "High Arrow" dam (which would result in flooding around the Arrow Lakes) and a "Low Arrow," which would lead to far less environmental disruption around the lakes.[19]

The IJC had not indicated which of the options was preferable – that was up to the treaty negotiators to decide. They agreed to a plan that featured the construction of the Libby dam in the US (but no diversion of the Kootenay) as well as three dams in Canada, at Mica, Duncan Lake, and a high dam for the Arrow Lakes. According to a mutually agreeable formula, Canada was to be paid cash for the flood control benefits and enhanced hydro power generation in the United States. It would likewise receive half the extra US electricity that the control dams would now permit because of the steadier flow. The Columbia River treaty, incorporating this scheme, was signed in January 1961.[20]

The treaty signing was rushed so that it could be completed before Eisenhower left office. Perhaps for this reason, the federal government mistakenly believed that Premier Bennett agreed with the terms. But that was not the case. Bennett was opposed mainly because he thought it would hinder the development of other plans he had in mind, and the premier was peeved about how the federal government had treated him. In a reversal of the frequent political stumbling block for Canada-US environmental agreements, the US Congress ratified the accord, while the Canadians delayed sending it to Parliament.

Bennett pursued a "two rivers" strategy that involved the development of the Columbia River in order to fund the development of the Peace River. After the derailment of the Kaiser plan, Swedish industrialist Axel Wenner-Gren had signed a preliminary agreement for a project in the northern part of the province, with a Peace River hydro development the centrepiece. Bennett announced in August 1961 that the province would take over Wenner-Gren's Peace company by nationalizing the private utility BC Electric. In its place, a public utility, the BC Hydro and Power Commission, was created. British Columbia then insisted it sell its downstream benefit under the Columbia treaty to the US, rather than repatriate the power, to fund the Peace project. But that contravened the federal government's policy against long-term power exports (which, as of 1959, was regulated by the National Energy Board, as the next chapter discusses).

Columbia progress was again at an impasse. After Pearson's Liberals won the 1963 election, they quickly reached an understanding with British Columbia about Canadian terms for the sale of the downstream Columbia power benefits to the American power utilities. That included allowing long-term energy exports. Instead of a new treaty, the Pearson government negotiated a 1964 protocol to alter the 1961 pact. This protocol spelled out several changes in financing and operations as well as clauses clarifying diversion rights. Under the protocol, Canada received half of the power made possible downstream in the United States but sold it off for the first thirty years for $254 million (passing that on to BC) and received another $64 million for the next sixty years of flood control benefits. The dam locations, and their sequence and schedule of development, remained as they were in the 1961 treaty. The river control provided by the treaty dams also enabled BC to later build the Revelstoke and Mica dams.

To its proponents, "the Columbia River Treaty serves as one of the most successful examples of a transboundary water treaty. It is lauded for equitably sharing the benefits of an international river system and for its durability and flexibility, allowing for significant flood control and hydroelectric development."[21] But in a book titled *Continental Waterboy*, published in 1970, Donald Waterfield called the Columbia agreement a "pusillanimous surrender" on Canada's part.[22] Many others agreed that the treaty was a sellout to the Yankees.

Moreover, after these dams were built a range of environmental and social consequences became apparent. Like other huge infrastructure projects, if the true costs to the impacted communities and local environments had been factored in, such plans likely would not have passed cost-benefit analyses. Reflecting the progress mindset of the era, officials did not effectively consult with the First Nations inhabitants or other area residents. The dam near Castlegar raised water levels by thirty-six feet, turning the Arrow Lakes into a massive reservoir. The rising waters would flood over 25,000 acres of arable land and fourteen lakeshore communities, displacing approximately 2,000 people.

The damming of rivers in the Columbia basin had deleterious repercussions along many of the same lines as the St Lawrence and Niagara projects: damage to aquatic species, pollution, erosion, and methane releases. As we have seen when discussing fish diplomacy, this region hosts perhaps the richest salmon stocks in the world. All the Columbia River dams served as mostly impassible barriers for these migratory fish (fish ladders were sometimes installed but were generally ineffective). Besides, their spawning grounds were often already obliterated. The lifeways of many different Pacific Northwest Indigenous groups, which revolved around fish, were severely disrupted by this type of ecological damage.

In addition to dams built on the mainstem of the Columbia River, other dams were built on its tributaries. On the Pend d'Oreille–Flathead River system, the US had built one dam before the war and several others in the 1950s and 1960s. Cominco, the Canadian mining-smelting conglomerate that ran the Trail smelter, wanted to build another dam on the Pend d'Oreille River, close to its junction with the Columbia and downstream from Trail, adjacent to the American border. In 1952 the IJC gave its approval, and the station was soon finished. In 1951, the US applied to the IJC to build the Libby dam on the Kootenay River, with a reservoir that would extend forty miles into Canada. The United States intended to offer monetary compensation for flooded lands but did not want to share the project benefits. The Libby dam proposal was withdrawn in 1953, reintroduced in 1954, and then the dam was built as part of the larger Columbia River project.

The Ross dam affair on the Skagit River was also contentious and protracted. Seattle City and Light originally built this dam in the 1930s. Then it proposed raising the structure. The initial dam had inundated a bit of Canadian land, but a High Ross dam would cause a much greater deal of flooding over the border. The IJC approved the application in 1942, subject to compensation and provided that the water level at the international boundary was not raised until there was a binding agreement between the City of Seattle and BC providing for indemnification for injury to the latter. BC passed legislation in 1947 authorizing the flooding. The dam was raised in 1953. This 540-foot-tall dam flooded 12,000 acres in Washington State, and another 550 acres in British Columbia. However, when Bennett came to power, his government found the compensation for land and property that would be flooded in their province insufficient. Seattle and the US section of the IJC tried to compel BC to accept the existing compensation arrangement. Further talks were postponed until the Columbia River Treaty was dispensed with, and from 1954 to 1966, Seattle City and Light and the Canadian province entered into annual agreements to authorize the flooding that had already occurred.[23] A more permanent resolution would have to wait until the 1980s (see chapter 9).

Several other water issues in the west also arose in the postwar period. The two countries had asked the IJC to examine the use and apportionment of the waters of the Waterton and Belly Rivers in the late 1940s. This stemmed from Alberta's plans to utilize most of the water from these rivers, both of which start in Montana and then join the Oldman River in Canada, for irrigation. But the two sides of the IJC were unable to agree, submitting conflicting national reports. Alberta went ahead with its irrigation plans. Sage Creek, which went in the opposite direction of the Waterton and Belly Rivers, also stalemated. In response to American complaints about water usage in Canada, the IJC recommended a formal apportionment of the stream along with a dam. But neither country thought the potential cost was warranted. Meanwhile, the Milk–St Mary water allocation continued to fester.

The St Lawrence, Niagara, and Columbia developments all involved drawn-out political and diplomatic debates. At times, the St Lawrence and Columbia were the most vexing issues in the bilateral relationship, even overshadowing discord about the Korean War. Though Canada and the US equally saw these waterbodies as resources to be controlled and harnessed, they also conceptualized them quite differently, especially when it came to the links between national identity and environments. Canada's approach to engineering transborder waters, for instance, was inextricably bound up in unique forms of hydraulic nationalism. This was often in opposition to what was perceived as American imperialism. Hydroelectricity was seen as a means of delivering Canada from its "hewer of wood servitude to American industry and its bondage to American coal."[24] That is, more domestic hydro power meant less reliance on American fossil fuels. Canadian hydro power development was therefore part and parcel of enhancing autonomy and natural security.

At the same time, self-interest, practicality, and political necessity compelled Canada to continue tying itself energy-wise to the United States. Infrastructure bound Canada and the United States together physically when it came to energy trade. This was certainly the case

Table 6.1
Canadian annual exports of electricity to the United States, 1940–58 (volume in millions of kilowatt hours).

Year	*From Ontario*	*From Quebec*	*From other provinces*	*Total Canada*	*Exports as % of Canadian production*
1940	1,471	637	28	2,136	7.1
1941	1,690	638	32	2,360	7.1
1942	1,767	655	32	2,454	6.6
1943	1,860	646	39	2,545	6.3
1944	1,919	629	37	2,585	6.4
1945	1,976	617	49	2,642	6.6
1946	1,824	618	40	2,482	5.9
1947	1,386	639	41	2,066	4.8
1948	1,041	653	49	1,743	4.1
1949	966	651	140	1,757	4.0
1950	1,046	642	238	1,926	4.0
1951	1,491	647	238	2,376	4.3
1952	1,577	665	251	2,493	4.2
1953	1,399	678	347	2,424	3.9
1954	1,847	659	212	2,718	4.1
1955	3,588	666	179	4,433	6.1
1956	4,384	675	45	5,104	5.8
1957	4,222	549	59	4,380	5.3
1958	3,404	526	145	4,075	4.2

Source: A.E.D Grauer, "The Export of Electricity from Canada," in R.M. Clark, ed., *Canadian Issues: Essays in Honour of Henry F. Angus* (Toronto: University of Toronto Press, 1961), 275.

for transmission lines and fossil fuel pipelines, as we will soon see. During the latter half of the Cold War, fossil fuel and hydro power exports would continue apace, and the former would become more important than the latter. But most of these fossil fuels did not come from the border area. Transborder diplomacy about border waters, for its part, would shift towards environmental protection in the 1970s.

Looking back on the first century after Canadian Confederation, the history of Canada-US hydroelectricity geopolitics and governance shows that the earliest large Canadian hydro power projects were built on, or planned for, border waters which, after the enactment of the Boundary Waters Treaty, legally required formal transnational coordination. Federal governments or agencies established some export policies, but the politics of subnational governments, special interests, and specific power projects played an equally decisive role in shaping the power trade. The result was a constantly evolving political and regulatory context, albeit one which trended towards cooperation and integration and, as we will later see, towards a reduced role for government regulation.

When completed, these hydro power megaprojects were hybrid envirotechnical systems that blended the natural and the artificial into new forms of infrastructure. The reconfigured Niagara Falls was perhaps the most striking example of this. A flowing façade fronted a waterfall much diminished in size and volume, its appearance and contours carefully choreographed in order to maximize water diversions for energy without sacrificing the aesthetic appeal for tourists. Turbulent stretches of the St Lawrence and Columbia, two of the largest rivers on the continent, were transformed into placid lakes-cum-reservoirs. By disguising the ecological aspects underpinning it, envirotechnical infrastructure denatured networked energy and democratic politics while simultaneously naturalizing expectations of persistent technological and economic growth.

7

Fossil Fuels after 1945

During the early Cold War period, Canada joined the United States as a principal producer of fossil fuels, which are formed by hydrocarbons. The discovery and exploitation of vast oil and gas deposits in Canada proved very consequential for modern Canadian-American relations. To be sure, the mobilization of these energy sources is one of the most important framers of modern Canadian politics. The 1950s and 1960s, the decades covered in this chapter, are sometimes labelled as a period of informal continentalism for hydrocarbon resources since Canada and the United States loosely coordinated the fossil fuel trade, doing so through a series of ad hoc decisions and preferences rather than permanent agreements. More entrenched and permanent exchange patterns would not become the norm until later in the twentieth century.

It bears pointing out that the policy regime for Canadian hydrocarbon exports that developed after the Second World War was conditioned by the crossborder hydroelectricity trade.[1] Concerns about long-term contracts involving electricity that could not be repatriated on demand had shaped the Fluid and Electricity Exportation Act, in turn influencing approaches to exporting fossil fuels. The material properties of hydroelectricity, water and electricity in particular, informed how energy was applied and governed; the same is true of the various fossil fuels. While oil, natural gas, and coal are all fossil fuels, they have different characteristics. Coal is a combustible rock, though types of oil and gas can be derived from it. By the mid-twentieth century, coal's primary uses in North America included heating, industrial applications such as steelmaking, and electricity generation. Oil is a viscous liquid, and natural gas is a lightweight, colorless, odorless gas (mostly methane), though it can be cooled and liquified for transport (known as liquid natural gas, or LNG). Oil and natural gas are variously used for heating, transportation, and electricity generation. Oil powers vehicular transportation; natural gas also powers vehicles, though it is not frequently used this way. Both are feedstocks to produce plastics, petrochemicals, and myriad other synthetic products. The chief application of natural gas in North America is for heating buildings and power generation. As with other energy forms, the various properties of fossil fuels both enabled and constrained technical options for their procurement, production, and use, which in turn altered the viable economic and political choices.

PIPELINES

Before the Second World War, Canada was a minor player in oil and natural gas. Oil wells had been drilled in southwestern Ontario around the time of Confederation, and refineries sprung up to process the different products derived from petroleum, such as kerosene. Some of the products were exported to Britain and the United States. Imperial Oil was one of the domestic Canadian producers. In 1897 it was bought by Standard Oil of New Jersey which soon consolidated the Ontario industry and expanded to other parts of the country. Refining was concentrated at Sarnia, where it could easily receive crude imports from the United States. Natural gas deposits had also been discovered in southern Ontario. During the 1890s, pipelines carried some of this gas to Detroit and Buffalo. However, these deposits were soon exhausted, and these first Canadian exports ceased for the next half-century, aside of small amounts of natural gas exported to Buffalo.[2]

Most fossil fuel exports in the first half of the twentieth century went in a northward direction. In 1941, the Portland-Montreal oil pipeline was completed; it transported primarily non-North American oil from Maine to Quebec. Pipelines were subject to international and domestic debates, as well as regulatory hearings about issues such as routes and the volumes that they could carry. The 1938 Natural Gas Act in the United States had given the Federal Power Commission responsibility for approving gas exports. In Canada, the Fluid and Electricity Export Act of 1907 underwent minor modifications in 1925 and 1955. In 1949 Ottawa passed the Pipelines Act which affirmed federal control over interprovincial and international oil and gas pipelines and exports. The Fluid and Electricity Export Act was superseded by the National Energy Board (NEB) in 1959. The establishment of the National Energy Board signalled the federal government's recognition that fossil fuels would likely overtake electricity as Canada's main form of energy export. Thus, this board was given broad powers concerning oil, natural gas, and electricity. The National Energy Board was responsible for the licensing of any energy forms sent across the border, as well as related infrastructure such as transmission lines and pipelines.[3] Any pipelines built in Canada also needed to be chartered by Parliament.

The creation of the National Energy Board reflected the fact that, by the 1950s, Canada was producing enough fossil fuels to export significant volumes. Many new oil and natural gas pipelines came to link Canadian and US markets.[4] A dual pipeline was built under the Detroit River to send US natural gas to Ontario. The Niagara River region was another natural gas gateway. Small amounts were exported between Montana and Alberta. In 1953, Canada gave its permission to an American pipeline that goes from Haines to Fairbanks, both in Alaska, but passes through a few hundred miles of Canadian territory along the way.

There were also talks of a pipeline to move gas from Alberta to Ontario, taking a shortcut through US territory. Different companies made different proposals, and a forced merger was brokered by C.D. Howe to build what came to be called the TransCanada Pipeline. This pipeline could run partly through the US since this would be shorter and cheaper. For nation-building reasons, and perhaps to help his own northwestern Ontario riding, Howe (and many Canadians) wanted the pipeline to be purely in Canada. This was part of a nationalist desire to link Canada in an east-west fashion, blunting the north-south continental pull, through megaprojects such as the TransCanada highway and the St Lawrence Seaway.

The American-born Howe was likely the most powerful figure in the St Laurent government. Dubbed the "minister of everything," he was a leading figure in Canadian-American relations and had extensive government and business ties in the United States. There are different schools of thought on Howe (and the Liberals in general): on the one hand, he is seen as a sell-out to the United States who nurtured Canadian-American integration. On the other hand, by the 1950s Howe seemed like a nationalist resisting further integration with the US (he was a chief proponent of an all-Canadian St

Lawrence Seaway). The answer may be that Howe was a political and economic pragmatist who believed that was good for industry and business was good for the country.

The TransCanada Pipelines company was having problems financing the all-Canadian section of the pipeline, which would go north of Lake Superior through the rocky Canadian shield. The Liberal government decided to advance a loan to cover up to 90 percent of the $80 million price for the western portion of the line from Winnipeg to Sudbury. But the company building the pipeline was half-owned by American interests. That engendered the Great Pipeline Debate of 1956 in the House of Commons. With a seasonal construction deadline looming – work needed to start before winter or wait until the following year – the Liberal government used a closure motion to end a parliamentary filibuster, causing an uproar. Nevertheless, the bill to help finance the company passed, and the pipeline was completed from Saskatchewan to Montreal by 1958. Soon after, TransCanada Pipelines became principally Canadian owned.

Other natural gas lines followed that were much less politically controversial. In 1957, the Westcoast Energy Inc system began delivering natural gas from northeastern British Columbia to the lower mainland and United States markets.[5] The Midwestern Gas Transmission Company proposed a pipeline connecting with the new TransCanada line in Manitoba, bringing gas to the US Midwest.[6] Its first attempt was denied, but then in 1960 it secured permission for a line to central Wisconsin. The Great Lakes Pipeline was built from the same Manitoba/Minnesota border junction, but by different private interests. Another pipeline opened in 1961 to bring gas from Alberta, crossing the international border in eastern British Columbia at Kingsgate. The NEB and FPC approved a pipeline to take natural gas from TransCanada's pipeline and send it to the Massena-Ogdensburg area by way of Cornwall. This short pipeline opened in the early 1960s, and by 1966 its licence allowed imports of 23,000 mcf per day. TransCanada also became a supplier for Vermont via a ten-inch pipeline that ran to Burlington.

Turning to oil, before 1945 almost all of this hydrocarbon consumed in Canada was imported from the United States. In the second half of the twentieth century, that trend would change. Both countries left the development of the oil sector mostly in private hands with some governmental oversight and involvement. As the western Canadian oil industry developed after 1945, the Canadian and Albertan govern-

Table 7.1
Canadian production and trade in crude petroleum, 1946–76 (quantities in thousands of barrels)

Year	*Production*	*Imports*	*Exports*	*Consumption*
1946	7,586	63,407	0	70,993
1948	12,287	75,559	1	87,845
1950	29,044	78,660	0	107,704
1952	61,237	81,200	1,424	141,013
1954	96,080	78,772	2,345	172,508
1956	171,981	106,470	42,907	235,543
1958	165,496	104,039	31,679	237,856
1960	189,534	125,560	42,235	272,859
1962	243,238	135,365	86,128	292,475
1964	274,479	143,835	101,718	316,596
1966	319,568	158,544	126,799	351,313
1968	378,403	178,415	169,230	387,588
1970	459,977	208,363	244,466	423,874
1972	560,468	288,781	348,431	500,818
1974	513,412	299,239	330,583	482,068
1976	479,397	265,743	174,291	570,859

Source: Statistics Canada.

ments actively encouraged American investment since US firms had the experience and capability Canadian companies lacked. American finance could also help, somewhat paradoxically, to make Canada less dependent on American fuels. But this also meant that foreign multinationals, which vertically integrated most of the oil industry, were able to influence Canadian energy policy.[7] The American-owned Imperial Oil remained the major oil company in Canada.[8]

American markets and companies shaped Canadian oil policy more than American officials or policymakers. Though American firms quickly swept into the prairie oil fields, the American government was not immediately overjoyed about the fossil fuel discoveries in the Canadian west; in the late 1940s, Washington believed it still had access to ample domestic oil reserves. US officials were concerned that Canadian oil imports might affect American producers or harm American-Venezuelan oil relations.[9] On the other hand, the 1952 Paley Report indicated that the US needed to secure greater supplies of oil and gas from reliable sources. American companies, therefore, continued investing heavily in the exploration and development of Canada's oil and gas resources.

Table 7.2
Canadian production and trade in crude natural gas, 1946–76 (quantities in millions of cubic feet)

Year	*Production*	*Imports*	*Exports*	*Consumption*
1946	47,900	836	0	48,268
1948	58,603	404	0	59,007
1950	67,822	6,433	0	71,076
1952	88,686	9,518	8,145	86,253
1954	120,775	12,482	7,148	119,823
1956	169,153	16,850	9,642	175,205
1958	337,804	34,716	86,972	288,548
1960	522,972	5,571	91,043	437,497
1962	775,887	5,575	319,566	461,896
1964	944,280	8,046	404,144	548,182
1966	1,106,643	43,551	426,224	723,969
1968	1,383,872	88,228	598,144	873,956
1970	1,851,095	11,878	768,113	1,094,860
1972	2,298,981	15,759	1,007,054	1,307,686
1974	2,420,138	9,228	960,713	1,468,653
1976	2,458,668	9,855	954,051	1,513,572

Source: Statistics Canada.

Two major liquid hydrocarbon pipelines to take Canadian oil south were built. The TransMountain Pipeline Company completed its pipeline from Edmonton to Vancouver in 1953 and then extended it into Washington State. The Interprovincial pipeline, constructed by the Interprovincial Pipe Line Company (IPL), carried oil from Edmonton to the head of the Great Lakes at Superior, Wisconsin. This line was completed in 1950, and in 1968 was replaced by Line 3. IPL itself was a subsidiary of Imperial Oil of Canada, which meant that it was controlled by the US-owned Standard Oil; it would remain that way until 1998 when IPL became Enbridge and Canadian owned. Initially, tankers carried crude from Superior to Sarnia during the ice-free shipping season, but another pipeline reached Sarnia in 1953 via Michigan, crossing that state's Straits of Mackinac. Before the decade's end the line reached to Toronto. In the 1960s, IPL built lines across the Niagara River to Buffalo, added to the loop network that passed through the greater Chicago area, and with financing from the federal government connected Line 9 to Montreal in the 1970s.

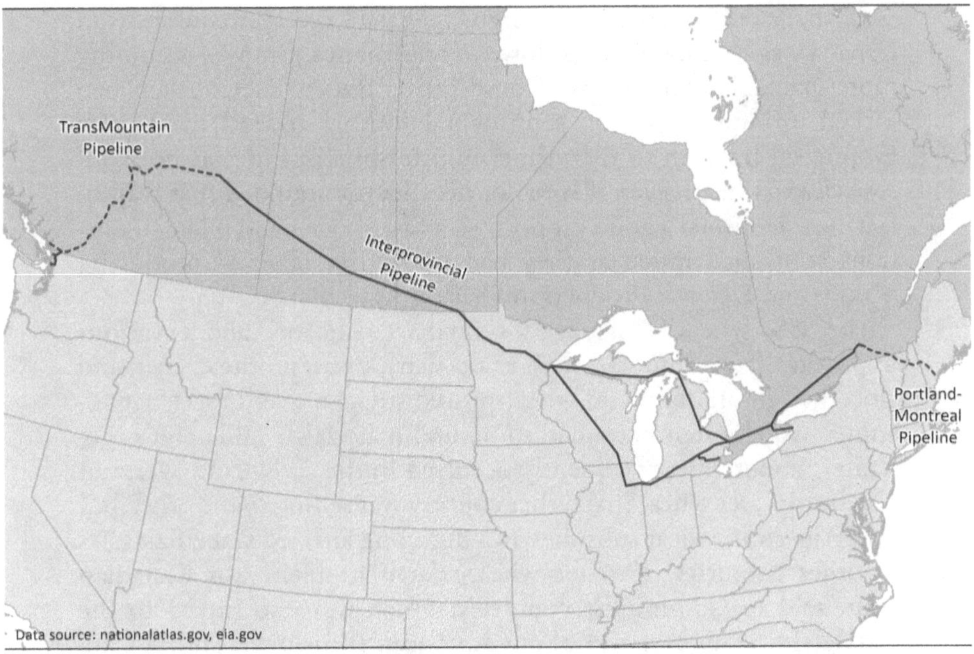

Figure 7.1 Crossborder oil pipeline network built prior to 1970.

OIL DIPLOMACY

The US kept high tariffs on foreign oil imports to protect its own producers. Ottawa asked for preferential treatment for Canadian oil – and eventually got it. The Voluntary Oil Import Program (VOIP) had initially not exempted Canada. But a month and a half later, Eisenhower amended VOIP to exclude oil arriving "overland" – that is, by pipeline, truck, or rail. Almost all oil sent from Canada to US arrived this way. Eisenhower decided to give Canada alone an exemption, which meant that Canadian oil was not subject to duties or taxes in the US.[10] This decision was based on his personal relationship with John G. Diefenbaker, who followed St Laurent as prime minister. In 1959, the US inaugurated the Mandatory Oil Import Program (MOIP) to restrict imported refined and crude oil products. Canada would again get an exemption.[11] US oil imports from Canadian sources increased steadily, from 4.9 percent of total US oil imports in 1958 to 11.7 percent in 1962, and 18.7 percent by 1967 (a figure which exceeded imports from the Middle East).

By the late 1950s, there were signs that the Cold War consensus in Canada was starting to break down. Anti-Americanism was becoming more palpable. Progressive Conservative leader Diefenbaker had picked up and played on sentimental feelings toward the British Empire on his path to the prime ministership. But he was not anti-American at heart, even if some of his rhetoric sounded that way. In fact, he established a good rapport with Eisenhower and bilateral relations continued much as they had under the Liberals, producing NORAD and Defence Production Sharing Agreements.

The US generally assuaged Canadian concerns about various import tariffs and quotas, such as on dairy, meat, produce, lead, and zinc, though uranium and wheat proved trickier, as did GATT negotiations (which often pertained to natural materials).[12] Bilateral negotiations about wheat frequently occurred in the early Cold War: not necessarily over wheat that either country was selling to the other, but how American wheat subsidies and dumping affected Canadian sales to other countries. Another wheat-related problem was Canadian grain sold to Communist countries, which was also linked to the extraterritoriality concerns about American firms operating in Canada but applying US laws.

Diefenbaker clashed personally with John F. Kennedy. Though the professional diplomats were largely able to act as shock absorbers, this personal animosity still led to some complications in Canadian-American relations, especially over the Cuban missile crisis and Canada's potential acquisition of nuclear warheads. By the end of his time in office, Diefenbaker was campaigning on starkly anti-American themes. Lester Pearson, Diefenbaker's replacement, got on well with Kennedy for the brief time both were leaders of their respective nations, but less so with Lyndon Johnson.[13]

The minority Diefenbaker government had appointed a Royal Commission in October 1957 to look into the state of the oil and gas industry. The Royal Commission on Energy, also known as the Borden Commission, produced two reports. The first made several recommendations concerning a National Energy Board to monitor the fossil fuel industry, including natural gas and oil exports and the related conduits. The second report stated that Canada had ample oil reserves to meet its national requirements and therefore deemed increased oil exports acceptable. The report recommended that Canadian oil serve all points west of the Ottawa River, supplied by a pipeline from Alberta; the part of the country east of the Ontario-

Quebec border was to continue to import foreign oil, subject to market conditions, chiefly from Venezuela. This split the country into two oil regions, with the Ottawa Valley the dividing line.

These recommendations were incorporated into the National Oil Policy (NOP) announced by the Diefenbaker government in 1961, which was largely designed around maintaining Canada's exemptions in the United States.[14] Instead of embarking upon a policy of national self-sufficiency in oil, this approach was a commitment to furthering a continental oil relationship. That reflected the wishes of American capital which controlled fossil fuel companies in Canada. These oil companies opposed a pipeline to Montreal, although smaller independent Canadian companies were in favour. The Diefenbaker government was happy, as had been its Liberal predecessors, to mostly leave the burden and risk of developing fossil fuel resources to the private sector.

The price for oil from outside of North America tended to be lower than the price at which Canada was selling its oil in the US. Essentially, Canada was using the oil it developed to supply the country west of the Ottawa River while selling most of the rest to the US at a higher price than the oil it was importing to supply eastern Canada. Consequently, the eastern part of the country became dependent on foreign oil. However, this east-west oil supply system had as much to do with the interests of the oil multinationals (e.g., ensuring a market for Venezuelan oil) as those of the Canadian state. Of course, in return, Canadian oil received an exemption in the US (though this again served the interests of the oil multinationals, Standard Oil specifically).

At the very least, it is safe to say that the options for Canada's national oil policy, and Canada-US oil relations, were limited by the oil majors. In some ways, this mirrors the general Canada-US diplomatic relationship: the asymmetry in favour of the United States sets the broad parameters in which Canada can operate, even if those parameters are not always explicitly stated. US parent firms of the oil multinationals had some means of controlling whether its Canadian subsidiaries or Canadian-owned firms could sell oil or expand abroad. That often limited international opportunities for the Canadian oil industry. Sometimes this worked to Canada's advantage, however, such as in countries where a Canadian company was more politically acceptable than an American one.

MOIP was in many ways a voluntary program, as it did not strictly regulate oil imports, leaving companies to operate as they chose without quotas. But there was no guarantee that the US would continue exempting Canada. Indeed, Kennedy was preparing to revoke Canada's exemption, partly to spite Diefenbaker. Kennedy did, in fact, stall approval for two pipelines (oil and natural gas) in 1962. But after the Liberals were elected, Prime Minister Lester Pearson convinced JFK otherwise at their Hyannisport meeting in May 1963.

Within a few years, the MOIP exemption existed on paper but not in practice, and Canadian oil imports were not accorded unlimited entry into the United States. Rather, imports were determined or limited by an informal understanding between National Energy Board officials and representatives of the US Department of Interior that Canadian oil would not unduly displace American domestic oil. Canada regularly exceeded these limits, however. The Pearson-Johnson tiff over the prime minister's 1965 Vietnam speech translated "into a cooler approach to the idea of a continental energy or oil policy between the US and Canada, and a persistent push to limit Canadian oil exports to the US."[15] In 1967, Canada and the US signed a secret agreement in which Canada agreed formally to limit exports, yet these too were exceeded.

Pearson's policy was to maintain both the NOP and Canadian exemption while continuing – hopefully increasing – Canadian oil exports to the US, balanced by importing cheaper foreign oil to eastern Canada. The policy for natural gas also continued as before: amounts that were surplus to Canadian use could be exported. Matters would continue much this way until Pierre Trudeau upended Canada-US energy relations.[16]

COAL AND CARS

During all of this, another important fossil fuel, coal, continued moving north. Coal is the dirtiest fossil fuel from a carbon emissions perspective. The mining process is ecologically destructive, and burning coal puts many different types of pollutants into the atmosphere, contributing to acid rain, air pollution, and climate change. In North America by this time, coal had two primary uses: electricity generation and metallurgical production. The US was Canada's main source of coal for steam-powered electricity generation, chiefly imported by central Canada (with Ontario Hydro a major consumer). Indeed, the United States was historically the world's foremost coal exporter.

In 1950, the US exported 25,468,000 tons of the sooty stuff, and 90 percent of it went to Canada – which accounted for about half of the coal burned in Canada at the time. Though total US exports went up over the next quarter century, the amount sent to Canada declined: 15,661,000 tons in 1965, but only two million tons less than a decade later.[17] Incidentally, the amount that Canada exported began rapidly increasing around 1970. After declining through much of the Cold War, Canada's total coal consumption rose again, peaking at seventy million tons at the end of the twentieth century, primarily thermal coal for electricity generation.[18]

Fossil fuel exports are linked to debates about foreign investment and the Auto Pact. Pearson had appointed Walter Gordon as finance minister, and he set out to reduce American financial investment in Canadian business.[19] As the 1972 Gray Report would later show, US investors controlled about half of Canadian manufacturing and mining/smelting, more than three quarters of the chemical industry, and virtually all the Canadian oil and gas industry. Gordon's demarche met with a host of obstacles. When the Kennedy government moved to impose a tax on American investment abroad, which would achieve many of Gordon's goals, Ottawa sought out and received a partial exemption. But there were still bilateral balance of payments problems, with a Canadian deficit in the auto industry. The solution was a 1965 trade agreement: the Auto Pact, as historian Dimitry Anastakis details, created a free trade regime for vehicles and auto parts.[20] Essentially, automobile manufacturers were allowed to sell as many vehicles in Canada as they produced in that country. The Canadian auto industry subsequently thrived, its success irritating the United States.

The Auto Pact concerns us here not only because of its impact on the general tenor of the Canada-US relationship and trade, but because of the environmental and energy impacts of automobiles. Cars, trucks, and vans collectively have consumed massive amounts of fossil fuels, requiring more and more fuel to be discovered, refined, and consumed. As much as burning petroleum has a large impact on climate change, the production stage of a vehicle also has a colossal ecological footprint. Manufacturing all the constituent parts of a vehicle – metal, glass, plastics – requires copious amounts of resources and energy. So even though the Auto Pact did not involve negotiations about a specific oil field, waterway, or type of transborder resource, it inherently had linked environmental consequences. Of course, had such a pact not been brokered, many vehicles would still have been produced; presumably, however, there would have been much less auto production in, and less economic benefits for, Canada.

We might say similar things about cultural diplomacy during this period: magazines, for example. Concerns about the domination of American media in Canada led the Pearson government to enact regulations on American periodicals (as well as films and television). Changes to the volume of magazines printed in either country of course had repercussions for the number of trees cut down for paper in Canada.

The early Cold War trade in fossil fuels demonstrates the extent to which energy and environmental diplomacy had affected the nature of the two countries and their bilateral relations. In studies of Canadian-American relations during this period, the hydrocarbon trade is usually mentioned, albeit subordinated to the international security politics connected to the ongoing capitalist-communist conflict. Yet fossil fuels arguably had longer-lasting significance for Canadian-American relations, given their contribution to continental integration, economic development, and global carbon emissions. As I will show in subsequent chapters, in the last decades of the Cold War and then the decades afterward, hydrocarbons would become even more important to Canada-US relations.

8

Great Lakes Issues

First Nations have historically borne the disproportionate brunt of North American hydroelectric developments. This hydraulic imperialism partly stems from the fact that water sites that had long attracted Indigenous groups often made ideal locations for hydroelectric installations. But the bigger factor is settler society's propensity to covet Indigenous lands and see the occupants as second-class citizens that could be removed or disenfranchised by the state for the ostensible collective benefit of the nation; that is, they were considered expendable barriers in the way of modernity and progress. This colonial narrative played out across the twentieth century and across the continent.

Pollution was an equally obvious way that hydraulic imperialism could hurt Indigenous communities. Water-borne toxics and pollutants were a ubiquitous threat to natural security by the latter half of the twentieth century. Most Canadians and Americans who lived near border waters were exposed, though First Nations were more proportionally susceptible because of the locations of many of their communities, their lifeways, and society's disregard for their well-being. Because pollution had become so evidently widespread in the Great Lakes–St Lawrence basin by mid-century, crossborder agreements were inked in the 1970s to address water quality there. In this chapter, I will focus on water quality, water levels, and invasive species in the Great Lakes–St Lawrence borderlands in the middle and later decades of the Cold War. The first Great Lakes Water Quality Agreement (GLWQA) in 1972 achieved quick success, albeit with limited objectives. The 1978 Great Lakes Water Quality Agreement, which is still in place, had a tougher task. New types of biological pollution – that is, invasive species – also appeared on the public's radar. So too did fluctuating water levels in the Great Lakes, and conflicting ideas about their causes and whether they could be controlled. In all this, we start to see changing ideas about environments and public safety, and growing concerns about the impacts of industrialization and progress, reflected in state-to-state relations.

Though hazardous chemicals, fluctuating water levels, and many types of foreign species have no intentionality to their actions – or, for those that can make choices, no cognizance of the political impacts of their movements – they are diplomatic actors because of the problems and damage they can cause. Chemicals move and change within natural environments, bioaccumulating within and poisoning biotic bodies. Their unpredictability, mobility, persistence, and frequent invisibility make them difficult to address and remediate. Those very qualities invite, even require, coordinated action if governance and regulations pertaining to border regions are to be effective. Collaborative action is also necessary for dealing with changing water levels and invasive species because of the ways they eschew borders. Thus, transboundary pollution, foreign biota, and fluctuating lakes force themselves onto the diplomatic docket and, in doing so, are prone to fostering cooperation over conflict.

GREAT LAKES WATER QUALITY

Much of Canada-US environmental relations is related to energy, directly or indirectly.[1] Many of the pollution concerns that became apparent in this era were the byproducts of energy production. Both nations have used and abused the Great Lakes without appreciable per capita differences. At the same time, because of its larger population, the United States contributed a greater amount of pollution to the Great Lakes than did Canada.

As early as 1912, the Canadian and US governments had asked the IJC to examine the general extent of pollution in the Great Lakes and to make specific recommendations for the St Marys, St Clair, Detroit, Niagara, and St Lawrence Rivers. The main concern of this investigation was the effect of waterborne diseases (such as cholera) on the shoreline populations. The IJC recommended sewage treatment and water purification for human waste. Each nation mostly ignored the commission's advice about restricting border pollution. As populations and industry increased around the basin, pollution eventually got out of hand. After the conclusion of the Second World War, it was obvious that something needed to be done. The two countries asked the IJC to investigate the state of the Great Lakes connecting channels (that is, the rivers connecting the Great Lakes). They found bacteria levels three to four times higher than during the 1912 investigation. And there was even more industrial waste than human waste entering the waters: two billion gallons of effluent daily versus 750 million gallons. The IJC addressed all this in a 1951 report.[2]

In 1956 the two countries began discussing a joint reference to the IJC about pollution abatement and control in the lower Great Lakes. The initial push came from the US, driven by complaints from the state governments of New York and Michigan over the pollution of Lake Erie. Canada responded slowly because of a lack of urgency, and a belief that the US side was the main culprit. Furthermore, Ottawa and Ontario disagreed about which level of government should pay for measures, such as sewage treatment, to reduce pollution. In 1960 the IJC appointed joint investigative boards for Lake Erie, Lake Ontario, and the St Lawrence River. These boards were made up of technical officials from the federal, provincial, and state levels. Their interim reports drew extensively upon earlier scientific studies and emphasized nutrient loading (especially phosphorous) as the cause of eutrophication in the lakes.[3]

All this was a response to the clear degradation of the Great Lakes. By the 1960s, Lake Erie was widely considered "dead." That diagnosis was the result of excessive eutrophication – the process in which nutrient loading causes too much algae growth, and the algae in turn uses up the oxygen in the water when it decomposes. As the shallowest and smallest by volume of the Great Lakes, Lake Erie was also the receptacle for many urban sewer outflows and industrial regions, such as Detroit and Cleveland. The latter's grossly polluted Cuyahoga River repeatedly caught fire in the 1950s and 1960s, including the most famous blaze in 1969. But other rivers throughout the Great Lakes basin, such as the Rouge, Buffalo, and Chicago, also went aflame.

In 1964, Canada and the United States formally asked the IJC to study pollution in the lower Great Lakes. The IJC issued three reports, in 1965, 1968, and 1970, that provided scientific evidence attesting to the seriousness of the situation. The 1965 report recommended measures to limit phosphorus inputs in particular. However, Ontario and the various American governments were not willing to consider such measures at that time, and the report was mostly ignored. The commission's final report in 1970 concluded that municipal and industrial pollution was occurring on both sides of the boundary to the injury of health and property on the other side. The report recommended several actions to the governments to improve water quality in the basin, including programs that would control phosphorus inputs into the lakes, new water quality objectives, and establishing institutions to coordinate an overall cleanup effort.

Based on the IJC recommendations, the United States and Canada began an intensive phase of negotiations. The Canadian and American governments formed a Joint Working Group in June 1971. One impediment was Canada's position that the 1909 Boundary Waters Treaty gave each country the right to contribute pollution up to half of the "assimilative capacity" of the waters, regardless of population. Following this line of thinking, the primary responsibility for pollution reduction would have fallen to the US since it was contributing more than half.

A Canada-Ontario Agreement, signed in 1971, cleared the way for Canadian participation in a comprehensive program to address Great Lakes pollution. It established formal mechanisms for cooperation and shared responsibility for pollution abatement. Ontario agreed to accelerate the construction of municipal sewage treatment facilities and trunk sewers in urban areas around the lower Great Lakes and the upper St Lawrence River. The federal government promised to loan Ontario two-thirds of the estimated $250 million cost.

Richard Nixon and Pierre Trudeau signed the Great Lakes Water Quality Agreement (GLWQA) in April 1972.[4] This GLWQA only applied to the two lowest Great Lakes, Erie and Ontario, as well as the international section of the St Lawrence River. The GLWQA committed each nation to develop common water quality objectives and regulatory standards for several pollutants, and to create and implement their own national programs to achieve these goals. The focus was point source pollution, chiefly excess nutrient loading. The main strategy to reduce the nutrient inflow involved improving municipal sewage treatment. A regional office was created at Windsor to help the IJC with its new responsibilities under the GLWQA, which included supervising implementation, monitoring, water boards, and data collection. However, the GLWQA was not binding – that is, it did not have the teeth of a formal treaty or diplomatic agreement. Rather, the agreement was a "standing reference" under the Boundary Waters

Treaty that provided a framework for coordinating water quality management of the Great Lakes.

Between 1972 and 1978, about US$10 billion was spent on upgrades to water and sewage treatment. The bulk of this was through the US Clean Water Act. In both countries, the federal governments subsidized actions and regulations taken at the provincial and state levels.[5] Total phosphorus concentrations for Lake Erie soon declined, and the effect on water quality was readily apparent. Nevertheless, all the phosphorous loading targets were not being met. Moreover, the 1972 GLWQA did not apply to the three upper lakes and it did not cover nonpoint sources of pollution nor hazardous toxics.

In 1978, the two governments replaced the 1972 agreement with a new GLWQA. The 1978 Great Lakes Water Quality Agreement built upon the foundation established in the earlier agreement and incorporated new scientific information. It encompassed all the Great Lakes, but again was not binding. Importantly, it shifted the focus from conventional pollutants, such as phosphorus and bacteria, to toxic and hazardous polluting substances. Persistent toxic substances remain in the environment for very long periods, accumulate in living organisms, and seriously impact the health of wildlife and humans. Through the 1978 Agreement, the two countries adopted a policy that the discharge of all persistent toxic substances be "virtually eliminated" in the Great Lakes and international section of the St Lawrence River. Timelines were established for municipal and industrial pollution abatement and control programs. The 1978 agreement also employed a broader ecosystems approach to basin management, recognizing that water, air, and land pollution were interlinked.

The 1978 agreement has remained in place up to the present. Rather than a new agreement, changes and additions were made to the 1978 GLWQA. Since the GLWQA was a good faith agreement – an "executive agreement" rather than a treaty – with no mechanisms for enforcement, it relied on the two countries to live up to its commitments. By the 1980s, however, they were already failing to do so. Industry refused to curtail its pollution further, and governments were not making them. The production of some toxic chemicals was phased out, but they tended to remain in the ecosystem plus new chemicals were always being developed. In 1987 an annex was added to the GLWQA. It created areas of concern (AOCs) for the most polluted parts of the basin, with remedial action plans (RAPs) to clean them up.[6]

Many of the pollutants befouling the Great Lakes came from industrial centres like Niagara Falls. The legacy of buried toxic waste was exposed in the 1970s by the tragedy of Love Canal in a suburb of Niagara Falls, New York. Heavy industry, including many abrasives and chemical concerns, had been located at Niagara since the nineteenth century because of cheap power. One of these firms, the Hooker Chemical Company, had dumped approximately 22,000 tons of toxic waste into an old, abandoned canal between 1942 and 1953. In 1953, Hooker sold the property to the Niagara Falls Board of Education for $1 and disclosed the chemical wastes there. The city built an elementary school on top of the canal and houses all around it. By the 1970s, the chemicals that had been leaching into nearby homes spurred a national health crisis. This brought awareness to the widespread problem of hazardous waste dumps across North America and sparked a series of policies, such as Superfund.

Love Canal was partially a Canadian concern since it was very close to the binational Niagara River. That waterway had long borne high levels of toxic pollutants, as there were many other discard sites in the area. The SCA Chemical Waste Services of nearby Lewiston, New York applied for and was granted a permit by the New York State Department of Environmental Conservation to dump up to one million gallons of treated chemical wastes per day that would end up in the Niagara River. This dumping became an issue in the Canadian federal election of 1980, and the Department of External Affairs sent diplomatic notes to object. Consequently, in early 1981 New York State revoked the permit.[7] But many other waste sites in the area continued to leach toxic chemicals into the river.

Incidentally, Canada and the United States each signed but never ratified the UN's Convention on the Transboundary Effects of Industrial Accidents, created in response to chemical spills in Europe. Instead, they signed a strictly bilateral arrangement in 1994, the Canada–United States Inland Pollution Contingency Plan.[8]

GREAT LAKES WATER LEVELS

Now we turn from one type of Great Lakes diplomacy, water quality, to another, water quantity. Water quantity policy often centres on lake levels – these fluctuate, predominantly because of natural forces but also from anthropogenic interventions such as diversions and dams. Debates over appropriate Great Lakes water levels divide as much along user-type lines as along national lines: shoreline property owners, navigation and shipping, hydroelectricity and energy, irrigation, and industry.

Emboldened by the various water megaprojects built in the post-1945 period, engineers promulgated even bolder water control plans that involved the bulk export of water to the US, especially the southwest. The two most infamous are NAWAPA and GRAND. NAWAPA is the acronym for North American Water and Power Alliance, which involved damming and diverting water from large rivers in Alaska, British Columbia, and the Yukon to create an enormous reservoir in the Rocky Mountain Trench. From there, water would be redirected to the western United States. Hostile public reaction and the question of feasibility quashed the idea. The Great Recycling and Northern Development (GRAND) Canal was a similar scheme. First advanced in 1959 by Thomas Kierans, this plan would dike James Bay (the bottom part of Hudson Bay), creating a freshwater lake. This water could then be sent to the Great Lakes and on to the southwestern United States and even Mexico. Like NAWAPA, this $100 billion scheme was wildly expensive and ecologically ridiculous. It did gain some important backers in the 1960s and 1970s, even if it never came close to happening. Nevertheless, both the GRAND and NAWAPA proposals continued to resurface from time to time and have recently been brought up again as solutions to southwestern water scarcity.

In the meantime, Canada and the Great Lakes states had continued to sporadically clash with Chicago and Illinois over the Chicago diversion. In 1967, the US Supreme Court established an average of 3,200 cfs limit for Chicago. In the 1980s, the Corps of Engineers studied an increase to 10,000 cfs. This was the maximum flow the canal could handle. Later, Illinois unsuccessfully requested the diversion go to that ceiling.

Wary of the threats posed by the likes of the NAWAPA and GRAND proposals, or smaller schemes to take water out of the Great Lakes basin such as the Chicago diversion, the US Great Lakes states, Ontario, and Quebec, signed the Great Lakes Charter in 1985. The purpose was "to conserve the levels and flows of the Great Lakes and their tributary and connecting waters; to protect and conserve the ecological balance of the Great Lakes Basin ecosystem to provide for cooperative programs and management of the Great Lakes Basin by the signatory States and Provinces." Any plan proposed in any Great Lakes state or province that involved new consumptive uses or diversions had to give prior notice to, and seek the approval of, all other states and provinces. However, this charter was a nonbinding good faith agreement, and there were serious questions about whether it could withstand a legal challenge.

As I have already shown, the outflows of Lake Superior and Lake Ontario had both been dammed, in the early twentieth century for the former and the 1950s for the latter, and the IJC regulates the levels of these lakes. Lake Erie is partially affected, though not officially regulated, by the Niagara remedial works and power diversions. There had been talk of doing the same for Lake Huron by installing works in the St Clair River, which would affect Lake Michigan as well since the two lakes are essentially one hydrologically.

Scientific understanding of "natural" lake levels had also fluctuated. By the immediate post-Second World War period, engineers and government experts had acquired a more solid understanding of the causes of Great Lakes oscillations. The IJC then completed several reference studies on Great Lakes water level issues. In 1964, when water levels were very low after high levels in the 1950s, the governments asked the IJC whether it would be feasible to maintain the waters of all the Great Lakes at a more constant level. This study was completed in 1973 when lake levels had risen to record highs. The IJC advised the governments in its landmark 1976 report "Further Regulation of the Great Lakes" that protection against high and low levels was best achieved through systematic management using all the tools available. It also recommended that the high economic and environmental costs of further artificial regulation of Lakes Michigan and Huron could not be justified by the benefits.[9] A 1983 IJC study about regulating outflows from Lake Erie reached a similar conclusion.

Taken together, these studies showed that engineering interventions in the Great Lakes–St Lawrence basin had cumulatively lowered water levels by several feet, but natural forces were still the prime determinant.[10] Depending on which lake one considers, the maximum range of water level fluctuations has only been about four to seven feet in the 150 years since records have been kept. The Great Lakes system experienced extremely low levels in the late 1920s, mid-1930s, and again in the mid-1960s. There were very high levels in the 1870s, early 1950s, early 1970s, mid-1980s, and mid-1990s. While cycles of low and high water levels follow a variable schedule that is not entirely predictable, they do follow general patterns (at least they used to: climate change has introduced a great deal of uncertainty into these cycles).

In 1985, the IJC submitted a report in response to a reference on consumptive uses and diversions. This study demonstrated that consumptive uses (agricultural irrigation, bottled water, and other packaged beverages), which had not been considered significant because the volume of water in the system is so large, could collectively have a noticeable impact. In fact, these cumulative "death by a thousand straws" scenarios probably withdrew more water from the lakes than diversions. However, the 1985 study concluded that climate and weather affect levels of the lakes far more than existing anthropogenic diversions and uses, recommending that governments not consider the manipulation of extant diversions to either intentionally raise or lower levels.[11] In 1986, during a period of record-high water levels, the governments asked the IJC to examine and report on methods to alleviate the adverse consequences of fluctuating water levels in the Great Lakes–St Lawrence River basin. The IJC's final recommendations in its 1993 report (when the high levels had receded) included a range of actions such as promoting shoreline management measures but recommended against further attempts to regulate the Great Lakes.[12]

GREAT LAKES INVASIVES

Chemicals were not the only potentially harmful things infiltrating the Great Lakes. Several types of foreign species, such as alewives and sea lamprey, had entered the Great Lakes before the St Lawrence Seaway was built, potentially via canals. The most notorious of these was the sea lamprey. These vampire-like creatures use their round mouths to suction onto fish, their sharp teeth making incisions so that they can drink body fluids. It is unclear whether sea lamprey were native to Lake Ontario or had come in through the St Lawrence or the Erie Canal. Regardless, Niagara Falls blocked the sea lamprey from entering the other Great Lakes until changes to the Welland Canal were made in the early twentieth century (though it is possible they may have been in the upper lakes before then). They were blamed for the demise of the whitefish, though this scapegoating conveniently overlooked the anthropogenic impacts that had hurt fish stocks, including pollution and overfishing.

A detailed transborder investigation of the Great Lakes fisheries, which began after the outbreak of the Second World War, reported on their sorry state. In April 1946, the two countries signed a convention creating the International Fisheries Commission for the Great Lakes. It was empowered to regulate many aspects of the fisheries: closed and open seasons, stocking, harvest limits, and gear. However, like so many other crossborder accords, US Senate approval was not in the cards. In 1955 a second convention, called the Convention on Great Lakes Fisheries, was signed to replace the 1946 version. This convention was shorn of most of the regulatory powers of its predecessor, though it did create the Great Lakes Fishery Commission.[13] The commission was given several tasks, but the one it is best known for its program to control sea lamprey. Searching for a comprehensive solution for sea lamprey eradication, the commission tested some 6,000 chemicals. By 1958, they found that TFM (a chlorinated compound) would work as a lampricide and kill juvenile lamprey in their spawning streams. It apparently did so without harming other organisms, although this benign impact is likely exaggerated. The lampricide substantially reduces, but does not eliminate, the sea lamprey; consequently, the chemical still needs to be applied annually.

The proliferation of lamprey had helped eliminate the predators of a small non-native fish called the alewife. These soon dominated the fish biomass in all the Great Lakes except Superior. Natural resources managers introduced Pacific salmon into Lake Michigan in the later 1960s in the hopes that they would reduce the alewives and provide an attractive sport fishery to replace the decimated stocks of other large species. The salmon did do this. But soon, there was concern that the alewife population was too low to sustain the salmon population, and later there were worries that these introduced salmon might be preventing native fish populations, such as trout, from rebounding.[14]

After it opened in 1959, the St Lawrence Seaway offered an aquatic highway for a host of foreign species, including mussels, round goby, Eurasian ruffe, water fleas, and tiny shrimp. The chief vector by which a multitude of new species came in was the vessels plying the Seaway. Few transoceanic ships utilized the Seaway, compared to what government planners had prognosticated, since the rise of container ships too big for the Seaway coincided with its opening. Those ocean-going ships that did come employed ballast water systems. Ballast refers to heavy substances placed in the bottom hold of a vessel to maintain its stability when not carrying a sufficient amount of cargo. Empty ships headed for the Great Lakes filled their ballast tanks with water before crossing the ocean. When picking up their cargo in the Great Lakes–St Lawrence basin, they dumped this ballast water. However, if this jettisoned water had been originally obtained from the Caspian Sea, for example, expelling it could release small foreign organisms that survived the journey.

Through ballast water, zebra and quagga mussels from Eurasia made their way into the Great Lakes. Zebra mussels were first discovered in Lake St Clair in 1988. They quickly colonized much of the rest of the lakes (and then spread across North America from this Great Lakes base). The zebras were then followed by the quaggas. These two types of mussels collectively unleashed ecological domino effects. They attach themselves to hard surfaces in the water, fouling beaches, docks, and boat hulls; sometimes power stations had to be shut off since mussels clogged their water intakes. Moreover, mussels are filter feeders, which changes the chemical composition of the water when done on a large scale, which was certainly the case. The clearer water that results lets sunlight penetrate deeper, allowing massive algae growth. That leads to eutrophication and toxic types of algal blooms, and mussel droppings also concentrate phosphorous and other potential pollutants at the bottom. In the twenty-first century, quaggas have replaced zebras as the dominant invasive mussel type in the Great Lakes.

Despite the knowledge that the Welland Canal had allowed species such as the sea lamprey and alewife to move between Lake Ontario and Erie, and then to the upper Great Lakes, there was apparently no consideration that invasive species could arrive via the Seaway and wreak havoc in the Great Lakes.[15] For the Seaway planners, "[t]heirs was an error of omission, not commission. They failed to consider the ecological risks of opening these freshwater seas to oceangoing freighters, even though it was obvious by the 1950s – before construction began on the Seaway – that the lakes were vulnerable to invasions by foreign species."[16] Yet the post-1950s Canadian and American regulators should take perhaps an even bigger share of the blame because they failed to clamp down on the invasives problem once it became apparent that ballast water was a conduit. Regulatory solutions to this problem were fairly straightforward. But the relevant parts of the American and Canadian governments were reluctant to force regulations on the shipping industry, which did not want to let rules get in the way of its profits. It took until the twenty-first century for more effective measures to be put in place, and even today there are still loopholes and blind spots.

While Cold War–era regulations to prevent Great Lakes invasive species were ineffective, the Great Lakes Water Quality Agreements stand out as much more successful examples of transborder cooperation. The GLWQA would prove to be a watershed for environmental protection of the Great Lakes, and it has been heralded as an international model for addressing transboundary pollution. Granted, it was much easier to come to a transborder agreement about the Great Lakes in the early 1970s when relatively few stakeholders were consulted and the focus was a few conventional point-source pollutants.

Moreover, after the 1970s, governmental funding, industrial regulations, and societal commitment did not keep up with the new Great Lakes problems. While the success of the GLWQA can easily be exaggerated, it is still noteworthy that these two countries were able to come to such agreements in the first place. Few other countries had cooperatively gone as far in limiting pollution to protect citizens and natural security. Indeed, the unpredictable ways that pollutants moved across borders and up trophic chains required collaborative and coordinated transnational efforts in order to be at least somewhat effective. To be sure, the qualifier "somewhat" is important here. After all, despite the governance advances represented by the Great Lakes Water Quality Agreements, people and other species in and around these inland seas are arguably more exposed to chemical threats today than at any point in the past.

9

Water from Coast to Coast

In addition to the water megaprojects covered in chapter 6, there were a wide range of other bilateral Cold War–era water issues, including hydro power, water control and flooding, and water quality. Large hydro projects continued to be built in Canada, though these moved away from the border and into the northern tier of the country. Nevertheless, a paramount motivation or justification for building many of these, such as in Manitoba, Quebec, and Labrador, was to export the power south to the United States. Yet again, we see the many ways that the desires of American markets helped determine Canada's engagement with its natural resources. Furthermore, we will see how seemingly regional projects, some of them fairly small, could take on a diplomatic importance out of proportion to their physical size or national relevance.

Whereas water policy in the Great Lakes basin is defined by water abundance, in the western interior, water scarcity is a more common problem (though, of course, flooding is a water abundance problem). In the Great Lakes, water forms the border, whereas in the western half of the continent and on the east coast, waterbodies more commonly cross the border. This latter situation frequently creates clear upstream and downstream riparians, which increases the perception of zero-sum conflicts. This was all further complicated by the selective invocation of the United States of its Harmon Doctrine, whereby the upstream state theoretically has full sovereignty to use waters as it wishes before the water crosses the border. This doctrine was beneficial to the United States vis-à-vis Mexico, but when it came to Canada, its application was as apt to hurt US interests as it was to help.

ELECTRICITY EXCHANGES

Between the 1920s and the 1960s, non-firm (i.e., interruptible) power sales dominated the Canada-US electricity trade. That changed to deal with the Columbia River agreements. In 1963, Canada's National Energy Board began allowing for the export of large blocks of electricity.[1] Such exports could take advantage of the growing crossborder electricity networks. During the Second World War, several major crossborder lines were established to move electricity. The Northwest Power Pool joined together several US states during the war, and British Columbia was soon added to the mix. The biggest member of this power pool, the Bonneville Power Administration, built a line to the border that met with a line from BC Electric, and others developed in the Northwest interior.[2] In the 1950s, Detroit Edison (Michigan) and Niagara Mohawk (New York) began exchanging electricity with Ontario Hydro.

In the following decade, these interchanges were formalized and made permanent in the Canada–United States Eastern Interconnection (CANUSE) power pool. It was extended to New England and came to involve thirty different power utilities, a group which produced about one-third of the continent's power.[3] In 1965, after the completion of the St Lawrence and Niagara power projects, Ontario Hydro and PASNY entered into long-term contracts for electricity interchanges, which included building the infrastructure to carry the juice. It is worth pointing out that there were several years in the mid-1960s when the US exported more electricity – not just hydroelectricity, but electricity in general – to Canada than did Canada to the US. Transborder electricity grids further proliferated in the 1960s; as of 1975, there were sixty-five international interconnections, six of which could be considered major connections, with a total transfer capability of over 6,000 megawatts.[4]

Most North Americans took these arrangements for granted whenever they flipped on a light switch. But the extent to which Canada and the US had intertwined their energy resources became readily apparent when energy was not available. The Northeast power blackout of November 1965, for example, involved a technical failure along a transmission line running from Ontario Hydro's Beck No. 2 station at Niagara that triggered a massive power loss along the Atlantic seaboard.

The Columbia River Treaty and the policy switch to long-term electricity exports have been accused of undermining any momentum for a Canadian national power grid. This grid idea was discussed during the late 1950s and early 1960s when it first became technically possible. Provinces had primary jurisdiction over hydro power and thus were the ones building or licensing dams, and most of the provinces were not interested in a pan-Canadian grid at the time. Almost all big post-1965 power projects would be built far away from the southern Canada–US border. The financing for many of these dams was predicated on agreements to export the power to the United States, further precluding the formation of a Canadian national grid at the expense of continental connections. Efforts by both the Diefenbaker and Pearson governments to create national grids were export-oriented anyway.[5] Sending power on long-term contracts across the border gave the American governments and utilities purchasing the power more influence over Canadian hydro power developments.

Prairie Water Issues

The Garrison dam was completed on the North Dakota stretch of the Missouri River in the 1950s (see figure 9.2). There were plans for an enormous series of canals and pumps to take water from the dam's reservoir, Lake Sakakawea, to irrigate huge swaths of agricultural land as well as some other benefits. The initial plans were scaled back, and Congress authorized a reduced Garrison Diversion Unit in 1965. As construction on the diversion unit began, the Province of Manitoba grew concerned that this diversion would result in the Missouri River watershed mixing with the Red River watershed. That might allow foreign biota, such as fish and microorganisms, as well as agricultural pollution (fertilizers and pesticides) that could cause algae blooms, into the Red River. From there, these pollutants and non-native biota could make their way downstream, potentially threatening fisheries and aquatic species in Lakes Winnipeg and Manitoba.[6]

Though it was considered a regional issue stateside, Garrison became more of a national *cause célèbre* in Canada.[7] Ottawa relayed diplomatic objections to the diversion several times, beginning with an aide-memoire in 1970, and then requested the matter be referred to the International Joint Commission. A referral took place in 1975. After studying the matter, the IJC recommended that certain aspects of the Garrison Diversion be modified or halted.[8] Following the IJC's recommendations, in the mid-1980s, a compromise allowed construction to proceed but significantly reduced the scope and size of the planned works while addressing some of Manitoba's concerns about the transmittal of invasive species. Since then, the Garrison matter has continued to simmer, approaching a slow boil whenever an expansion of the diversion unit is proposed. Currently, there are plans to pipe treated water to the Red River Valley, though irrigation is no longer a primary purpose.

The Souris River was linked to the Garrison dispute, but it is also its own separate transboundary environmental affair. The Souris River rises in Saskatchewan, flows through North Dakota, then recrosses the border into Manitoba before draining into the Red River. The Souris was the focus of a 1939 water apportionment reference, and a 1948 reference on the Souris and Red Rivers. In 1959, the IJC created an International Souris River Board of Control to oversee remedial works. Since 1945, both countries have built various dams on this waterway. In 1989, Canada and the US entered into an Agreement for Water Supply and Flood Control in the Souris River Basin. That agreement permitted the construction of two large dams in the Saskatchewan portion of the watershed, the Rafferty dam and the Alameda dam. Despite the placement of the Rafferty-Alameda dams in Saskatchewan, the primary purpose was to provide flood control benefits for North Dakota (though the dams never stopped Minot from flooding in 2011).[9] These dams also created a reservoir to provide water for crop irrigation, cool the Shand coal-fired power plant, and offer recreation opportunities.

The Red River begins in the United States before flowing into Manitoba and Lake Winnipeg. It drains a fertile agricultural region, but its flatness allows flood waters to spread far beyond the riverbanks. The Red, and its tributaries, have been the subject of both water control (flooding) and water quality (pollution) concerns. A disastrous flood struck in 1950, resulting in evacuations in Winnipeg. The city responded by completing the Greater Winnipeg Floodway in 1968. But floods happened that same year and again in the following three decades, including a huge flood in 1997. Working through the offices of the IJC, further remedial works were built on each side of the border. Water quality has arguably been an even pricklier bilateral issue here. Most of this concerns nonpoint source pollution from agricultural runoff and food processing, such as sugar beets and potatoes. This pollution was pernicious enough that a reference went to the IJC in 1964.[10] The two countries accepted the IJC's recommendations for water quality objectives and monitoring, creating the International Red River Pollution Board.

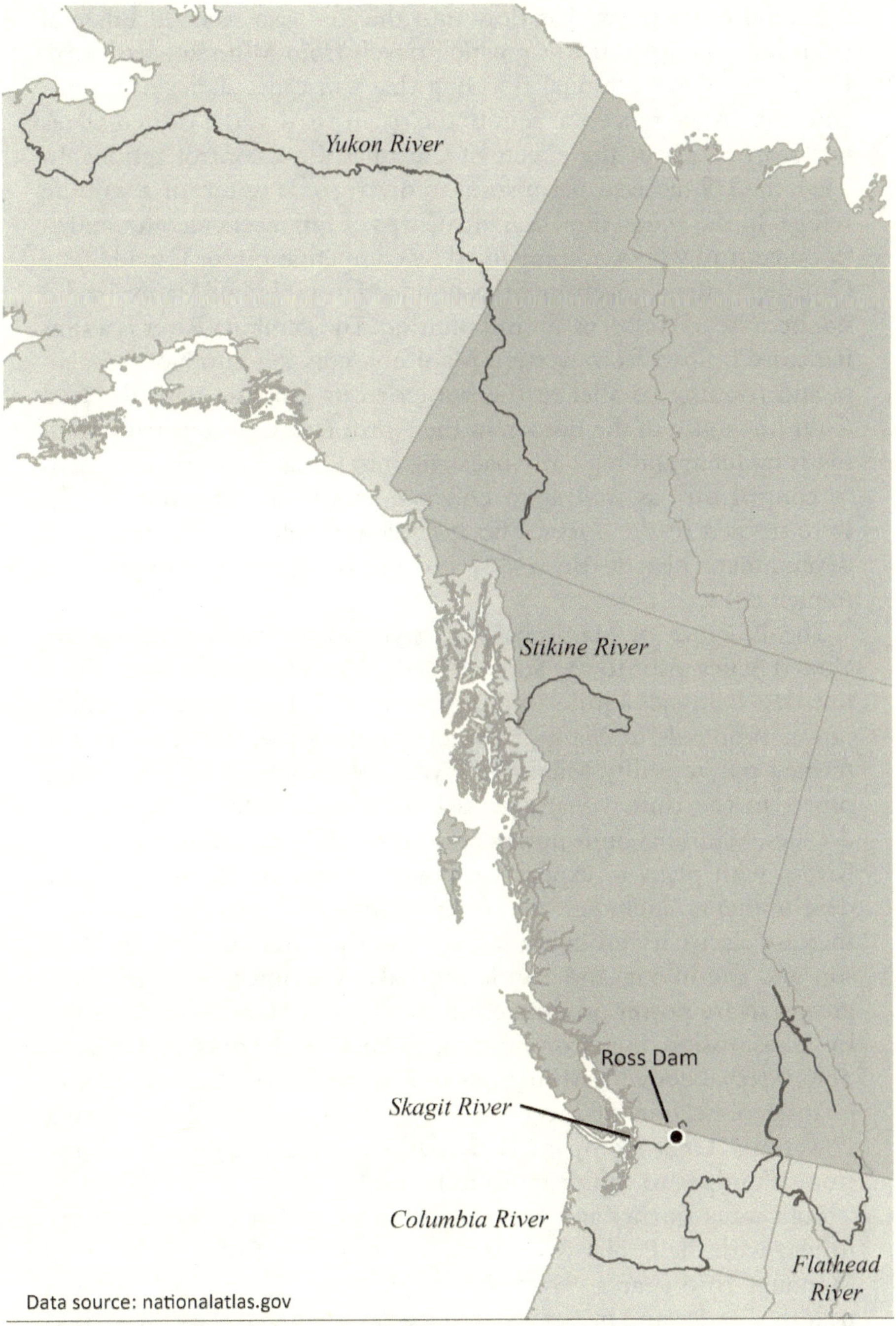

Figure 9.1 Transborder water issues on the west coast.

Several other rivers that flow into the Red also received bilateral attention. The Roseau River, which travels from Minnesota to Manitoba, experiences seasonal flooding that can cause damage in both countries. A reference was sent to the IJC in 1929, as the United States was worried about the effects of Canadian flow control actions. In 1949, the US received permission to divert some water for a wildlife refuge. In the 1960s, the US Army Corps of Engineers recommended flood control works, accompanied by compensation for Canada. The Canadian federal government responded favorably, but Manitoba did not because of concerns about pollution. The Pembina River is a similar story. It flows from western Manitoba, crossing into North Dakota and running parallel to the border to its juncture with the Red River just south of the border. In the North Dakota watershed, flooding is frequent and regularly backs up into Canadian territory. Works to control this, as well as to enhance irrigation and water supply, were studied in the 1950s. The IJC recommended a comprehensive development plan in the 1960s, but the two governments did not implement it.

The Province of Manitoba first exported hydroelectricity to the United States prior to the Second World War, albeit with a very short line (less than half a mile) and on a very small scale. As part of hydro power proposals in Manitoba's north during the 1960s, the newly formed public utility Manitoba Hydro began talks to export hydro power to the United States on a much larger scale. In subsequent decades, Manitoba built power projects on the Churchill and Nelson Rivers, with plans to export the power to the United States. These developments included major environmental manipulations to increase electricity production: diverting the Churchill into the Nelson and modifying and regulating Lake Winnipeg so as to allow greater hydro power production in the Nelson. Manitoba built a 230 kV transmission line from Winnipeg to Grand Forks to facilitate power exchanges with Minnesota and North Dakota utilities. Another interconnection of the same voltage was built with Minnesota Power and Light Company of Duluth; an even bigger 500 kV line from Winnipeg to Minneapolis followed.[11]

Both water quality and water quantity (as well as air quality) were in play with the Poplar River, which crosses from Saskatchewan into Montana. In this area, Saskatchewan has large lignite coal deposits near the border, and in 1973 Saskatchewan proposed a large coal-fired power plant, the Poplar Generating Station. Montana objected on several grounds. This station became the object of two separate references to the IJC: the first on water apportionment (the coal plant would withdraw cooling water from the various branches of the Poplar River), and another on transborder water quality stemming from coal waste pollution. Several years of diplomatic talks through the IJC produced a complex agreement on water apportionment. But water quality, such as boron contaminants, remained an even bigger problem. Montana was concerned about a variety of transborder pollutants that would result from various aspects of mining and burning coal. The IJC created the International Poplar River Water Quality Board, though this board took several years to release findings. In the meantime, the Poplar River issue reached "a new low point diplomatically."[12] By the early 1980s, however, and before the board had made controversial recommendations minimizing the pollution threat, a diplomatic agreement was reached. This joint accord largely involved data and monitoring. The Milk–St Mary problem, for its part, continued to simmer.

WEST COAST WATER ISSUES

In an earlier chapter, I discussed the Ross dam on the Skagit River, which was raised in 1953. In 1967, BC agreed that Seattle could raise the dam to its full height, with the Ross Lake reservoir flooding 5,189 acres in BC, for ninety-nine years, in return for cash compensation of $34,566 annually. In 1970, Seattle filed an application with the US Federal Power Commission for an amendment to the 1927 licence so that it could further raise the Ross dam to generate additional power, which would flood additional acreage.

But strong local opposition arose in the area prescribed for inundation, and after the replacement of Bennett's government, British Columbia angled to get out of what it considered a poor deal. The federal government also opposed the High Ross dam. The involved parties had already referred the matter to the IJC for a nonbinding Article IX reference. The resulting study concluded that the economic consequences of the flooding would not be inordinate, but that severe ecological consequences would result in the Upper Skagit Valley. The IJC now had qualms about the wisdom of extending the dam's height. Negotiations ensued about compensation and plan alterations, and BC tried to induce Seattle to give up on raising the dam.

In the early 1980s, the IJC issued a supplemental order suggesting that Seattle City and Light not raise the dam further and accept compensation in exchange for the additional electricity it would forego. After more tough bilateral negotiations, with the IJC as a sort of mediator, all sides tentatively accepted this formula in 1983. BC would provide Seattle with the electricity it would lose out on, and a commission and funding would be created for recreation and conservation purposes in the Skagit Valley. An IJC order, and a Canada-US treaty, formalized this new understanding in 1984. The High Ross dam was ultimately not built. This was one of the first transborder cases where environmental concerns helped stop the expansion of hydroelectricity.[13]

About the same time that the Skagit controversy was concluding, the Sage Creek Coal Company began developing a coal mine around Cabin Creek and Howell Creek, both tributaries of the Flathead River in British Columbia. The Flathead crosses from Canada into the United States, running through the Waterton-Glacier International Peace Park (the world's first international peace park, which was jointly created by Canada and the US in 1932).[14] The lifeways of several Indigenous communities depend on this river basin. The pollution from a coal mine would obviously impair the water quality, so the matter was sent to the IJC.

An IJC board conducted several years of detailed studies. But there was not enough baseline information about the local ecology, nor enough detail in the Sage Creek Coal Company's proposals, to arrive at definitive findings. Nonetheless, IJC investigations tended to show that the effect of coal mining would be adverse and recommended that the plans not be approved, though it did outline some potential pathways for approval of a revised proposal. The BC government was unhappy with the findings, but the company voluntarily withdrew its plans in 1989. Though other proposals for different types of mines in the Canadian portion of the Flathead River were forwarded, in 2010 BC and Montana inked a memorandum of understanding that could prohibit mining activities in this basin.

Further north, several other potential crossborder developments did not come to fruition but bear mentioning: hydro power projects on the Stikine and Yukon Rivers, for example, and various types of mining that might send pollution across the border.[15] Worries about supertankers transporting Alaskan oil led the United States and Canada to sign the 1979 Canada-US Vessel Traffic Management Agreement. Its non-binding stipulations about traffic lanes applied to the

BC–Washington State coastal area. The siting of potential oil ports in this area, which would receive Alaskan oil via pipeline, also concerned regulators and officials. Canada felt it bore the brunt of the risk while receiving few benefits. Around this time, the United States and Canada entered into talks about hydrocarbons exploration in the Beaufort Sea in the north as well as the Georges Bank in the Atlantic.

EASTERN WATER ISSUES

On the Atlantic coast, other water matters attracted bilateral attention. Ambitious American plans to harness the tides of Passamaquoddy Bay by damming it for tidal power date back to the early twentieth century. The idea was that receding tides could spin turbines and produce electricity as water left the bay. This proposition even had the support of President Franklin D. Roosevelt, who summered on a nearby island (which later became an international peace park: the Roosevelt-Campobello). Canada and New Brunswick opposed this undertaking on the grounds that the power structures placed in the water would harm the herring and sardine fisheries. The Canadian government was nonetheless pressured into joining an IJC reference on the matter in the late 1940s.[16] The IJC reported that though a Passamaquoddy development was technically feasible, there were still questions about its economic feasibility. On the latter score, Canada declined to participate in another reference.

Meanwhile, the federal and provincial governments looked into hydro power development on the St John River. This waterway has its source in Maine, then flows through Quebec and New Brunswick. Power dams might push a reservoir across the border. Worried that the US might go to the IJC unilaterally over the Passamaquoddy and concerned about the spill-over effects for other bilateral developments such as those on the St Lawrence and Columbia, Canada reluctantly joined in a 1956 St John reference. After additional study, the IJC linked the Passamaquoddy and St John power developments. However, the commission also found the tidal power economically unattractive, at least under existing conditions. Despite President Kennedy's support, further US pressure in the 1960s for Passamaquoddy as a TVA-style development was not enough to move the project forward.[17]

Interest in St John power development remained. But the potential location of the dams moved further south along the river, where a reservoir would not back up over the border. Maine looked at building the Dickey and Lincoln dams on the St John River. These structures would generate hydro power in Maine and provide flood control there and downstream in New Brunswick. Water quality was also a concern on this river. The chief pollution culprits were the pulp and paper industry. In 1972 the two countries established the Canada–United States Committee on Water Quality in the St John River, composed of representatives from various levels of government. The committee was tasked with studying the water quality problems along the international stretch of the river. The IJC was asked to review the committee's work and submit recommendations to the two federal governments. It did so through a 1977 report that endorsed specific water quality objectives. Though Congress approved this undertaking, the Dickey-Lincoln dams were ultimately not built, with the environmental opposition playing a role.[18]

In 1972, the Pittston Company announced plans for an oil refinery and marine terminal at Eastport, Maine, on the border with New Brunswick. The facility would receive crude oil from the Middle East, refine it, and then distribute it. However, the passage to Eastport is through a channel in Canadian waters. This narrow channel is perilous for larger tankers because of navigation obstacles such as shoals, islands, extreme tides, and strong currents.[19] A crash by an oil tanker here would be disastrous. Maine's Board of Environmental Protection approved the Pittston application, albeit with qualifications that included the approval of Canadian authorities. But Canada objected, through formal diplomatic channels and other avenues, pointing to the potential risk to the environment and fisheries. The Canadian government also enacted regulations intended to make ship passage unfeasible and asserted that the channel was internal waters. Consequently, the Eastport project did not continue, though proposals for liquid natural gas terminals have recently been made.

QUEBEC-US WATER ISSUES

Quebec had several ongoing water issues with the United States. Lake Memphremagog lies mostly in that province, though the bulk of its watershed is in Vermont. This lake experienced a noticeable decline in water quality, as high anthropogenic nutrient inflows caused algal blooms. A bilateral ad hoc group was established to study the problem, and it recommended a program of pollution control abatement in both

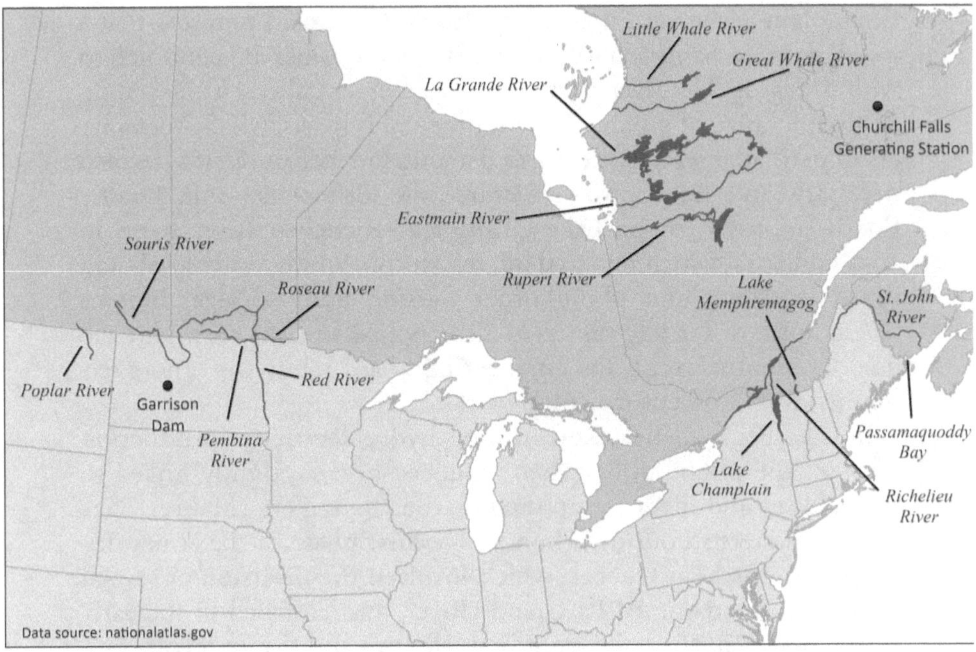

Figure 9.2 Transborder water issues in the central and eastern part of the continent.

countries. In 1989, the governments of Vermont and Quebec signed an Environmental Cooperation Agreement on Managing the Waters of Lake Memphremagog. However, there was little improvement.

Similar attempts, and results, bedevilled nearby Lake Champlain. Its northern tip is in Quebec, with the southern part bisected by the New York–Vermont border, and it debouches into the Richelieu River, which flows north to the St Lawrence. Flooding occurred regularly in the Champlain-Richelieu corridor; that was not a problem, so long as the floodplains were just used for farming. In 1937, the IJC approved remedial works on the Richelieu River to control flooding. Construction started on the Fryers Island dam, but other elements were not completed because of the Second World War. Thus, the full extent of the envisioned flood control was not achieved.

After the war, floods were less severe for an extended period, allaying worries about building in the floodplains.[20] High water returned in the early 1970s. Ottawa and Washington asked the IJC to examine the feasibility of regulating the levels of Lake Champlain and the Richelieu River in 1973. The commission created the International

Champlain-Richelieu Engineering Board. This board reported that a gated dam at Saint-Jean-sur-Richelieu was feasible in conjunction with dredging. However, there was disagreement about its desirability, given a range of potential environmental impacts, which Vermonters in particular were quite worried about. Further study was deemed necessary, and no control structure was ultimately built. Drastic floods occurred in the Lake Champlain–Richelieu River basin in 1992 and 2011, which renewed interest in controlling water levels and raised worries about phosphorous causing harmful algal blooms (these nutrient loading concerns also applied to Lake Memphremagog). In summer 2022, the engineering board released a report recommending different structural works.

In Quebec's Quiet Revolution, hydroelectricity production through the public utility Hydro-Québec became tightly linked to nationalism and identity, captured by the rallying cry "Maîtres Chez Nous" (masters in our own home). The first phase of the James Bay project in northern Quebec, which involved the diversion of several rivers into the dammed La Grande River, was launched in the early 1970s. When finished, the eight powerhouses and five reservoirs produced about 12,000 MW. Though these James Bay power developments were obviously far from the border, some of the surplus electricity was sent to the United States.

The La Grande project had gone forward without an environmental impact assessment and without consulting local Indigenous Peoples. The Cree and Inuit of northern Quebec secured an injunction in 1973 to stop construction; that was quickly overturned, however. Government officials and those affected by the megaproject then turned to negotiating a settlement. The James Bay and Northern Quebec Agreement (JBNQA) was signed in 1975 by the Government of Quebec, Government of Canada, Hydro-Québec, and northern Quebec Cree and Inuit. It established environmental and social protections and exchanged certain Cree and Inuit rights in the agreement territory (though trapping and hunting rights remained) for monetary compensation and other rights, recognitions, and benefits.

The second phase of the James Bay hydro development launched in 1989. This involved new power stations on the Great Whale River, as well as the diversion of the Little Whale River. This Great Whale development was predicated on exporting the electricity to New York State on a firm and long-term basis. But the project met with stiff resistance from the affected Cree, who had expanded their alliance with environmental NGOs, including some organizations in the US. This opposition, and changes to the electric utility market and long-term contracts in the United States, led the New York Power Authority to cancel an 800 MW purchase agreement for Great Whale electricity. In 1994 the newly elected Parti Quebecois announced that it was stopping the Great Whale project indefinitely.[21] The Cree and Quebec government signed the Paix des Braves in 2002, building on the previous JBNQA. That agreement cleared the way for hydro development on the Eastmain River. Two years later, the same parties signed an agreement authorizing the diversion of the Rupert River to the Eastmain and La Grande watersheds, and new generating stations on the Rupert. These were completed in 2012.

Quebec's ability to export power to the United States was further enhanced by the influx of power from the Churchill Falls Generating Station in Labrador. It was built between 1967 and 1974 by the Churchill Falls (Labrador) Corporation, which is a joint venture between the Newfoundland and Labrador Hydro Corporation and Hydro-Québec. At the time of completion, Churchill Falls was the largest underground power station in the world. Hydro-Québec contracted for 90 percent of the resulting electricity for several decades at prescribed rates. This became a political problem in Newfoundland and Labrador when energy prices rose and Hydro-Québec was able to sell power to the US for noticeably higher than it had paid Newfoundland for Churchill Falls electricity.

After 1970, Ontario, Quebec, BC, Manitoba, Newfoundland, and New Brunswick exported large amounts of power to the United States. Control of hydro power and electricity transmission was central to the political economy of these provinces. Many provinces were more amenable to a national grid, or regional grids, in the 1970s or 1980s; none of these came to fruition, though specific provinces sometimes traded electricity. As new hydro sources came online, such as the James Bay, Nelson, and Churchill projects, even more energy was sent to points south, even if the total percentage of Canadian electricity that was exported did not change much. These various energy projects collectively illustrate that northern North American interchanges could have profound impacts on the continent's ecosystems and natural security.

Hydroelectricity exports were not the only way that water put itself on the diplomatic docket in the second half of the twentieth century. Pollution and flood waters moved across the border at various spots along the international divide, whether on the west coast or east coast or multiple points in between. Many of these were large developments, several qualifying as megaprojects. But many were smaller developments which, despite their size, turned into political problems that sometimes garnered more crossborder controversy than their larger brethren.

10

Energy and Minerals

In the 1970s, scholars began paying more attention to the ecological aspects of Canada-US relations. This was particularly true amongst political scientists and legal scholars, who, in this decade, frequently published journal articles and book chapters surveying the leading issues in Canadian-American environmental relations. By the 1980s, a spate of books on Canada-US energy and environmental relations had appeared.[1] That trend continued into the 1990s and up to the present.[2]

Fossil fuels and minerals were prominent in this early literature. During the latter half of the Cold War, the period covered in this chapter, Canadian oil and gas became an even higher-profile part of the bilateral relationship. After all, fossil fuels were extremely lucrative and had national security dimensions, and American interests were heavily invested in the Canadian industry. The growth in Canadian fossil fuel production also coincided with the rise of the North American environmental movement and new forms of Canadian nationalism. As this chapter will show, the concerns of both environmentalists and nationalists would, directly and indirectly, impact continental fossil fuel and mineral relations during the Cold War.

Fossil fuels and minerals influence societies in numerous ways. Hydrocarbons, of course, have tremendous energetic ability and, along with electricity, are defining features of modern society. Likewise, minerals such as uranium, bauxite, potash, and phosphates underpin contemporary living standards: fertilizers for crops, fuel for nuclear power generation, and metals for all sorts of applications. But, when refined, smelted, or burned, these can threaten human health through pollutants, radiation, and greenhouse gases. Thus, these natural resources can become objects of diplomatic concern twice over: at the harvesting and trade phase as well as dealing with the cross-border hazards that result.

ENVIRONMENTAL MOVEMENT

Lester Pearson had assumed the prime ministership of Canada when the environmental movement was just beginning to take hold in the United States. Rachel Carson's *Silent Spring*, published in 1962, was one of the indispensable texts of the movement, but there were many other forces at play. No one mistook Lester Pearson, or his prime ministerial predecessors, for an environmentalist. He did show some concern about radioactive fallout and test ban negotiations. Nevertheless, Pearson was "apt to view the environment through the lens of the development and utilization of natural resources and the freest possible flow across the Canadian-American border of oil, gas, strategic metals and minerals, and electricity."[3]

Silent Spring received attention and adherents in Canada, but the environmental movement was much stronger south of the border. It was also more apparent in American politics. President Kennedy appointed a secretary of the interior, Stewart Udall, who wrote a book on the blight of pollution. Lyndon Johnson's "Great Society" program included many environmental and beautification facets, and more than three hundred laws to protect the environment were passed during his presidency. The 1970s have been labelled the "green decade," and it was kicked off in 1970 by several ground-breaking, and ground-protecting, federal pieces of environmental legislation, as well as the first Earth Day. Explicitly environmental departments and agencies were created within the US government, becoming another set of actors in transboundary diplomacy. New types of environmental NGOs and interest groups appeared on the scene, joining older organizations like the Sierra Club and the Audubon Society. The fact that much of this transpired under Richard Nixon, no friend of environmental regulations, showed how far ecological concerns had permeated the mainstream in the United States.

Canada also created governmental departments or agencies that focused on environmental issues, generally following the American example. Institutional and constitutional differences led the two nations' environmental regulations down different paths.[4] That speaks to some of the differences between the environmental attitudes of the two nations. Americans were generally quicker than Canadians to form groups and pass legislation to protect environments; at the same time, they were also the frontrunners when it came to promoting the kinds of the economic and consumption systems that undermined ecological protection efforts. The Canadian economy's long reliance on the exportation of staples meant that the desire to preserve landscapes if they could also be economically productive frequently found less purchase in Canada than in the United States.[5] That said, put in a global comparative perspective, the similarities are much more apparent than the differences when it comes to Canadian and American attitudes toward the natural world.

The 1960s and 1970s witnessed the rise of not only a North American environmental movement, but a new nationalism in Canada critical of American designs on Canada's resources. The rising tide of environmentalism, and the growing importance of multilateral environmental diplomacy by both Canada and the United States, was signposted by the 1972 UN Conference on the Environment, also known as the Stockholm Conference. Even in those types of multilateral settings, however, Canada's position was often determined by continental priorities. Ottawa's approach to the Stockholm Conference, for example, was shaped by its concerns about its Arctic Waters Pollution Prevention Act vis-à-vis the United States.[6]

The Pierre Trudeau government attempted to distance Canada from the United States in the 1970s. While Trudeau, who was prime minister for most of the period between 1968 and 1984, had definite international ideas, domestic affairs concerned him more than foreign relations.[7] Trudeau had considerably different notions of, and goals for, the Canada-US relationship than previous prime ministers, whether they were Liberal or Conservative. Indeed, he was wary of the US, and his "third option" policy aspired to reduce Canadian trade dependence on the US and seek new international partners. This new direction preceded Richard Nixon's stated ambivalence about doing Canada any favours and the president's suggestion that there was a need for a more "mature" bilateral relationship. Nixon's measures to deal with the balance of payments concerns, and an unwillingness to exempt Canada, created additional friction in bilateral relations.

Indeed, many commentators point to the Nixon-Trudeau dyad as the end of the Canada-US special relationship. The 1970s was a time of diverging national interests after an extended period where they had mostly converged. Canadian nationalism and anti-Americanism were on the rise, fuelled by American policies towards the Vietnam War, Cold War militarism, and Civil Rights. Trudeau was opposed to nuclear weapons, though he did consent, albeit reluctantly, to the American testing of cruise missiles in the Canadian north. But he was not as opposed to free trade as some of his nationalist policies might suggest.

Trudeau had mixed personal relationships with subsequent Republican presidents: the prime minister enjoyed a warmer rapport with Gerald Ford than with Nixon or Ronald Reagan. Ford's Michigan background meant he had some understanding of Canada's importance to the United States, and Reagan did at least genuinely seek a closer relationship with Canada. Trudeau got on reasonably well with Jimmy Carter, a Democrat. "No president ever worked harder than Jimmy Carter," wrote historians John Herd Thompson and Stephen J. Randall about the president from Georgia, "to understand the issues in Canada-US relations."[8]

NATIONAL ENERGY PROGRAM

From the 1940s through the 1970s, both countries fluctuated between protectionism and liberal trade with each other on energy resources. US corporations and their Canadian subsidiaries controlled the majority of the Canadian petroleum industry. The shift to allowing long-term arrangements for electricity exchanges had paved the way for the oil and gas trade to move from "informal continentalism" to the contemporary "integrated, harmonized, and liberalized energy trade."[9] Responsibility for energy policy in the US shifted from the states to the federal government; in Canada, this responsibility remained bifurcated between the provinces and Ottawa, with certain fossil fuel-producing provinces angling to enhance their jurisdiction and control over hydrocarbons policy.[10]

At first, the Trudeau government pushed hard for an increased US market share for Canadian hydrocarbons. The exemption in the US that Canadian oil had enjoyed ended in 1970. Preliminary talks for a continental energy agreement, which the United States wanted, were underway in 1969 and continued for the next few years. They ultimately went nowhere. The Canadian government did not want to lose its option to buy cheaper Venezuelan and Middle Eastern oil for the eastern part of the country while selling more expensive western Canadian oil to the rest of Canada and the United States. It also wanted the latitude to cut off exports to the US when necessary. At the time, with oil prices high, Canada was reaping the rewards of sending record amounts of petroleum south.

Then came the energy crisis in the wake of the 1973 OPEC oil embargo. Both countries were partially reliant on oil from outside North America and the energy crisis, even if it was exaggerated and exploited by fossil fuel interests, had lasting reverberations.[11] The US became more amenable to importing Canadian oil but, at the same time, Trudeau began phasing out oil exports to the US in order to ensure sufficient domestic oil supplies, dashing American hopes for a formal oil agreement.

Trudeau then set off on a major policy switch to make Canada less dependent on foreign oil, increase Canadian ownership in the energy sector, and give the federal government a bigger share in Canadian oil production. Oil exports to the US were reduced, and an export tax was imposed. This led many Americans, including some in Congress, to wonder whether Canadians only cared about the "special relationship" when it benefitted them.[12] The Trudeau government also announced the creation of Petro-Canada and proposed building a pipeline from the Great Lakes to Montreal in December 1973. These and other policy interventions were designed to keep domestic gas prices low, compared to the volatile world market, which western producers perceived as benefitting eastern Canada at their expense.

In 1980, the Trudeau government announced the National Energy Program (NEP) to increase domestic control – considering that over three quarters of the domestic fossil fuel industry was American-owned – thereby achieving economic self-sufficiency and increasing Canadian energy independence.[13] Natural gas exports were frozen, oil exports were reduced, and domestic oil prices were kept low. Any production had to be done by a firm that was at least half Canadian-owned, and strict regulations and taxes were applied to development on lands owned by the federal government. Not adequately forewarned about the NEP, the US government formally protested this perceived discrimination (and complained about the Foreign Investment Review Agency, a federal agency created in 1973 to screen American investment).[14] Alberta did not like the NEP either, to put it mildly. Though it was not the main goal, a side-effect was an increase in US investment in fossil fuel exploration and development in Canada. At the same time, the NEP did serve to jumpstart the Canadianization of domestic fossil fuels: Canadian ownership rose to a third of the industry.

Nevertheless, with the NEP in place, Canada-US relations reached a low point in the early 1980s, egged on by a severe recession that even led the Trudeau Cabinet to explore sectoral free trade options. More than a decade of multilateral leanings and nationalist-tinged policies toward the US had purportedly brought about a decrease in Canadian prosperity. But relations improved after Brian Mulroney came to power in 1984. He enjoyed a good personal relationship with Reagan. Their penchant for summit diplomacy led to an agreement to expand northern air defence infrastructure, renewal of the NORAD agreement and the Defense Development and Production Sharing Agreement, and addressing acid rain.[15]

Mulroney retreated from economic nationalism and protectionism, preferring an open market-based approach. Along with Reagan, he embraced policies that paved the way for the neoliberal financial revolution that has come to define North American economies. He welcomed foreign direct investment in Canada. The Mulroney government quickly dismantled the NEP and privatized Petro-Canada. Mulroney also moved to satisfy the Reagan administration's desire for something more comprehensive and binding than the previous informal understandings that had characterized oil and gas relations. The way to do this was to include fossil fuels in the ongoing negotiations for a free trade treaty. Those talks became the basis for the energy chapter of the 1988 Canada-US Free Trade Agreement (CUFTA), which would later essentially be folded into the 1994 North American Free Trade Agreement.

The CUFTA represented the first formal and comprehensive continental energy agreement, and it created a stable playing field for bilateral oil and gas relations.[16] Neither country could impose price controls on oil and natural gas or impose import or export charges without doing the same domestically. Neither country could discriminate against the other or arbitrarily cut off exports; the controversial proportionality clause held that any reductions in energy exports had to be matched by reduced domestic consumption. Canada gained secure access to the American market and Alaskan oil; the United States got stable access to Canadian energy, entrenched within a rules-based system.[17] The CUFTA represented a retreat on the part of the federal governments, giving more latitude to subnational units and the market to determine fossil fuel policy.

Exactly when Canadian fossil fuel exports to the United States became more important than electricity exports is debatable, depending which measurement is used (e.g., total value, percentage of supply, importance to national security). Nevertheless, we can certainly state that fossil fuels were firmly ensconced as the cornerstone of Canada-US energy relations long before the 1988 and 1994 free trade agreements. The US imported over 1.3 million barrels of Canadian petroleum per day in 1973, but then the numbers fell; by the early 1980s, it was under half a million barrels per day. By the end of the Cold War, with free trade in place, the US consistently imported more than one million barrels of petroleum a day from Canada. By the end of the millennium, that number had tripled because of the expansion of the western Canadian tar sands, which I will explore in a later chapter.

PIPELINES AND TANKERS

Conduits were needed to move all of these fossil fuels. In the late 1960s, the US government had tried to get Alaskan oil and natural gas to the lower forty-eight states. Overland pipelines would need to cross Canadian territory to make that happen. The National Energy Board conducted hearings on a proposal by the Foothills Pipe Lines Ltd for a natural gas pipeline along the route of the Alaskan Highway; this line received a positive recommendation. On the American side, the Alaska Natural Gas Transportation Act of 1976 changed the US Federal Power Commission "from an autonomous regulatory body to an advisory committee."[18]

In 1977, the two countries entered into a formal treaty, the Canada–United States Agreement on Principles Applicable to a Northern Natural Gas Pipeline, to facilitate the planning and construction of a pipeline along the recommended route. They also entered into the Transit Pipeline Treaty that same year. According to this agreement, both countries would not interfere with any transborder hydrocarbon flows. The main reason for the treaty was to protect a pipeline that originated and ended in the same country but crossed into the territory of the other along the way – natural gas pipelines from Alaska to the contiguous US in particular.

In addition to a diplomatic agreement about the best route, Ottawa and Washington also needed to work out compromises on other related aspects. Canada's new Northern Pipeline Agency was given oversight of the 800 km pipeline, built between 1978 and 1982, from central Alberta to two locations on the Canada-US border. The Foothills pipeline through the Yukon was given an easement and passed environmental and social impact assessments; it was delayed for economic reasons, however.[19] In 1985, the Interprovincial company did complete a pipeline to carry light crude oil from Norman Wells to Alberta. This was the first permanent buried pipeline in the Canadian Arctic.

Huge petroleum reserves had been discovered on Alaska's north slope, at Prudhoe Bay, in the 1960s. The main options for moving it to market were running a pipeline to the southern Alaskan coast, where it would be loaded onto tanker ships, or moving it to the lower forty-eight states entirely by pipeline, which would cross through Canadian territory. Canada was worried about a potential oil spill along the Pacific coast and wanted to convince the Americans to move the oil by pipeline through Canadian territory, the Mackenzie Valley specifically, so it could link up with Albertan pipelines. Over the span of several years in the early 1970s, Ottawa tried to convince the Nixon administration to do just this, with no success. At any rate, the 1977 Berger Report recommended a pipeline moratorium for ten years to settle outstanding Indigenous land claims and environmental issues. Instead, a trans-Alaska pipeline was built. In 1989, the infamous Exxon Valdez oil spill would befoul the southern Alaskan coastline near Anchorage.[20]

In 1969 and again in 1970, the Humble Oil Company sent a tanker, the *Manhattan*, through the Northwest Passage. This was a test of sorts to see whether a tanker offered a viable transportation method for Alaskan and northern fossil fuels. Canada considered the Arctic Archipelago, including the Northwest Passage, to be part of its historic internal waters; the United States viewed this passage as an international strait with a right of free transit. The US had informed Canada beforehand of this voyage but did not ask permission. The *Manhattan*'s trip raised a sovereignty furor in Canada amongst nationalists, in addition to provoking environmentalists. In response, Canada passed the Arctic Waters Pollution Prevention Act (AWPPA), which claimed that Canada's need to prevent pollution gave it functional jurisdiction of one hundred nautical miles (expanded to 200 nautical miles in 2009).[21] Truthfully, the AWPPA was as much, or more, about asserting Canada's offshore jurisdiction as it was about preventing pollution.

Canada's claim to sovereignty in the Arctic is relevant here because of the potential implications for environmental and energy relations, such as exploration for and the transportation of hydrocarbons.[22] But those implications have remained mostly theoretical. In 1985, another US voyage through the Northwest Passage, the *Polar Sea*, again raised hackles about what constituted internal waters. Consequently,

Figure 10.1 "... Surely we can work out some mutually agreeable means of friendly pollution of the Arctic." Editorial cartoon about Canada-US Arctic relations, *Vancouver Sun*.

a Canada-US Arctic Cooperation Agreement was signed in 1988. This offered a pragmatic approach, if not a resolution, as the US agreed to ask permission to transit Canada's Arctic waters. Canada's claim to these seas as inland waters is debatable and has lately become a pointed issue as climate change makes fossil fuel exploration and vessel transits here more viable.

OTHER TRADE

In addition to natural gas, fertilizer requires phosphate rock and potash. Though Canada had ample natural gas and potash, since the 1950s it had imported most of its phosphate supplies from the United

States. Conversely, the United States acquired most of its potash from Canada – the former imported around 300,000 tons of potash from the latter in 1963, but over five million tons by 1975. From the mining to the processing, the production of these different fertilizer components is energy intensive and environmentally disruptive because of the chemical byproducts. Asbestos is similar to potash in that Canada has some of the world's largest reserves, one province became the leading producer, and Canada was the principal supplier of this mineral to the United States. Asbestos has a wide range of industrial applications, but it is also a known carcinogen.[23]

Aluminum, like potash and asbestos, had been dominated by American capital. But this was also one of the resource industries where Canada did some fabrication and manufacturing rather than just exporting raw materials. Granted, Canadian aluminum production needed to import bauxite, an essential part of the smelting process (a process that relied on cheap hydro power). Since the start of the twentieth century, American interests had controlled a great deal of the Canadian aluminum industry – through Alcan – though independent Canadian producers appeared in the 1950s. By the later 1950s, Canada regularly sent almost 200 million tons of aluminum per year to the United States. More than twice that amount was exported to the US annually during the 1970s.

Though the United States produces more copper than Canada, its requirements are also much higher. Hence, Canada sent noteworthy volumes of this metal to the US during the first three decades of the Cold War. Copper mining has environmental impacts, notably on nearby freshwater, but the most widespread environmental degradation is air pollution from the smelting process, which releases particulate matter and SO_2. Canada supplied the US with many other minerals and materials, such as zinc, lead, and cobalt. It remained a major provider of uranium to the US up until the mid-1960s when the US began excluding foreign uranium. Canada responded by sending this resource elsewhere – using the exportation of nuclear materials, technology, and expertise as a lever in the pursuit of various Cold War international diplomacy goals, such as non-proliferation and containing communism. Nuclear exports and sharing became parts of Canada's relations with countries such as India, Pakistan, and Romania, and with international institutions such as the United Nations and the World Bank.[24] By the later 1970s, the US had started to relax its measures against uranium imports from Canada.[25] At the end of the

Cold War, most of Canada's uranium exports were again going to the United States.

American imports of pulp, paper, and lumber came predominantly from Canada into the 1970s. In that decade, coal, phosphates, food and agricultural products, and iron ore were the four primary commodities Canada imported from the United States. Taking 1977 as a representative year, the preponderance of agriculture commodities Canada sent to the US were still wheat and wheat-related products, followed by barley, canola, meat, and distilled alcohol and beverages.[26] Foodstuffs are not only environmental diplomacy but, in a way, energy diplomacy as well since they end up being consumed by humans and animals to create muscle power.

Most of those imports and exports carried on with little fanfare or public debate. Some of the energy topics covered in this chapter, such as the National Energy Program, did become the type of punctuated bilateral dispute that garnered newspaper headlines and the frequent attention of diplomats. Many of the other energy affairs in this period, such as pipeline agreements that largely flew under the public's radar, became controversial only later on, once the ramifications of pumping massive amounts of carbon dioxide and methane into the atmosphere became widely known. To be sure, these are emblematic of the seemingly ordinary and constant types of environmental diplomacy that progressively added up to something bigger than the sum of their parts.

11

Crossing Borders

Borders, whether accepted or contested, complicate environmental and energy relations. One might think that the Canada-US border has long been well-established, but certain maritime borders – in the Pacific, Atlantic, and the north – were disputed for much of the last half of the twentieth century. The placement of maritime demarcations has implications for determining control over valuable fisheries, as well as harvesting rights for extensive fossil fuel and mineral deposits. When it comes to other parts of the Canada-US border, such as through the Great Lakes or along the 49th parallel, different species and pollutants frequently disregard the line, forcing nation-states to respond to the situations and problems they create. Moreover, the physical properties and behaviours of these different resources and species determine the range of diplomatic options: in other words, the type of chemical in an airborne pollutant, or the dietary predilections of a certain fish, have political implications. In this chapter, I will start with Cold War discussions about the Law of the Sea and then turn to various fisheries and other migratory species. Then I will consider air pollution and acid rain towards the end of the Cold War. Many of these concerns dominated diplomacy for extended periods, proving once again how critical environmental and energy topics were to the general state of the bilateral relationship.

LAW OF THE SEA

After the Second World War, maritime jurisdiction attracted the attention of Canadian diplomats, particularly after Newfoundland and Labrador joined Confederation in 1949. In this realm, Canada's interests often differed from those of the United States, with the result that there was some butting of heads over prospective maritime laws. The Louis St Laurent government explored ways to strengthen the existing three-mile territorial sea limit and extend it to offshore fisheries up to a twelve-mile limit. At the 1958 and 1960 United Nations conferences on the Law of the Sea, which sought to codify the use of ocean resources, the Diefenbaker government promoted international cooperation but also aggressively pursued Canada's interests as a coastal nation. Ottawa pushed unsuccessfully for control of fisheries and continental shelf resources to twelve miles offshore, favouring multilateral agreements so long as those seemed the best way of protecting Canada's coastal interests.[1]

The Lester Pearson government's 1964 Territorial Sea and Fishing Zones Act abandoned the effort to reach an international agreement and, in its place, set out a national strategy that claimed Canada's right to establish an exclusive fisheries zone along the whole of the country's coastline. To obtain international recognition for this baseline scheme, the government entered into a lengthy, and ultimately futile, process of diplomatic negotiations and public relations.[2] A 1970 amendment to the 1964 act created a twelve-mile territorial sea and used fishery-closing lines to cut off certain areas from foreign intrusion. Canada and the United States also signed the Agreement on Reciprocal Fisheries of 1970.[3] That same year Canada announced the Arctic Waters Pollution Prevention Act to create a 100-nautical-mile pollution zone (see the previous chapter).

Ted McDorman identifies 1970 as the transition point after which international law, and the Canada–United States saltwater relationship, moved into the modern era.[4] The United States preferred internationalizing coastal areas, which played to its national interests. Canada found its interests better served by aggressive positions that enhanced national sovereignty over continental shelf zones. Both countries brought these stances to the United Nations discussions during the 1970s. This process, the United Nations Convention on the Law of the Sea (UNCLOS) III, was enshrined in a 1982 treaty. Canada signed this convention. The United States did not sign, opposed in particular to its deep seabed mining regime, though it has generally honoured UNCLOS.[5]

Ottawa and Washington each unilaterally declared a 200-mile extension of their territorial seas in 1977. These exclusive economic zones (EEZs), as they were known, created exclusive fishing zones within that extension. This rendered moot many bilateral points of contention, such as the twelve-mile-territorial sea, but created other overlapping conflicts over fisheries, hydrocarbons, and borders by theoretically bringing formerly international territory under national jurisdiction.[6]

After declaring the 200-mile maritime extension, Canada and the United States appointed Special Negotiators to hammer out agreements about the range of conflicting border claims about fisheries and hydrocarbon issues in the Gulf of Maine.[7] These negotiators produced a report that offered specific and innovative solutions to overlapping claims. This led to the East Coast Fisheries Resources Treaty (1979) and a treaty about the international maritime boundary in the Gulf of Maine. President Carter lacked the political capital to push these two pacts through the US Senate, however. The east coast fisheries treaty stalled, even though Canadian secretary of state for External Affairs Mark MacGuigan called it Canada's top foreign policy issue, with Trudeau's National Energy Program poisoning the well to some extent.[8] Reagan withdrew the treaty in the face of domestic opposition. This irked Canadians, and the Canadian Navy even sent some warships and a submarine to keep out American fleets.[9]

These negotiations did pave the way for the two countries to submit the Gulf of Maine boundary to international arbitration. In the 1960s, offshore hydrocarbons had been a matter of contention, but fishing then evolved into the bigger problem. The US claimed all the Georges Bank fishing grounds, while Canada claimed the northeastern part. The matter was then turned over to the Special Negotiators, who recommended an agreement on fisheries and submission of the Gulf of Maine boundary to the International Court of Justice. This court's 1984 ruling established the maritime boundary, giving Canada about one-sixth of the Georges Bank.

The ruling did not address some disputed territory: the so-called "grey zone" with Machias Seal Island (and the nearby North Rock) at the centre. Jurisdictional claims over this island predated Canadian Confederation, as New Brunswick had installed a lighthouse in the 1830s. Whichever country controlled the island would have jurisdiction over the adjacent lobster fishing grounds, the "grey zone." The two countries engaged in low-grade diplomatic sparring over this island at several points in the twentieth century, with access to the surrounding fisheries the main point of contention. In the 1970s, the United States suggested taking the Machias Seal Island matter to the International Court of Justice. But Canada opted to exclude the question of sovereignty of Machias Seal Island from the Gulf of Maine case sent to the court.[10] When lobster stocks declined in the early twenty-first century, local strife about this zone made national headlines.

IGNORING BORDERS

Canada and the United States had signed several different fisheries treaties in the first half of the twentieth century. Although fish became comparatively less central to environmental diplomacy after the Second World War, that is not to say that fish fell off the diplomatic agenda. In the decade following 1945, halibut and seal conservation were frequently discussed, but no new agreements were arrived at.[11] As mentioned above, expanding maritime boundaries through law of the sea negotiations in the 1960s and 1970s had repercussions for coastal fisheries. The extension to a 200-nautical-mile fishing zone (the EEZ) also brought US and Canadian claims into conflict at a number of points along the Pacific, Atlantic, and Arctic coasts.

When it came to Pacific salmon, the last diplomatic accord had been the sockeye agreement of 1930. Negotiations continued in the early Cold War period, and in 1957 that agreement was extended to pink salmon.[12] Both Canada and the United States lobbied to include an article on anadromous fish in the 1982 Convention on the Law of the Sea, specifying that countries should retain the right to harvest the fish that spawned in their national waters. This principle became a basis for the 1985 Pacific Salmon Treaty.[13]

Under this treaty, each country receives a proportion of the quota equal to the proportion of the salmon that spawn in its territory. This is based on the idea that a salmon that spawns in one country's river belongs to that country, which should be compensated if fishers from the other nation intercept those fish. The treaty created the Pacific Salmon Commission to scientifically estimate the maximum sustainable yield and recommend quotas for the various species of Pacific salmon. However, Joseph Taylor III points out problems with the bilateral salmon arrangements. Technologies and techniques evolved faster than the regulations, while commercial fishing outfits were more concerned with short-term gains than the long-term sustainability of the stocks. Furthermore, those regulations were sometimes based on flawed assumptions about salmon behaviour and on a level of abstraction that turned fish into irrational blocks of stock owned by one political jurisdiction in a way that did not reflect reality. Thus, the succession of salmon agreements "actually codified inequalities and perpetuated irrational management."[14] Many of these critiques applied to fisheries management throughout the continent, and many other types of species.

The 1985 treaty measures were intended to depoliticize the co-management of salmon stocks.[15] Instead, the 1985 treaty soon proved dysfunctional, with Canada claiming that catches were imbalanced in favour of the United States. For much of the 1990s the two sides remained acrimoniously deadlocked over these fisheries management arrangements. In 1997, Canadian fishing boats even blockaded an Alaskan ferry.[16] This debacle was mostly smoothed over by revising parts of the 1985 treaty via a 1999 agreement. That was more or less a truce recognizing the depleted nature of the stocks. It shifted the emphasis away from "equitable balance of interceptions" and towards conservation, with the harvest rates more closely tied to actual species abundance. The US also agreed to some reduction in the percentage of Fraser River fish it intercepted, and trust funds were created to improve habitat and protection measures. Though the 1999 agreement defused the situation, it has not removed all points of contention. Another agreement was signed in 2008, carrying the modus vivendi forward with some slight alterations.

The unique case of Yukon River salmon bears mentioning, too. Given Indigenous uses of salmon from this river for non-commercial purposes, it was left out of the 1985 agreement. In 2002, Canada and the US made the Yukon River Salmon Agreement through an exchange of notes, and it was appended to the Pacific Salmon Treaty. The primary purpose of this agreement is to ensure that adequate numbers of salmon are allowed to reach Canada to spawn in their natal streams, and also to protect and restore salmon habitat.

Like salmon, tuna have occasionally created bilateral conflict on the west coast. In 1979, Canadian authorities arrested nineteen US tuna vessels for fishing in Canadian waters. The US responded with a brief tuna embargo. These frictions led to the 1981 Canada–United States Albacore Tuna Treaty which allowed reciprocal fishing rights. In response to US complaints about Canadian vessels overcrowding American waters, amendments in 2002 put limits on certain reciprocal rights. The next year, the two nations also arrived at an agreement on Pacific Hake and Whiting, giving the US about three-quarters of the harvest.[17]

When it came to Pacific Halibut, whose management has been less controversial, the 1953 Convention remained in effect. A protocol to the 1953 agreement was added via a 1979 Protocol. Responding to the 1977 EEZs declaration, this protocol stated that fishers could only harvest in their political jurisdictions. The International Pacific Halibut Commission regulates or prohibits fishing in certain areas, establishes closed seasons, collects data, puts limits on fish sizes and catch quantities, and regulates the type of permitted technologies.

Turning to inland waters, the Great Lakes Fishery Commission formed in 1954 still applies today.[18] Aided by this commission, various US and Canadian agencies signed a 1981 agreement called a Joint Strategic Plan for Management of Great Lakes Fisheries (and updated it in 1997). Though nonbinding, this scheme worked through the Great Lakes Fishery Commission in pursuit of shared conservation goals across the basin. Each of the five lakes has its own committee, forming the Council of Lake Committees. Though best known for its sea lamprey control program, the Great Lakes Fisheries Commission's activities also include other biodiversity preservation efforts.[19]

In the latter half of the twentieth century, commercial fish harvesting in the Great Lakes basin was not nearly as contentious as it used to be. That had little to do with the governance systems put in place going back more than a century: rather, there was not much to argue over, relatively speaking. Certainly, there seemed to be a greater cross-border willingness to cooperate when it came to preservation measures. But most fish populations in the Great Lakes basin were severely depleted compared to their historical populations, while non-native species had proliferated, and a significant share of the tiny commercial catch is rightfully reserved for Indigenous harvesters. Recreational fishing, worth some $7 billion annually, has long been more lucrative than commercial harvesting.[20]

Thus, fisheries relations in the twenty-first century, across the board, are characterized more by cooperation and less by the competitiveness that marked earlier periods, aside from some little skirmishes and posturing. The situation on both coasts benefitted from the 1990 signing of a Canada-US Fisheries Enforcement Agreement, which made it an offence for vessels from either country to operate illegally in the waters of the other.

Canada and the United States are also party to a range of multiparty international agreements on ocean stocks: the North Pacific Fisheries Convention, which was signed in 1952 and replaced in 1993 by the North Pacific Anadromous Fish Stocks convention; the Northwest Atlantic Fisheries Organization (NAFO); and the International Commission for the Conservation of Atlantic Tunas (ICCAT). Both northern North American countries are also signatories to a number of other multilateral conservation agreements. They joined the International Whaling Commission, established in 1946, though Canada withdrew in the 1980s over Inuit treaty rights to hunt whales. Both countries were amongst the five nations that signed onto the 1973 agreement for the conservation of polar bears, which prohibits unregulated sport hunting and the use of aircraft and large motorized vehicles. Broader multilateral agreements that include Canada and the US are the Convention on the International Trade of Endangered Species (CITES), which entered into force in 1975, and the 1993 United Nations Convention on Biological Diversity (though the US has never ratified the UNCBD).

Besides fish, many other species cross the Canada-US boundary frequently or seasonally. But there is little transnational coordination outside of a few isolated cases. That is partially because the Canadian provinces have more responsibility for species at risk; the federal government has jurisdiction for some migratory birds, certain aquatic species, and species on federal lands. US federal wildlife laws, meanwhile, take precedence over state regulations. By the later twentieth century, countless governmental and nongovernmental actors were involved in crossborder wildlife activities. But few of these involved direct diplomacy, though there were some transboundary partnerships and efforts through NAFTA's Commission for Environmental Cooperation (discussed in more detail in chapter 12).[21] Nongovernmental organizations are responsible for ecoregional conservation zones such as the *Yellowstone to Yukon* and *Algonquin to Adirondack* initiatives that try to create connective habitats for roaming species.

These types of initiatives reflect a partial shift towards protecting regional ecosystems rather than specific species or parks. Early twentieth-century efforts to protect transborder birds had focused on conserving species with economic value to humans. The 1916 Migratory Bird Treaty was a partial exception since aesthetic concerns were also at play. By the last decades of the twentieth century, the goal was mostly to preserve species and biodiversity for the sake of ecosystem services; in general, the two countries care about conservation more for instrumental reasons than intrinsic ones.

Declining duck populations and habitats motivated Canada and the United States to establish the North American Waterfowl Management Plan (NAWMP) in 1986. The goal was returning duck populations to their 1970s levels by restoring habitat through a variety of public-private partnerships. Within this framework NAWMP had a coordinating role, such as monitoring and data gathering, while hands-on activities were downloaded to different levels of government and civil society groups such as Ducks Unlimited.[22] NAWMP has been updated several times, with Mexico added in 1994, and the plan received a fundamental revision in 2012. Like most other North American transnational preservation agreements, conditions for the affected species have improved even though the stated protection goals have not been fully met.

The year after the NAWMP was signed, the two countries inked an agreement on the Porcupine caribou herd. These animals migrate annually between Alaska, where much of the calving range is in the Arctic National Wildlife Refuge (ANWR), and the Northwest Territories and the Yukon. Various First Nations rely on these caribou for sustenance and cultural uses. The 1987 International Porcupine Caribou Agreement coordinates the protection of this herd and its habitat through an international board that collects data, makes recommendations, and monitors impacts. The herd went from an estimated 169,000 caribou in 2010 to 218,000 by 2017; the story for caribou throughout the rest of the continent, however, is not so rosy.[23] The Obama administration banned fossil fuel production in the ANWR, which helped the Porcupine herd. But the Trump administration had begun reversing this policy before leaving office. It also worked to open up mining in the ANWR as well as the Boundary Waters Canoe Area Wilderness in Minnesota. The Biden administration has moved to reverse these Trump-era policies.

AIR QUALITY

In the later Cold War, crossborder air pollution burst onto the diplomatic scene. This was not the first time. The Trail Smelter had been a political lightning rod, and then early in the Cold War, pollution across the Detroit and St Clair Rivers attracted the attention of officials. Atmospheric pollution could cut both ways. While acid rain is generally perceived as a situation where the United States inflicted harm on Canada, there are also many cases where air pollution originating in Canada afflicted the United States.

In the first decade of the Cold War, air pollution across the Michigan-Ontario border in the St Clair–Detroit River corridor raised concerns. The United States and Canada sent several different references to the International Joint Commission about air quality in the Port Huron-Sarnia and Detroit-Windsor regions.[24] Determining the precise sources of this pollution was of paramount importance. Sarnia's Chemical Valley south of the city had already developed into an enormous petrochemical complex that befouled both air and water. Detroit's industrial base along the water included polluting steel and automobile manufacturing. The IJC formed a joint St Clair–Detroit Air Pollution Board in the 1960s. This board's 1972 report found that sulphur dioxide and particulate matter from Detroit was crossing over to Windsor, aided by prevailing winds. Along the St Clair River, it turned out that the main victims of Sarnia's air pollution were not in Port Huron but in Ontario. The IJC recommended that the two federal governments create pollution boards and establish national air quality standards.[25]

During the 1970s, the volume of air pollutants decreased by about half because of industry's modernization efforts. But it still was not close to the IJC's recommended levels. Further committees and IJC references followed, resulting in air pollution targets and a binational committee to monitor the situation. However, the targets were overly optimistic, and the state and province did not sufficiently reduce their emissions. Ongoing air pollution problems throughout North America, as well as acid rain, served to distract attention. Furthermore, the two federal governments were worried about IJC activism and maneuvered to sideline the commission when it came to bilateral talks about air quality.[26]

Around this time, Ontario was involved in several other transboundary air quality disputes. Ontario Hydro built a large coal-fired power station at Atikokan in the northwest part of the province. This was close to cherished recreational areas at the international border, such as the Boundary Waters Canoe Area Wilderness in Minnesota. The Reynolds aluminum smelter at Massena, New York was accused of contaminating the nearby binational Mohawk community, including the parts in Canadian territory.[27] Eventually, these various air quality issues either fell off the public's radar or became

Figure 11.1 Aerial view looking southwest over Sarnia's Chemical Valley and the St Clair River towards Michigan. Note the emissions coming from the smokestacks.

subsumed within wider debates about acid rain and national air quality agreements.

In the early 1970s, acid rain was an issue no one had heard of; by the 1980s, "acid rain not only dominated the Canada-US environmental relationship, it dominated the entire bilateral relationship."[28] Acidified precipitation, or acid rain, is created when sulphur and nitrogen oxides (SO_2 and NO_x) emissions are transported through the atmosphere and transformed into sulphuric and nitric acids. This acidified precipitation fell onto terrestrial and aquatic environments where it had a range of short- and long-term negative consequences. Don Munton, a leading scholar on air pollution and acid rain, notes that "[t]he impact is particularly strong during the spring run-off period when melting acidic winter snows produce an 'acid shock' in streams."[29]

Coal-fired plants, smelting, and other industrial processes are the chief emissions culprits. Both countries generate acid rain that falls in the other. Acid rain originating in the US and falling in Ontario was the biggest problem, though the smelters in the Sudbury region certainly contributed to acid rain within the province. That acid rain affected cottage country north of Toronto further helps explain why the issue gained so much public traction. Soon after acid rain was publicly recognized as a nuisance, diplomatic talks got underway. The United States and Canada formed a scientific committee to study the matter, named the Bilateral Research Consultation Group on the Long-Range Transport of Air Pollutants. This group produced an interim report in 1979, the same year that Canada and the US, along with many European countries, also signed the Convention on Long-Range Transboundary Air Pollution. Ongoing bilateral studies demonstrated the widespread extent and damage of acid rain, establishing that 70-80 percent of it originated in the United States. The two countries signed a memorandum of intent calling for a transboundary air quality agreement in 1980. Working groups produced reports, but the two sides could not agree on all the recommendations, such as the need for emission limitations and controls. In 1982, Canada proposed that each country reduce its SO_2 emissions by half.

The Reagan administration rejected the Trudeau government's proposal (though New York State and Quebec signed their own subnational acid rain agreement). The United States was more reluctant since it was the prime contributor and, as such, would have to bear the brunt of any necessary changes. Matters were not helped by the ideological unwillingness of the Reagan administration to impose any environmentally motivated regulations on economic activity, such as through the Clean Air Act; in fact, the US was going backward in that respect. The president himself did not seem to even believe that acid rain was caused by human activities. Washington stalled the talks, calling for more research. At the 1985 Shamrock Summit, after the election of Brian Mulroney's Progressive Conservatives, the US disingenuously agreed to appoint special envoys to study the problem. At summits in 1987 and 1988, Mulroney demanded a bilateral pact on acid rain. Informal talks and public diplomacy continued – what political scientist Stephen Clarkson called "the largest effort Canada has made to attempt to shape the policy of another country."[30] But the Reagan administration's stonewalling continued. A frustrated Ottawa pulled out of formal negotiations, awaiting the president's successor.[31]

The US proved more amenable to addressing the problem after George H.W. Bush entered the White House in 1989. Some scholars contend that this shift was attributable to Canadian pressure, but it was probably driven by other factors.[32] Bush moved to reform domestic air pollution laws, and the ensuing compatibility of American air pollution laws helped clear the way for movement on a Canada-US accord. Negotiations began on what would emerge as the 1991 Canada–United States Air Quality Agreement (AQA). National differences remained, but a compromise was broached. Canada wanted something with more concrete commitments and teeth; the United States, for its part, did not want to put any promises on paper.[33]

In the Air Quality Agreement, SO_2 emissions were permanently capped at approximately 13.3 million tons by 2010 in the US and 3.2 million tons in Canada. But the latter did not achieve one of its major goals: to get an American agreement to reduce deposition in Canadian territory. The US would not make any commitments beyond its borders. It did commit to following the requirements of its recently enacted Clean Air Act, which had the potential to reduce the emissions that created acid rain which eventually went across the border. Canada "had to accept on faith that transboundary flows and acidic deposition in Canada would be reduced by the measures Washington adopted."[34] The 1991 Air Quality Agreement also established a research and monitoring network and a bilateral coordinating committee. The AQA had similarities to the 1972 Great Lakes Water Quality Agreement, including the fact that it relied on provincial and state regulations supported by federal subsidies. At the same time, compared to the GLWQA, the AQA had even less transparency and enforcement mechanisms, featured a very minor role for the IJC, and contained no outright pledge that pollution from one country would not cause environmental harm across the border.[35]

The results of the 1991 Air Quality Agreement were mixed.[36] In 1996, the Canadian co-chair of the IJC, Adele Hurley, resigned in protest of the American failure to live up to its acid rain commitments. In the longer run, neither country has fully followed through on its commitments. However, SO_2 emissions did go down by almost 70 percent. Granted, this decrease probably had more to do with domestic regulations and technological changes instituted in each country than the international agreement.

The Air Quality Agreement also created a framework for addressing other air pollution issues, such as particulate matter and ozone. Ground-level ozone results from the reaction of nitrogen oxide and volatile organic compounds in the troposphere, fostered by sunlight and warm temperatures. When combined with particulate matter, it creates smog. Scientists knew that ozone had effects on vegetation, synthetic materials, and textiles, and that long-term exposure was linked to human health problems. They also recognized that, like acid rain, the emissions creating ozone problems could originate in one country but harm the other (especially in the Great Lakes region). In December 2000, Canada and the US signed an "Ozone Annex" to the Air Quality Agreement. Acknowledging that its economy, and its emissions, were tied to the United States, Canada "timed its phase-out mechanisms to parallel those adopted by the United States, thus ensuring a level playing field between the two states."[37]

A different type of ozone problem – the hole in the ozone layer – involved Canada and the United States in bilateral and multilateral diplomacy. Both were adherents to the Vienna Convention for the Protection of the Ozone Layer of 1985. The Reagan Administration had been initially dismissive of the ozone hole problem, but both the United States and Canada were key to the outcome of the 1987 Montreal Protocol on Substances that Deplete the Ozone Layer. This protocol is one of the few success stories in terms of global environmental agreements. The signatory countries agreed to phase out chlorofluorocarbons (CFCs) by 1996.[38] By the end of the twentieth century, CFC production had been mostly eliminated, and the hole in the ozone layer was shrinking. Canada was initially aggressive on carbon dioxide emissions, too: the international ozone talks in the 1980s included discussion of what would eventually be known as climate change. However, we will leave that for a future chapter.

A 1986 Canada-US Agreement on the Transboundary Movement of Hazardous Waste established a bilateral notification and consent program for the crossborder mobilization of hazardous waste. This was amended in 1992 to add provisions for municipal solid waste. The trade of waste materials is also governed by the two nations' domestic legislation and other international conventions on waste movement. At the time the 1986 agreement was signed, the vast majority of US hazardous waste exports were sent to Canada. In 1988, for example, about 85 percent of the 140,000 tons of hazardous waste the US exported went to its northern neighbour.[39] Large volumes of nonhazardous waste also crossed the border. The various transborder agreements only helped manage the flow of hazardous material, not limit it. To illustrate, in 2004 Canada exported approximately 340,000 tons of hazardous waste to the United States, which in turn sent 450,000 tons back.[40] The US Congress has looked into banning foreign waste, going so far as passing a bill to that effect in 2007. However, it was never implemented. Recently, American opposition helped stop an Ontario proposal for a deep underground nuclear waste repository close to Lake Huron. However, both countries have other nuclear waste storage facilities dotting the Great Lakes.

Sticking with toxic byproducts in this region, in 1998 the United States and Canada inked the Great Lakes Binational Toxics Strategy. The goal was the "virtual elimination" of targeted toxic substances in the Great Lakes basin, such as DDT, PCBs, and mercury. A few years later both nations were signatories to the Stockholm Convention. In this United Nations accord, many countries agreed to reduce or eliminate the so-called "dirty dozen," a list comprised of the twelve most dangerous persistent organic pollutants (POPs), all of which were also included in the 1998 Great Lakes Binational Toxics Strategy.

The topics covered in this chapter spanned from détente to the end of the Cold War and beyond. There were many cases where seemingly domestic concerns, such as pollution or fish, thrust themselves into binational relations by ignoring the border. In this way, more-than-human nature shows itself to be a powerful historical actor with its own forms of agency. For North Americans living through it, the Cold War turning hot seemed like the more immediate and existential threat. But, with the benefit of historical hindsight, the environmental diplomacy issues addressed in this chapter collectively posed equally grave, and longer-lasting, threats to humans and ecosystems alike.

12

Trading Resources

In the second half of the twentieth century, the Canadian economy became less dependent on exporting raw materials and foreign investment, at least by certain metrics. Between the 1970s and the 1990s, Canadian manufacturing made noticeable strides, and many of the resources that were exported – such as aluminum or paper – were at least partially processed before leaving the country. A few years after the end of the Cold War, and for the first time in the nation's history, unprocessed resources accounted for less than half of the total value of Canadian exports. Since then, the needle has been moving back from whence it came – that is, towards the extraction and export of natural resource staples.[1]

After the interventionist and nationalist policies of the Pierre Trudeau era, the pendulum swung towards free market policies. The fall of Soviet Communism buttressed and emboldened the globalized neoliberalism that characterized the 1990s. That trend was particularly apparent in North America, where Jean Chrétien's Liberals and Bill Clinton's Democrats – both centrist to centre-left parties – deferred to the free market in much the same way as had their right wing predecessors of the 1980s. Foreign affairs was not Chrétien's main focus, but he was interested in cultivating an image that he was more distant from the United States than Brian Mulroney. Nevertheless, his personal relations with Clinton were relatively friendly during their overlapping years (1993–2001).

The free trade agreements of 1988 and 1994 were defining aspects of late twentieth-century North American history. In many ways, free trade represented the age-old Canadian conundrum of prosperity versus sovereignty. This chapter will explore the environmental and energy facets of the free trade agreements as well as other aspects of the bilateral natural resource trade, such as softwood lumber, and other issues that extended into the twenty-first century, such as water and invasive species. Exploring these topics confirms that energy and environmental issues remained pre-eminent parts of Canada-US relations.[2]

FREE TRADE

Unpacking the free trade agreements requires returning to the Brian Mulroney years. His personal history is intertwined with crossborder resource diplomacy: he grew up in Baie-Comeau, a company town founded by the owner of the *Chicago Tribune* and its extensive pulp and paper empire, and went on to become the president of the Iron Ore Company of Canada, another resource industry that initially had significant American involvement. While Mulroney had not always favoured an intensified integration of North American economic and environmental resources, those defined his outlook by the time he occupied 24 Sussex Drive. Furthermore, his neoliberal views were well suited to the growing forces of international globalization. Mulroney got on well with Reagan and Bush, the two Republican presidents he encountered while prime minister.

In the lead-up to the 1988 free trade agreement there was plenty of handwringing within Canada about the benefits and drawbacks. Both the proponents and opponents envisioned that the free trade regime would dramatically restructure the Canadian economy and society; where they differed was over the question of whether that would be a good thing. The major benefit of this agreement for Canada may have been a negative one: preventing an American retreat into tariffs and protectionism.

As the early October 1987 deadline for an agreement approached, the two countries seemed at an impasse. But over the course of a dramatic weekend, an accord was hammered out.[3] The Canada-US Free Trade Agreement (CUFTA), formally enacted in 1988, had myriad environmental dimensions. As the name suggests, this agreement created free trade area arrangements between the United States and Canada for most industrial products as well as many services and types of foreign investment. It locked in the Auto Pact system while making some changes to it. Canada could not convince the United States to get rid of countervailing or anti-dumping duties. Binational dispute settlement panels were created. Agriculture, such as farm subsidies and import quotas, was so controversial that it was mostly exempted.

I have previously mentioned the fossil fuel aspects of the 1988 Canada-US Free Trade Agreement: it essentially barred price controls for oil and gas trade and integrated these sectors. A few years after the agreement, Canada exported one million barrels per day to the United States. That figure had quadrupled within a quarter century (accounting for about 40 percent of total American petroleum imports), the rise largely driven by production from the western tar sands.[4] Non-discriminatory electricity trade was included in the CUFTA, as each country granted national treatment to foreign electricity. The CUFTA, and later the North American Free Trade Agreement, also promoted restructuring, deregulation, and "continental integration in the energy and electricity sector at an administrative level, thereby making it more difficult for future governments to backtrack."[5]

The result was less federal control in both nations over the electricity trade. National Energy Board requirements to hold public hearings on electricity exports from Canada were reduced. Stateside, the Federal Energy Regulatory Commission (FERC), which had replaced the Federal Power Commission, encouraged greater choice and competition in the domestic electrical industry, as well as continental integration.[6] Notably, the regulation of the import and export of natural gas moved to the new federal Department of Energy. Numerous Canadian public utilities, such as BC Hydro, restructured to qualify for FERC licences to sell surplus power in the United States. Other public utilities, such as Ontario Hydro, moved towards privatization. The FERC and Canada's National Energy Board coordinated their regulatory approaches to better facilitate energy exchanges. In 1990, electricity exports between the two countries were roughly equal. By the start of the twenty-first century, Canada sent south more than four times the electricity that it received from the United States. Overall, since the initiation of free trade, Canada has become a net exporter of energy. Despite producing far greater volumes of fuels than Canada, the United States still needed to rely on importing large amounts of energy to meet its consumption requirements. Canada was the most secure and reliable source.

CUFTA was soon subsumed within a broader North American pact. The United States and Mexico wanted free trade with each other, and the way to do this was to widen the 1988 agreement. Though Canada was ambivalent about a trilateral deal, it did not want to be left out. The North American Free Trade Agreement, or NAFTA, was signed in 1992, fine-tuning the terms of the 1988 CUFTA and extending it to include Mexico. After NAFTA was signed, but before it was enacted, Chrétien and Clinton replaced Mulroney and Bush as leaders of their respective countries. Though both new leaders initially expressed skepticism, each eventually assented to NAFTA, and it took effect in 1994.[7] Mexico did not open up its fossil fuel industry to the United States to the same extent Canada had in the CUFTA. Some changes were made to the Auto Pact. NAFTA also dealt with aspects of economic integration that were not just about trade and industrial goods. It set rules on what types of domestic legislation each country could pass, liberalized foreign investment opportunities, and made the border more porous for people and firms.

As part of dealing with Chrétien and Clinton's seeming misgivings, the three North American countries negotiated and signed an environmental side agreement to NAFTA. Called the North American Agreement on Environmental Cooperation, it envisaged a broad range of objectives that would be the responsibility of the Commission for Environmental Cooperation (CEC). This side agreement did not assuage many environmentalist anxieties about the free trade agreement, however. For example, many were concerned that NAFTA could transform freshwater in its natural state (i.e., not packaged or bottled) into a commodity. This potentially opened the door to bulk water exports to the US, which Canada could not prohibit without violating NAFTA stipulations about non-discrimination and equal national treatment. In 1993, during the negotiations, the three North American governments issued a statement declaring that water was excluded from NAFTA. Nonetheless, given that many NAFTA terms are open to interpretation and court challenges, legal experts continue to debate how NAFTA (as well as other trade regimes such as GATT) might apply to water and its commercialization. There were, and still are, considerable concerns that once freshwater is exported or deemed a tradeable "product," a precedent under existing international trade law will have been set that would limit the ability to stop future exports, as well as worries connected to chapter 11 (the Investor-State Dispute Settlement Mechanism) and Article 315 (the proportionality provision).[8]

In 2020, the United States–Mexico–Canada Agreement (USMCA), essentially an updated NAFTA, came into effect. The USMCA eliminated some of the controversial investor-state dispute settlement provisions and added new environmental protections. However, this NAFTA 2.0 enshrines and continues the same neoliberal trade and market-based practices that prioritize profits over all else and stimulate overconsumption, arguably the main drivers of our ecological problems, inhibiting meaningful action to address the current climate crisis.

There is certainly an argument to be made that globalized trade has helped prevent armed conflicts. But it is difficult to avoid concluding that, overall, the free trade agreements were anything but bad for North American environments.[9] Even though NAFTA has led to some environmental coordination, chiefly through the CEC via its role as a credible information clearinghouse, the CEC has been underfunded and given little real enforcement power. The ecological damage resulting from the sheer expansion and scaling up of cross-border manufacturing and trade, as well as the outsourcing of economic activities to areas where environmental regulations are laxer, puts paid to any notion that the liberalization of trade regimes has increased environmental protections. Advocates claimed that the rising tide lifts all boats. But the only rising tide seems to have been literal rather than metaphorical, with all the additional economic activity spurring on sea-level rise by pumping more greenhouse gases into the atmosphere.

SOFTWOOD LUMBER

Several other trade issues with implications for bilateral energy and environmental diplomacy had their roots in the Mulroney-Reagan era. Softwood lumber, which is generally used to construct buildings, is a prime example. Canadian exports of wood and paper had been increasing even before the 1988 free trade agreement, a trend which trebled after the accord. Conflicts about softwood lumber had also preceded the CUFTA and, after 1988, this emerged as one of the most enduring trade disputes in recent Canada-US relations.

The heart of the dispute is the claim that the Canadian lumber industry is unfairly subsidized by the federal and provincial governments (especially BC). Since this matter involves endless minutia, convoluted trade regulations, and mind-numbing repetitiveness, there is, to repurpose a quote used earlier about the many bilateral fisheries agreements, a tiresome iteration about the question of softwood lumber. I will therefore endeavour to sketch out only the most salient points.

The first of several rounds of softwood negotiations began in the early 1980s. These involved complex and sometimes acrimonious negotiations, including court challenges and rulings. The perennial issue was the US contention that stumpage fees, the tax charged by a provincial government for the right to harvest timber, were artificially low and thus constituted illegal subsidies if the timber was exported to the United States. In 1982, in what is known as Lumber I, a group of US lumber producers petitioned for a countervailing duty, a type of trade penalty on a foreign exporter under WTO rules, on Canadian timber. Four years later came Lumber II: the United States petitioned for a 15 percent tariff, or countervailing duty, to offset low Canadian stumpage fees. Canada appealed the tariff, but before a NAFTA or WTO ruling was made, the two countries entered into a memorandum of understanding (MOU). Under this, Canada imposed a 15 percent export tax on lumber shipped to the United States, which settled the matter for the time being.[10] The MOU remained in place until Canada withdrew in 1991, leading to Lumber III (1991–94). The United States immediately imposed a cash deposit requirement to replace the duty. Canada successfully challenged American actions under the General Agreement on Tariffs and Trade and the binational panel of the Canada–United States Free Trade Agreement.

Eventually, the two countries arrived at a negotiated settlement: the 1996 Softwood Lumber Agreement.[11] This involved tariff-free quotas, with Canada agreeing to limit exports to a certain amount while the US refunded about half a billion dollars in duties collected during Lumber III. But that 1996 agreement soon ran into problems and expired in 2001 when Canada elected not to renew it. The subsequent Lumber IV phase saw the US heighten its countervailing rates and introduce anti-dumping penalties. Both countries challenged the other through NAFTA and World Trade Organization (WTO) panels,

Table 12.1
Canadian exports to the United States (in billions of dollars).

Year	*All products*	*Energy products*	*Forestry products and building and packaging materials*
1971	18.4	1.3	3.0
1976	39.1	5.0	6.5
1981	86.1	10.2	12.7
1986	125.0	9.7	18.2
1991	147.3	13.7	20.2
1996	279.3	25.4	39.5

Source: Statistics Canada, CANSIM tables 376-0006 and 376-0107 (https://www150.statcan.gc.ca/n1/pub/11-630-x/11-630-x2017005-eng.htm)

which tended to find that American duties were too high. Prime Minister Paul Martin threatened to restrict oil exports in retaliation, though nothing came of it.

This contentious phase was only ended by a 2006 bilateral softwood lumber agreement which involved the US returning more than $5 billion in duty deposits to Canadian companies. This 2006 accord was then extended by two years, and it expired in October 2015. Canada again moved to legally challenge American duties. In late 2020, the US Department of Commerce set a new duty rate of 8.9 percent on average, down from the 2017 average of 20.2 percent, to the satisfaction of Canadian authorities.

Similarly, the US has claimed that the monopoly powers of the Canadian Wheat Board are inconsistent with Canada's WTO obligations and disadvantage US international wheat sales. The United States does not import much wheat, but the preponderance is the Canadian hard red spring and durum varieties. This trade grew in the wake of the 1988 CUFTA. After problems in the 1990s, in the early 2000s the US pursued anti-dumping allegations and contended that Canadian wheat was unfairly subsidized. Some sanctions were initially imposed on Canada through the NAFTA framework, then reversed under appeal. A memorandum of understanding on the grain trade was signed in 1994 but expired the next year. The two countries arrived at a similar understanding about areas of agriculture trade in 1998. A WTO dispute settlement panel found in 2004 that Canadian wheat trading practices were acceptable, though some marketing practices contravened WTO rules. The CUFTA and NAFTA also removed corn tariffs, and by the early twenty-first century, considerable volumes moved from the US to Canada. The latter accused the former of unfairly subsidizing their corn exports but dropped the charges to await the outcome of WTO trade negotiations.

Similar debates have concerned the beef, live cattle, and meat trades. A few "mad cow" cases in the prairies resulted in the US market closing to Canadian beef for several years. As controversial as these various trade disputes were, they were mostly not allowed to creep into other aspects of the lucrative Canada-US economic relationship. To be sure, the total dollar value of that relationship was so substantial that even billions in softwood lumber duties or lost beef sales were not much more than drops in the continental bucket. But they certainly hurt the affected producers. Moreover, they probably disproportionately affect the perceptions of the average citizen about the state of relations with the other country, and disproportionately absorb the time of diplomatic and trade officials.[12]

As the above makes clear, many agricultural and meat products are exported and imported between the two nations. The corollary is that an enormous swath of acreage in both countries has a transnational dimension in that land uses, and the attendant environmental impacts, are partially subject to the vagaries of Canada-US economic relations and trade. This can take the form of diplomacy, such as tariffs, multinational trade agreements, or prohibitions against diseased meat. But one of the indirect ways that the US can affect Canadian landscapes and resource use on a large scale is through domestic policies and subsidies.

WATER ISSUES

The reader might recall the 1985 Great Lakes Charter discussed in an earlier chapter. Worries that various locales outside the Great Lakes basin – some close by, others as far away as the US southwest – might come calling for Great Lakes water led the US states surrounding these sweetwater seas to seek out a more watertight legal defence against such diversions or withdrawals. (And the Great Lakes were not the only potential source of bulk water exports: the premier of Newfoundland and Labrador, for instance, publicly mused about sending freshwater to the United States.) A 2001 annex to the 1985 charter resulted from fears of bulk water exports, galvanized by the Nova Group's 1998 proposal to send Lake Superior water by tanker to Asia. The annex committed the signatory states to develop binding regulations to ensure no net loss of Great Lakes water through diversion, consumption, or adverse impacts on water quality. The result was an interstate compact (a legally enforceable contract among US states approved by Congress) detailing how the Great Lakes states can manage and protect the basin, providing a framework for each state to enact laws for this protection.

This Great Lakes–St Lawrence River Basin Water Resources Compact, or Great Lakes Compact for short, was signed in 2005 and then enacted into law in December 2008 after approval by the US Congress and the legislatures of the involved states. Its principal provisions included a ban on new water diversions as well as measures for limiting and monitoring water use within the Great Lakes states. However, there were controversial exceptions to the new diversion rules, such as for counties straddling the watershed and a potentially dangerous loophole allowing unlimited water exports provided it was in containers less than 5.7 gallons. The Compact's provisions were extended to the Canadian provinces of Ontario and Quebec by the Great Lakes–St Lawrence River Basin Sustainable Water Resources Agreement (GLSLRBSWRA). This international good faith agreement, which also created the Great Lakes–St Lawrence River Water Resources Regional Body, came into effect in 2009.[13]

Illinois's refusal to consider any changes to the Chicago diversion nearly sank the decade of interstate negotiations for the Great Lakes Compact. The Chicago diversion through the Sanitary and Ship Canal was lamentably grandfathered in, meaning that the prohibition on large diversions did not apply to it. Chicago had repeatedly exceeded its withdrawal limit in the previous decades, sometimes intentionally, sometimes accidentally. But it made up for the excess water it had taken and has since apparently stayed within the legal limits.

The compact created a council to oversee its provisos, and the first prominent case it dealt with involved Waukesha, Wisconsin, located on the edge of Milwaukee. This city's request to divert some water from Lake Michigan for municipal use was approved in 2016, provided that an equivalent volume of water was returned to the lake. A similar diversion was approved for New Berlin, which borders Waukesha County. Racine, another Wisconsin city not far from Milwaukee, was putting out feelers for a seven million gallon per day diversion, chiefly for a potential Foxconn factory, but this has seemingly fizzled out.

Lately, water levels in the Great Lakes have seesawed much more rapidly, compared to historical norms, because of climate change. While low water levels, such as those experienced in Lakes Michigan-Huron in the early 2010s, left docks high and dry, elevated water levels have been even more problematic for infrastructure (though, as an aside, the answer to high water levels should often be *less* infrastructure, not more). This has been particularly pronounced on Lake Ontario in recent years. The control works built as part of the St Lawrence Seaway and Power Project afford the ability to partially control water levels, but only within a certain range. This leads riparian property owners to believe that the high water levels negatively affecting them can be fully controlled by the International Joint Commission. In the 1950s and 1960s, New York State residents with property that was damaged by high Lake Ontario levels attempted to sue Canada because of the changes to the flow regime of the lake caused by modifications to the St Lawrence River; Canada eventually settled out of court for $350,000.[14] In the last few years, property owners on Lake Ontario's south shore have been vocal in their dissatisfaction with Plan 2014, the recently implemented IJC method of regulation for water levels.

The areas of concern (AOCs) and remedial action plans (RAPs) under the Great Lakes Water Quality Agreement have been a mixed success. Since the last two decades of the twentieth century, the Canadian and US governments have not consistently kept up their funding for the IJC nor for measures to address areas of concern, essentially Great Lakes pollution hotspots. Consequently, only seven of the forty-three AOCs have been delisted. In some cases, remediation work is complete at an AOC, but only time and natural processes can complete the job. In 2012, a new protocol to the Great Lakes Water Quality Agreement added, among other things, new measures for AOCs and RAPs.[15] On the United States side, large pulses of funding have come via the Great Lakes Restoration Initiative, first launched in 2010.

Many of the drastic Great Lakes problems of the Cold War period have started to return, some aided by climate change. Toxic algae, caused by agricultural run-off and sewage effluent, is rearing its head again. Invasive mussels are still a problem. Pollutants, including some banned decades ago, still regularly show up in organisms and ecosystems. Plastics and microplastics now account for 80 percent of the pollution in the Great Lakes, and plastic particles are now found in everything from fish to beer to the human body. And we have discovered new dangerous pollutants, such as endocrine disruptors and PFAS/PFOA (the "forever" chemicals). Prohibitions against eating fish are still common throughout the basin.

Another type of pollution – biological pollution – is a perennial concern in the Great Lakes–St Lawrence basin. Many non-native species were anthropogenically introduced to North America via European settlers. Some did not take hold; others did become established, with the support or acceptance of humans, while others became a problem or a nuisance from an anthropocentric perspective. I have previously described several types of aquatic nuisance species that arrived in the Great Lakes and the different transborder responses, such as the Great Lakes Fishery Commission's sea lamprey program. Other responses in the late twentieth century included the Great Lakes Commission (which created the Great Lakes Panel on Aquatic Nuisance Species) and NAFTA's Commission for Environmental Cooperation. In the 2012 revision of the Great Lakes Water Quality Agreement, an annex specifically addressed invasives. A range of other non-governmental networks without formal enforcement capabilities track and catalogue continental invasive species, identify potential vectors, and raise awareness.[16]

One invasive on the cusp of entering the Great Lakes is Asian carp. That is a catch-all name for several different types of carp, with bighead and silver carp the most worrisome. These up-to-a-metre-long fish are resilient and prolific: they reproduce at astounding rates (i.e., up to a quarter-million eggs per year), live for several decades, and can daily eat 20 percent of their weight, which ranges up to one hundred pounds. During the 1970s, they were purposefully introduced into the southern US to act as natural vacuums in fish farms. By the 1990s, the carp had escaped through mismanagement and human error; they have been inexorably working their way northward up the Mississippi River and are now in Great Lakes tributaries. The most likely means, or vector, for the carp to get into the Great Lakes is via the Chicago Sanitary and Ship Canal.

The carp do not eat other fish but devour plankton or plant material. As a result, these carp can out-compete native fish species, causing repercussions along the food chain. They could be disastrous for specific Great Lakes ecosystems and human uses such as tourism, recreation, and the fishing industry. Silver carp also notoriously jump en masse out of the water when startled by watercraft engines, smacking boaters. The main preventative measure to keep carp from infiltrating further up the canal is electric underwater barriers, installed by the US Army Corps of Engineers at Joliett, Illinois, just miles from Lake Michigan. The Canadian government and other US Great Lakes states have tried various diplomatic and legal means of forcing Illinois to take stronger action to prevent carp infiltration, such as hydrological separation or the re-reversal of the Chicago waterway system. At the time of writing, it looks like additional carp prevention infrastructure at Joliett is moving ahead.

While restricting the movement of certain invasives is a goal of environmental diplomacy, encouraging the movement of other species is sometimes the aim. In 1997 the US and Canada signed a "Framework for Cooperation between the US Department of the Interior and Environment Canada for the Protection and Recovery of Species at Risk" that included ten species. But this never amounted to anything substantial.[17] Collaborative governance when it came to the whooping crane, however, was more successful. After signing a 1990 memorandum of understanding, Canada and the US inked the 2007 International Recovery Plan for this impressive bird. The following year, the North American Monarch Conservation Plan was signed – though this butterfly recently went on the endangered list. Several existing agreements about fish have been altered or extended since the end of the Cold War. Conservation agreements for other species also remain in effect. Additionally, there are numerous transborder collaborative efforts in this realm that do not operate at formal governmental levels.

Outside of the Great Lakes–St Lawrence basin, some of the historic water conflicts have recently flared up. In 2004, the Governor of Montana requested the reopening of the 1921 order concerning the Milk–St Mary apportionment and a task force was set up to explore the matter. The order was not reopened, and the existing apportionment remains an ongoing albeit uneasy truce. Granted, it has prevented water use conflicts here from getting worse.

Devils Lake in nearby North Dakota has been controversial. This lake has no natural outlet. With its levels on the rise in the later twentieth century, leading to localized flooding, North Dakota considered building an outlet to alleviate the problem. Like the Garrison Diversion, this would take water to a tributary of the Red River, potentially sending foreign pathogens and pollutants into Manitoba. Canada signalled its disapproval of the outlet early in the twenty-first century. But it declined the American invitation to take the issue to the International Joint Commission since no formal proposal had yet been promulgated. When the project advanced in 2003, Canada suggested an IJC reference; the State Department countered that Canada had already declined that option. The involved jurisdictions entered into diplomatic talks aimed at fulfilling the requirements of the Boundary Waters Treaty, but North Dakota did not want to invoke the IJC because of its Garrison experience.[18] Since it was clear that North Dakota would continue with the Devils Lake outlet regardless of any opposition, that state, along with the federal governments and Manitoba, worked out a 2005 deal that included some mitigation measures. These included filters and testing. Granted, this was not a formal diplomatic arrangement, and some commentators have characterized the whole affair as a "deeply flawed process."[19]

Later in 2005, the outlet opened with a temporary filter. However, it was quickly halted because of high sulphate levels, and the promised permanent filter still had not been installed. Faced with rising levels in Devils Lake, North Dakota built a second outlet in 2009. Both outlets were opened in 2012. At various intervals, Manitoba sought a legal injunction in US courts and through the diplomatic channels offered by the federal government. This seemingly intractable problem dragged on and is still unresolved. Lake levels have been marginally reduced, while Manitoba's worst fears have yet to be realized.

Several other flashpoints in the western part of the continent bear mentioning. Recently concerns have been raised about western Canadian pollution moving into the US, such as from the Teck mine, Trail smelter, and the Tulsequah Chief mine.[20] In 2015, Alaska and British Columbia signed a memorandum of understanding calling for a working group to protect transboundary waters, particularly from mining pollution. The treaty entitlements from the Columbia River Treaty are currently being renegotiated as well.[21] As the Shakespearian aphorism goes, what's past is prologue. Of course, the history of past environmental relations has done much more than merely set the stage for contemporary and future events. In profound ways, the history of these relations, and nature itself, continues to restrict options, create path dependencies, and frame political choices.

13

Energy and Climate Change

The 2001 Supreme Court ruling that made George W. Bush the president, rather than Al Gore, brought rougher waters to the Canada-US relationship. The new president was more than willing to act unilaterally. Jean Chrétien's aloofness towards the United States only increased, with significant support from Canadians, after Bush turned his sights on Iraq as part of the post-9/11 "War on Terror" and a new missile defence system. Canada demurred on those scores, though it did join the war in Afghanistan. Canadians denounced US imperialism while gobbling up American television, music, and goods; Americans criticized Canadian timidity while consuming Canadian fuels, minerals, and resources. Despite these frictions and contradictions, the value and volume of bilateral economic relations and trade remained strong, riding the wave of the free trade agreements.[1]

Bilateral talks about a changing climate went back to the 1980s. As I will show in this chapter, even though climate change is generally seen as a multilateral issue, it factored heavily into bilateral Canada-US relations in the twenty-first century – along with fossil fuels, the primary contributor to climate change. But climate change and reducing reliance on fossil fuels could not have been much lower on Bush's agenda. The same could be said of Stephen Harper and his Conservatives, who followed several years of the Paul Martin–led Liberals after he succeeded Chrétien. Harper won minority governments in 2006 and 2008 before securing a majority in 2011. Barack Obama, elected as president in 2008, sounded like the closest thing to an environmentalist that had occupied the Oval Office. His administration inherited the Great Recession and used a huge stimulus package to push for a number of green initiatives while taking some steps to curb the country's carbon emissions.

However, the Obama administration did not make much of a dent in the American dependence on fossil fuels. In fact, it was the opposite in some respects: during Obama's watch, American fossil fuel exports, which had been banned for four decades, began again, and the US massively expanded natural gas production while falsely touting it as a climate-friendly fuel that could help bridge the transition from hydrocarbons to renewable energy. Hydraulic fracturing (or fracking) and horizontal drilling became increasingly common ways to acquire natural gas and oil deposits that had been previously inaccessible or uneconomic. Fracking techniques involve pumping water, sand, and chemicals under high pressure to fracture rock to get at hydrocarbons. In addition to potentially poisoning groundwater, copious amounts of methane, a potent greenhouse gas, are liberated.[2]

With a power base in Alberta, the Harper government was committed to expanding the development of that province's tar sands. Tar sands are a form of heavy petroleum deposit where the oil, also called bitumen, is found in mixtures of sand, clay, and water and is in a semi-solid or tar-like state. In addition to emissions resulting from their end use, tar sands hydrocarbons have varying environmental impacts at different stages along the supply chain – including at the acquisition stage, which harms nearby Indigenous communities. A great deal of energy is required just to separate and upgrade this matter into a usable form, producing greenhouse gases in the process. Up until around the start of the twenty-first century, when production really began ramping up, both "tar sands" and "oil sands" had been used interchangeably. Then the fossil fuel industry, along with Ottawa and certain provincial governments, began framing "tar sands" as an improper label in an attempt to quell criticism. But regardless of which term is used, tying Canada's national security to this industry is incompatible with long-term natural security.

ENERGY EXPORTS

By the end of the twentieth century, tar sands investment and development were intensifying since Canada had used up most of its conventional sources of crude oil. Canada was the largest supplier of oil to the US. (See table 12.1 in previous chapter.) Both Canada and the

US became petro states – meaning that fossil fuels have an outsized influence on their political economy – to at least some degree.[3] Indeed, the evolution of Canada, and certain provinces, into a type of petro state is one of the most powerful exemplars of nature influencing politics. Many aspects of the Canadian state and political economy, particularly in provinces like Alberta, were dictated by the desire to develop and export oil and gas. The resulting investments and infrastructure then created momentum, or path dependencies, that all but ensured that fossil fuel considerations would continue conditioning politics and economics.

Less tangible, but equally weighty, is the expectation of energy and material abundance fostered by fossil fuels. Both Canada and the United States in the twentieth century were societies and economies based on plenitude and consumption – of many types ranging from water to wood to electricity to minerals and beyond – but the integration of Canadian fossil fuels into the American system, along with the wider free trade of resources, is likely the defining feature of the contemporary bilateral relationship.

More pipelines were laid to move the increased production from the tar sands. In 1997 the Express Pipeline came online, transporting crude oil from Hardisty, Alberta to markets in Montana, Utah, Wyoming, and Colorado. The Alliance Pipeline started taking natural gas from northeastern British Columbia and Alberta to Illinois three years later. In 2000, the Maritimes & Northeast pipeline opened. This line runs natural gas from offshore Nova Scotia to Massachusetts, with lateral lines supplying communities along the way.

TransCanada Pipelines began transporting crude oil on its newly built Keystone pipeline from Alberta to Oklahoma in 2011. The subsequent Keystone XL proposal involved a more direct route than the already existing line to send an estimated 830,000 barrels of crude daily to the Gulf Coast. But it became a line in the sand for climate change activists since the sunk costs of pipelines ensure that the owners need to operate them for decades to recover their investment. Two massive oil spills in 2010, the BP Gulf spill and Enbridge's Line 6B Kalamazoo River spill, demonstrated the risks and galvanized opponents. Proponents greatly exaggerated the number of permanent jobs the Keystone XL pipeline would bring. Moreover, most of the fossil fuels sent through that pipeline expansion were destined to be exported abroad.[4]

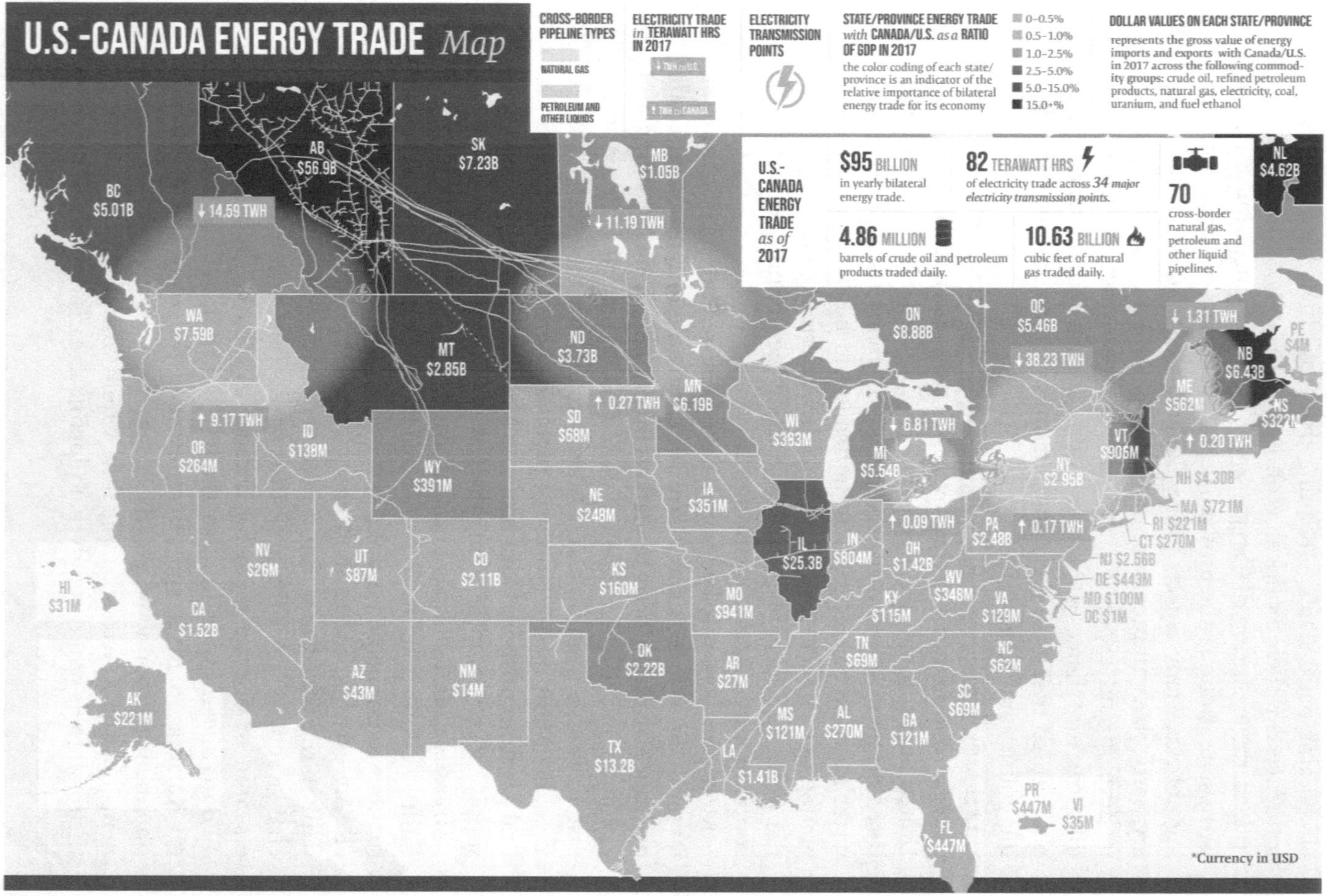

Figure 13.1 Map of the US-Canada energy trade as of 2020 showing transmission lines and pipelines.

Stephen Harper's government pushed for Canada's oil expansion, but in the United States, Obama's administration, hearing the opposition, seemed reluctant to approve the Keystone expansion. As a transborder pipeline, it was subject to the approval of the State Department, which slow-walked the process. Before leaving office, Obama declined the permits for the Keystone XL. But Donald Trump gave it the green light in early 2017. Construction soon began, though court rulings in 2020 on permits stalled the project. Then Joe Biden issued an executive order cancelling it.

The story is similar for Line 5, the Enbridge pipeline that carries Alberta fossil fuels underneath the Straits of Mackinac, connecting Lakes Huron and Michigan. This would be perhaps the worst possible spot in the Great Lakes for an oil spill. The governor of Michigan announced in early 2021 that her state would revoke the easement for Line 5, though Enbridge and the Canadian government have challenged this. In October 2021, Ottawa formally invoked the 1977 Pipeline Transit Treaty. The placement of the pipeline also ignored Native American treaty rights that were disregarded when the pipeline was first installed.

Enbridge did recently finish a replacement line for Line 3, which runs from Alberta to the head of the Great Lakes. In 2021, protestors were out in full force trying to prevent this upgraded pipeline. Indigenous activists have been at the forefront of opposition to Lines 3 and 5, Keystone XL, and the Dakota Access Pipeline; in forcing changes, delays, or cancellations, they asserted themselves as important diplomatic actors and rightsholders. Other pipeline proposals have recently been in the news too. The owners of the Portland-Montreal oil pipeline floated the idea of reversing it in order to export Canadian crude. Efforts to resurrect the Mackenzie Valley Pipeline Project made some progress, receiving federal Cabinet approval, but ultimately it seems to have again proven to be a pipe dream. On top of the many ecological impacts of pipelines, and the dependence on carbon-emitting fossil fuels they stimulate, their construction in northern permafrost environments is problematic because of disruptions to delicate ecosystems.

Pipelines spills are legion. Crossborder pipelines owned by Enbridge (formerly the Interprovincial Pipe Line Company) that move Alberta fossil fuels have experienced breaks large and small. In 1967 alone the Interprovincial Pipeline spilled almost three million gallons of crude oil; there were several spills in 1970–71, with one pipeline leak spilling a little over one million gallons; between 1973 and 1975, the Interprovincial pipeline spilled about five million gallons of crude in Alberta and Minnesota.[5] Enbridge's 1991 Line 3 spill in Minnesota was the largest inland oil spill in US history. In 2010, over one million gallons of diluted bitumen went into the Kalamazoo River from a busted Enbridge pipeline. Given that experience, and Enbridge's poor response and safety record, it is no surprise that getting Enbridge's Line 5 out of the Straits of Mackinac is an animating goal for many environmentalists in Michigan and the wider Great Lakes.

And those spill episodes that make headlines are just the most notorious. Even when pipelines do not experience catastrophic breaks, they constantly leak. A 2007 Alberta Energy Utilities Board report on pipeline performance found that between 1990 and 2005, the province's pipeline system suffered 4,769 releases of hydrocarbon liquids (most of which were crude oil or synthetic crude). Of those releases, 4,717 were less than 100 cubic metres (one cubic metre = 1,000 litres), forty-six were between 100 and 1,000 cubic metres, and six were between 1,000 and 10,000 cubic metres. Another study by Sean Kheraj found that between just 1999 and 2008, Enbridge recorded 610 oil and gas spills.[6] In addition to these constant discharges, processing and refining fossil fuels releases all types of pollutants and toxics. And, naturally, pipelines facilitate the burning of fossil fuels at the consumer end, which puts greenhouse gases into the atmosphere, causing global warming.

Shifting briefly to another energy form, at the close of the twentieth century, 60 percent of Canada's electricity production came from hydro power, 19 percent from coal, 13 percent from nuclear energy, 7 percent from gas, and less than 1 percent from other renewable energies.[7] The total amount of exported electricity increased after the free trade agreements. By 1996, over one hundred international lines connected Canada to the US, thirty-seven of which were bulk interties, capable of transferring 18,900 MW; the major inter-provincial connections in operation had a total transfer capability of 10,245 MW.[8] Canada now exports about 10 percent of its domestically produced electricity.

Scholars have identified several key features of Canada-US energy relations since the 1980s, the roots of which can be located in earlier hydroelectricity and fossil fuel export patterns: market-based, harmonious, and integrated regional markets; Canada as a net exporter; and multilevel, trans-governmental, and informal governance.[9] The various strands of energy policy remain highly fragmented within both countries. The same goes for crossborder energy trade regimes, though continental integration has clearly increased since the free trade agreements of 1988 and 1994. Granted, commentators have suggested that it was really the Federal Energy Regulatory Commission, much more than the free trade provisions, that "exercised the dominant policy influence on the US importation of natural gas and electricity from Canada."[10]

CLIMATE CHANGE

This binational energy context helps explain the attitudes of upper North American governments toward climate change. The United States' role in encouraging fossil fuel use, and frequently hamstringing international climate change efforts, has been well documented. Ottawa's international position on climate change is tightly linked to the domestic fossil fuel industry, the provinces, and the country's status as a major hydrocarbon producer. Of course, Canada's modern fossil fuel industry has historically been American-financed and much of the product was exported south.[11] Consequently, the United States has also directly or indirectly influenced Canada's climate change stance.

As I noted earlier, international ozone talks in the 1980s included discussions of what would eventually be known as climate change. At the 1988 Toronto Conference, sometimes cited as the start of international diplomacy on climate change, Prime Minister Mulroney touted a law of the atmosphere. However, this did not have American support.[12] Nevertheless, both countries participated in the meetings that created the United Nations Framework Convention on Climate Change (UNFCC) in 1992.[13] Canada, but not the United States, committed to limiting greenhouse gases (including CO_2) not covered by the Montreal Protocol to 1990 levels by the end of the millennium. Still, Mulroney's enthusiasm for climate action seemingly waned during his later years as prime minister. He had demonstrated a belief in environmental protection – and has been called Canada's greenest prime minister, though this is certainly debatable[14] – but the type of neoliberal measures he espoused have ultimately led to unsustainable results in the long term.

Busy reducing budgets and implementing austerity measures, Jean Chrétien's Liberal government was much less keen about attending to greenhouse gases (though the prime minister did seem to get a little more interested during his last term in office). During the 1990s, Canada moved from being an early proponent of combatting climate change to one of the obstacles. Rather than greenhouse gas emissions going down, as Canada had previously pledged, they went up. Chrétien's government did sign the 1997 Kyoto Accord, committing to a 6 percent emissions reduction below 1990 levels by 2012. But this seems to have been done primarily for the optics of keeping pace with the US and the Clinton government, plus the Canadian government claimed that it should get credit for the extent to which its forests acted as a carbon sink. The Liberals did not ratify Kyoto until 2002 and never seriously tried to hit its targets. Of course, that had a lot to do with intergovernmental relations between the federal government and the provinces, which is a perpetual stumbling block on climate issues.

Direct Canada-US climate relations did not really escalate until the late 1990s and, even then, talks occurred more at regional and subnational levels of government.[15] Provinces and states were reaching out to each other while the federal governments dithered.[16] In particular, the northeast area, comprised of Atlantic Canada and New England, pursued forms of collaboration through a Regional Greenhouse Gas Initiative, which limited emissions from power generation. The Western Climate Initiative, a state and provincial cap-and-trade system, also started up.[17]

Many politicians and commentators argued that Canadian industry and economic growth would suffer if Canada limited carbon emissions while the US did not. Moreover, given that the United States was historically the largest total emissions contributor (until 2006 when it was passed by China, a country that now has a population more than four times bigger than that of the US), many insist there is not much point in trying to hit climate change goals if the biggest countries in the world do not sign on. Consequently, the Canadian government has often tied its stance to that of the US. When the United States supported emission reductions, Canada looked bad if it did not commit to the same. However, if the US did not pledge to limit emissions, neither did Canada.

The Harper-led Conservatives were, like Bush, beholden to the oil patch. Both were agnostic, or outright denialists, about whether climate change was human-induced; certainly, neither was going to compromise any facet of economic growth for the sake of curbing emissions. The Harper government purposefully dragged its feet on climate change to sabotage the process, and the Obama administration's efforts were blocked by Congress.[18] Harper dangled a Canada-US treaty on climate change that Obama spurned since the former's motivations were disingenuous. Until his government won a majority in 2011, at which point they could dispense with the pretense that they cared about climate change, Harper used US inaction on reducing greenhouse gas emissions as an excuse for Canada to avoid action.

The recession in the wake of the 2008 subprime mortgage meltdown, and then Obama's delay on the Keystone XL pipeline, further hindered climate talks between the two countries. Canada's pledge to reduce emissions under the nonbinding 2010 Copenhagen Accord mirrored those of the United States (though neither country hit the target of reducing emissions to 17 percent below 2005 levels by 2020). A Clean Energy Dialogue was at least created to expand shared research and development into new technologies, and both countries managed to legally designate carbon dioxide as a pollutant.

A few years later, Justin Trudeau's government produced a lot of nice-sounding rhetoric about addressing climate change. But it also promoted the antithesis: fossil fuel expansion and new pipelines. Trudeau's Liberal government was active in the negotiation of the 2015 Paris Climate Agreement, a treaty through the UNFCC, and quickly signed on to the final package. The Paris Agreement was predicated on limiting global warming to two degrees Celsius (preferably 1.5 degrees). Domestically, the Trudeau government introduced a federal floor on carbon pricing for all provinces that had not set a carbon tax on their own. But it had to buy a pipeline to get Alberta, the biggest emitter, to sign on to this Pan-Canadian Agreement. (Plus, carbon pricing is at best an initial step as the minimal emissions reduction benefits would almost certainly be counteracted by the operations of a new pipeline.) Then Ottawa spent a lot of diplomatic capital fighting to save the Keystone XL and Line 5, even though any new pipeline infrastructure would make it virtually impossible to reduce the country's carbon emissions in line with the Paris Agreement. Mobilizing oil and gas is not only bad for the climate. It is also bad for business and taxpayers since investments in allied infrastructure such as pipelines will likely become stranded assets.[19]

In 2016, the three North American governments signed the North American Climate, Clean Energy and Environment Partnership. The ambitious goals of this partnership included sustainable growth, reduced emissions, and half the power generation coming from clean sources by 2025. But the chances of the US addressing climate change at the national level became nonexistent when Donald Trump was elected president. Trump quickly withdrew the US from the Paris Agreement, insisting that the terms would have to be renegotiated in order for his country to rejoin. The Trump government signalled its resistance to anything resembling action on the climate crisis at the expense of the economy – indeed, Trump was simultaneously advocating for increasing the use of dirty fossil fuels, such as coal (though coal use actually went down during his time into office, reflecting the economic competitiveness of renewables). On inauguration day, Joe Biden announced that the US would rejoin the Paris Agreement and reversed a variety of other Trump-era environmental rollbacks. Nevertheless, there are worries that Trump's bull had wrecked the regulatory china shop for decades to come.

Looking to the future, climate change and fossil fuels are sure to remain pivotal aspects of Canada-US environmental and energy diplomacy. The Arctic, too, will remain a hot topic, forgive the pun. In the twenty-first century, climate change and hydrocarbon exploration mean that a range of countries and concerns have increased interest in accessing resources in the north. Canada and the United States are likely to be diplomatically involved here. However, that may come through multilateral forums involving other northern countries, such as the Arctic Council, which was formed in 1996. To be sure, Canada habitually prefers dealing with the United States in such multi-country settings for pragmatic and strategic counterweight reasons.[20]

More directly, the legal dispute between the two nations over the legal status of the Northwest Passage continues, with Canada claiming it as internal waters that it has the right to control. There is also an ongoing debate about the location of the Beaufort Sea boundary between Alaska and the Yukon. In the early twenty-first century, the US made moves to claim this contested area. On that note, several other bilateral boundary disputes outside of the Arctic remain technically unresolved; the two countries have compartmentalized these cases and kept them from spilling over into other aspects of the bilateral relationship. Many interests have not given up on the prospect of building more pipelines to bring oil and gas south. The potential for American drilling in the Arctic National Wildlife Refuge, and the resulting impact on caribou herds, continues to attract attention. All these simmering problems, and others, seem likely to rise to a boil as climate change makes new fossil fuel reserves more accessible.[21]

CONCLUSION

The Nature of the Relationship

In the twenty-first century, Canada and the United States are, to varying extents, petro states. That is, they are both countries whose economies are heavily dependent on the extraction and sale of fossil fuels – despite the fact that fossil fuels henceforth need to stay in the ground if we want to have even a chance of avoiding the worst impacts of climate change. Consequently, Canada and the US are both climate villains. Since the Second World War, the US and Canada have consistently been at the top of the list of carbon emitters per capita.[1] Until 2006, when it was passed by China, the United States was the largest global contributor of carbon dioxide emissions. Canada is now the world's tenth-largest emitter of greenhouse gases – despite the fact it is only the thirty-sixth-largest country in the world by population. As of 2020, Canada accounted for 2 percent of global carbon dioxide emissions, and the United States 15 percent. However, such figures do not attribute to Canada its considerable fossil fuel exports, which are burned in the United States and therefore count towards that country's emissions.

The United States is, of course, an international superpower by virtually any measurement. When it comes to energy, contemporary Canada is a global power, bordering on a superpower.[2] Canada and the United States trade more resources than any two other countries in the world and likely have cooperatively modified the landscapes of their shared border areas on a larger spatial scale than any two other adjoining nations. Of course, the environmental impact of Canada-US relations is not limited to the border regions but extends to landscapes and waterscapes across upper North America, from the oceans to the far north and many points in between.

Natural resources were an important part of the bilateral relationship from the beginning. Most of the early direct diplomatic relations between the United States and the newly created Dominion of Canada revolved around the natural world, particularly fish and water. Environmental diplomacy in the half-century after Canadian Confederation was central to a Canadian-British-American "cleaning of the slate" and creating an amicable continental relationship (as well as better US-British relations). Many of these agreements have proven to be well-known precedents in the history of global environmental governance. Environmental diplomacy negotiations demonstrated that Canada was capable of independently controlling its foreign policy, symbolized by the 1923 Halibut Treaty. Ottawa confirmed this independence by negotiating a series of water development accords during the interwar years (though most of these could not get through the US Congress), as well as handling the Trail Smelter case.

The bilateral harmony created by environmental and energy diplomacy paved the way for rapid Canada-US integration during and after the Second World War. As the scope of subjects dealt with by the two diplomatic services markedly widened, so too did the range of environmental issues. With the completion of several hydro power megaprojects in the early Cold War, as well as the beginning of Canadian fossil fuel exports, energy became an even more crucial facet of the bilateral relationship. Cold War environmental diplomacy frequently involved other resources critical to national security and nation-building, such as steel, aluminum, nuclear materials, and minerals.

Interestingly, just as decades of binational hydropolitics reached their apogee with the construction of megaprojects on the Niagara, St Lawrence, and Columbia Rivers, plus many smaller hydroelectric projects elsewhere, oil and gas were superseding hydro power as the foremost concern of energy diplomacy. Fossil fuels were the most contentious form of energy relations during the 1970s, when the Great Lakes Water Quality Agreements were cardinal achievements. Acid rain and air pollution became not just major environmental problems but top diplomatic problems, where they were joined by Law of the Sea and other maritime issues, fish and invasives, and the Arctic. In some respects, the 1988 and 1994 free trade agreements, along with the end of the Cold War, reset the nature of Canada-US environmental and energy diplomacy. Energy integration and trade accelerated significantly while new challenges, such as softwood lumber and climate change, rose to the fore.

Looking at the history of the Canada-US relationship through an environmental and energy lens brings into stark relief the ecological impact of bilateral diplomacy: liberating fossil fuels, mining uranium, cutting trees, and reconfiguring border waters. The history of northern North American interchanges had a profound impact on the continent's ecosystems. It is impossible to quantify precisely the environmental impact of Canadian-American relations – but it is enormous.

The environmental impacts of the Canada-US relationship have conspicuously ramped up since the mid-twentieth century. These two countries were at the vanguard of what has been called the Great Acceleration, the dramatic post-1950 global surge in the growth rates of human socio-economic systems including population, energy use, production, consumption, and so on. This acceleration goes hand-in-glove with the Anthropocene, the start of which many commentators date to the mid-twentieth century. This term refers to a new geological epoch defined by humanity as the dominant influence on environmental and climatic change. Anthropogenic interventions have undoubtedly produced hybrid envirotechnical systems that blend the human and non-human. The Anthropocene concept highlights the extent to which humans have noticeably altered parts of not only the planet's surface, but areas above (climate) and below (geology) it, from carbon emissions and radioactive material to strata full of plastic, garbage, and concrete. By that criteria, few countries deserve the title of Anthropocene nation more than Canada and the United States.[3]

CONTEMPORARY ECOPOLITICS

We cannot properly understand the current state of North American ecosystems without invoking the history of continental ecopolitics. Nor can we properly understand the contemporary Canada-US environmental relationship without knowing how and why that relationship evolved. Essentially, many of the products, resources, and technologies – fossil fuels, electricity, metals, and minerals – that enable and structure modern lifestyles are heavily exchanged between the two countries. Though it may no longer always be in the form of unprocessed staples, Canada remains reliant on sending natural resources to the United States.

Political scientists have identified salient factors influencing the policy formation process in both countries when it comes to contemporary environmental diplomacy. However, many of the prime factors changed over the time period covered in this book, making it difficult to generalize; policy influences were very different in 1867, 1920, 1945, 1988, and 2010. Nevertheless, many current aspects of Canadian-American environmental and energy relations have long been formalized, incorporated, and diffused across levels of government. Environmental and energy diplomacy had become so common, widespread, and complex by the later twentieth century that issues were frequently handled by subject experts and technocrats in conjunction with diplomats and politicians.[4] This can limit the extent to which the changeover of political leaders can quickly alter or reverse policies, for better or for worse.

There has been an increasing number of subnational or civil society actors that influence diplomacy: not only states and provinces, but business and financial interests, nongovernmental organizations, and other interest groups. Indigenous communities are another type of diplomatic actor with unique nation-to-nation relationships. Informal networks and institutions are now far more common parts of binational environmental governance than they used to be and, some argue, more effective. Others might counter that governance is now much more fragmented. Multilevel governance was partially a response to the growing realization that environmental protection requires integrating many different factors from the local to the national to the international. But it can also lead to an offloading of responsibilities and costs. Furthermore, in recent decades there has been a destructive neoliberal pattern of deregulation and leaving matters to the free market and private enterprise.

Even before Canada became a petro state, it was a "hydro state" since hydroelectricity, especially from the border regions, was so disproportionately important to the political imaginary and political economy of the nation. This was particularly true of provinces that rely more heavily on hydro power, such as Ontario, Quebec, and British Columbia. Since many of the earliest sites of large hydroelectric development were along border waters with the United States, a distinct form of North American energy diplomacy emerged during the twentieth century. Hydro power and fossil fuels together fostered a political economy of abundance, an expectation of growth that manifested itself in external relations and domestic politics.

Canada and the United States today carry on an enormous range of energy exchanges – consequential not just for the economies and politics of the two nations but for global carbon emissions and climate change. Canada is the largest source of US energy imports and the second-largest destination for US energy exports (behind Mexico).[5] In 2020, the US consumed an average of just over eighteen million barrels of oil per day. Of this, 3.7 million barrels per day were imported from Canada, constituting more than three-quarters of Canada's oil production and 99 percent of its exports.[6] That comprised approximately half of American oil imports. Almost half of Canadian natural gas is sent to the United States, accounting for just shy of 10 percent of American consumption but almost all of its imports. More than half of Canada's uranium production, chiefly from Saskatchewan, is shipped to the United States, representing over 20 percent of American consumption and imports. In the other direction, Canada gets around a quarter of its crude oil and natural gas from the United States, and one-fifth of its coal.

Canada and the US arguably have the most integrated electricity market in the world. Most Canadian provinces both import electricity from, and export it to, the United States. About one-quarter of the electricity that moves across the border does so as part of long-term fixed contracts, while the remainder is traded on the power market. There are now more than three dozen sizeable transmission interconnections across the US-Canada border.[7] Over the last decade or so, BC, Alberta, Saskatchewan, and Nova Scotia imported substantially more electricity than they exported. Quebec, Ontario, and Manitoba did the reverse. New York State and Washington State were in the top five within the United States of both electricity exports from and imports to Canada.[8] In 2014, a total of 58,555 gigawatt hours (GWh) was sent from Canada to the US grid, while 12,808 went north; in 2015, Canada exported over 68,000 GWh (though this had dipped to 52,000 GWh by 2019). In 2020, the leading electricity exporting provinces were Quebec (24,300 GWh), Ontario (17,600 GWh), and British Columbia (12,000 GWh). Quebec primarily relays electricity to Vermont and New York, and some to Maine. Ontario chiefly sends electricity to New York and Michigan.

Granted, Canada's electricity exports to the US are proportionally small relative to total domestic production in both countries: less than 10 percent of the electricity generated in Canada is sent across the border, constituting only 1 percent of the electricity used in the United States.[9] However, this does not mean that the total amount of electricity sent over the border is tiny or insignificant; rather, such statistics point to the gargantuan amount of electricity consumed on the continent.

Quebec had plans for a new transmission line to New Hampshire, but that was abandoned in 2019. There are various transmission lines at different stages of planning, as well as several hydro power projects in Canada that are nearing completion – such as Site C, Keeyask, Muskrat Falls, Lower Churchill, and additional northern Quebec hydro power developments – which plan to export power to the US.[10] But crossborder lines are increasingly running up against resistance. In addition to New York State's earlier cancellation of a transmission line, voters in Maine rejected a new Quebec power transmission line in late 2021 (though the legality of that referendum has been challenged in court). Nonetheless, construction is set to begin on the Champlain Hudson Power Express, which will send electricity from Quebec to New York City. Hydroelectricity as a form of producing electricity has become a controversial enterprise in the twenty-first century. On the one hand, it is a carbon-free method of generating power; on the other, large hydro power project cause enormous ecological and social dislocations, and big reservoirs can emit greenhouse gases from decomposing material.

NATURE OF THE RELATIONSHIP

Environmental and energy diplomacy has deeply affected not only the nature of North America, but the nature of the Canada-US relationship. Environmental and energy factors help us better understand the general patterns and tenor of Canada-US relations over the past century and a half. An environmental diplomacy perspective brings in a unique array of foreign policy actors and factors, ranging from fish to waterfalls to acid rain. Of course, environmental diplomacy alone cannot explain the whole Canada-US relationship. The inverse is equally true: detailing the history of Canadian-American relations without emphasizing environmental and energy factors fails to provide a full picture of the bilateral relationship. This history helps us understand not only the many ecological and sustainability challenges we face today, but the very nature of the bilateral relationship itself, both the positive and the negative.

Frequent diplomacy and contacts about natural resources served as shock absorbers during times of bilateral conflict; at the same time, certain natural resource negotiations became punctuated controversies that dominated government-to-government relations. At many intervals, environmental and energy subjects have been among the top issues in Canada-US diplomacy: various fisheries treaties; St Lawrence Seaway and Power Project; Columbia River treaty; Great Lakes Water Quality Agreements; acid rain; fossil fuel exports. These types of energy and environmental files were also often linked to, or became levers for, influencing the opposite country on other matters. Though there are many cases where the Canadian and the American diplomatic services have prevented squabbles over one issue from affecting another, there are also many examples where progress in one area was linked to satisfactory results on a different subject. Indeed, it could be in the realm of environmental and energy relations that this type of linkage most commonly occurs. Perhaps that is because many different environmental issues already seem inherently or intuitively linked – or in some cases, they are actually physically linked, such as different waterbodies in the Great Lakes–St Lawrence basin.

The use of soft law, such as nonbinding agreements, has been a common refrain in Canada-US environmental relations since governments do not want to give up much sovereignty. Such pacts could be difficult to maintain if not for a belief in their legitimacy or a desire to preserve the harmony in the wider relationship. But nonbinding agreements can also provide more flexibility and are sometimes the only politically feasible options.[11] Indeed, many of the most consequential and durable Canada-US environmental and energy agreements have been nonbinding. Many have also been formal treaties, and it is worth pointing out that the United States has rarely played the type of power politics where binding accords are ignored or broken by the stronger nation when they become inconvenient.

The history of bilateral environmental diplomacy helps explain why, despite the power imbalance, Canada often does so well in direct negotiations with the United States government. Canada puts its top officials on the US file, which the State Department does not. Canadian officials invariably know more about the United States than their American counterparts do about Canada, and invest greater governmental resources into bilateral relations, which includes mastering the technical minutiae of fish and kilowatts. That is, Canadian diplomats have more reason to be intimately familiar with the cubic feet-per-second flow rate of a particular border water or, to paraphrase the Henry Kissinger quote employed earlier, with the sex life of salmon. Knowledge and expertise can be partial correctives to asymmetry.

Bilateral environmental diplomacy is proportionally much more important to Canada. Entire elections in that country have hinged on potential agreements with the United States. The executive branch and bureaucracy (mainly the Department of State) of the US government often took Canadian sensitivities into account – or humoured Canada – in large part because of Canada's geographic and trade significance. But the US Congress, with its powers over treaties, repeatedly showed itself more than willing to ignore or override Canadian interests; the history presented in the preceding pages suggests that one of Canada's frequent obstacles has been the US Senate. Pulling the various strands of environmental and energy diplomacy together reveals just how often the Senate and its Foreign Relations Committee, motivated by domestic concerns, affected or nixed bilateral agreements.

Another frequent impediment for treaties and agreements was Canadian nationalism. Concerns about sovereignty are usually pan-Canadian in that such sentiments are spread across the country. At the same time, environmental and energy diplomacy was informed by local concerns since the development of a specific power project, preservation of a distinct fish run, or crossborder pollution had evident repercussions for those living and working nearby. Consequently, certain domestic sectors, constituencies, and interests oftentimes had a disproportionate voice in shaping foreign policy and major diplomatic consultations. Recall the role of local discord in influencing regionally specific problems, such as maritime fisheries or acid rain, which were elevated to the top of the diplomat docket.

Such discords aside, in the long view of things, the upper North American relationship is marked more by cooperation than conflict, in large part because of resource statecraft. Looking at Canadian-American international relations through an environmental and energy lens reveals the extent to which cooperation is heavily predicated upon practicality, coinciding national interests, and shared environments. Constantly negotiating over subjects that moved across or constituted the border has fostered the peaceful relationship of these "natural allies." Geography and proximity made Canada much more important to the US than would otherwise be the case. Canada's cornucopia of natural resources made smooth Canada-US relations very desirable from the American perspective, as did the extremely long border which presents a security challenge for the US (mostly in terms of the potential for other nations penetrating the United States via Canada). These factors sometimes provide Canada with more political and economic leverage than outsiders might assume, given the power imbalance between the two countries.

At the same time, there has been much mythmaking concerning the "special relationship" between Canada and the US. While there is certainly truth to that label in the immediate post-1945 period, both nations have traditionally acted in their respective self-interests; proximity, strategic concerns, economic goals, and US power meant these self-interests lined up, particularly during the early Cold War. The Donald Trump presidency, conversely, underlined some of the ways that Canadian and American interests can diverge.

Asymmetry, or one-sidedness, is a perpetual theme in Canadian-American relations: how much freedom does Canada have vis-à-vis the United States? I am of the view that the inherent asymmetry in favour of the United States establishes the parameters within which Canada can act. The Canadian government had the agency to make independent decisions, but often made those decisions aware of the explicit or implicit limits set by the United States. We routinely see Canadian officials proactively self-censuring once it becomes apparent what would be acceptable to the United States.

America's power meant that it could influence Canada, whether it meant to or not. That is what Pierre Trudeau was getting at when he said, "Living next to you is in some ways like sleeping with an elephant. No matter how friendly and even-tempered is the beast, if I can call it that, one is affected by every twitch and grunt." This aphorism is even more appropriate for the purposes of this book since Trudeau invoked an animal simile. Even though Canada–United States relations generally dealt with creatures other than pachyderms, the point is that a change to a congressional subsidy or a tariff could mean the difference between Canadian producers going bankrupt or enjoying a banner year.

The Canadian and American governments generally created the conditions conducive to the interests of industrial capital, believing (or claiming) that these interests were synonymous with the public interest. Sometimes, perhaps often, those governments were captured by or beholden to industry and finance capital. What has been characterized as American imperialism, or Canadian dependency, was sometimes transnational corporate and capital interests acting on their own and not necessarily following the designs of the US state. American capital was typically following its own profit imperatives – imperatives that might be shared by certain Canadian interests. American firms and multinationals did hold disproportionate sway over Canadian resource sectors such as oil and mining, and to various extents in other sectors. But this was not the result of a purposeful long-term strategy by the American government or foreign service, which essentially had no long-term or coherent strategy for Canada, especially prior to the free trade agreements. In some instances where Washington purportedly coveted Canadian resources, American officials actually wanted to keep out Canadian imports in order to protect US domestic producers.

Environmental and energy relations, therefore, tell us a great deal about the American view of empire in relation to Canada. In those Canadian sectors where the US came to directly or indirectly dominate, Canadian policymakers and elites generally were not coerced or forced into it. On many occasions they initiated or invited American involvement. Canadian governments and financial leaders entered into transborder arrangements with eyes wide open – and sold it to the masses as the rising tide lifting all boats. American involvement meant quicker economic gains in Canada. Decreased sovereignty was the trade-off for increased prosperity. Decision-makers in provinces like Alberta were happy to bring in US finance and management to develop hydrocarbons since there was little expertise and capital in Canada. Many provinces were more than happy to export their electricity to the United States, predicating new developments on the ability to sell the resulting power to the American market.

We might ask what realistic alternatives there were to this history of massive resource extraction and crossborder trade? Canada could have exported far less to the United States or put greater limits on American finance and investment in Canada; at times, there were strong nationalist movements pushing for exactly those sorts of measures. However, that likely would have meant less of, or higher prices for, the material goods and lifestyles that most Canadians wanted. And there is no guarantee that Canada's ecological footprint would have been lower if it had not economically integrated itself with the US: the same amount of natural resources might have been developed but just used domestically (e.g., western oil and gas could have supplied the country east of the Ottawa River) or traded elsewhere. Given the type of capitalist ethos prevailing in northern North America during the temporal period covered in this book, choosing to limit material progress and economic growth for the sake of ecological protection was not something political and economic elites, nor the majority of people in either country, were likely to do. Even today, in an era where environmental concerns get more purchase, North Americans and their political leaders exhibit few signs of willingly putting limits on their consumption despite the climate and ecological crises staring them in the face.

As I have already stated, part of the reason that Canada and the United States have so much in common, from a global perspective, is their many shared geographies and ecological settings. Indeed, from the perspective of non-North Americans, the distinctions between the two nations trumpeted by many Canadians and Americans, but particularly the former, might well be considered the narcissism of small differences. At the same time, the two nations have some very different geographic and environmental mythologies. Many of the earliest scholarly theses to explain and justify the American and Canadian nations spreading across the continent – staples, Laurentian, frontier, metropolitan-hinterland – verged on, or were outright, environmentally determinist. Even if we now eschew the extreme tautologies and determinisms built into those classic interpretations, these spatial explanations point to a bigger truth: the environment not only sets the parameters within which human history plays out but can exhibit types of agency.

Drawing partly from those classic theses, both the United States and Canada have manifested different forms of environmental nationalism – perceptions of the links between natural environments and national character and identity – and these have influenced crossborder relations. Canadian environmental nationalism, which interlinked with sovereignty concerns, was frequently a complicating factor in bilateral relations; American nationalists, by contrast, rarely paid attention to Canada. Nevertheless, when provoked,

American nationalism, or its regional variants, could be vociferous and protectionist.

In this book, I have tried to provide a framework for understanding the broad history of Canada-US environmental and energy relations. In many cases, I have drawn on the detailed work of others, and I hope that providing this framework can make it easier for other scholars to fill in the gaps. Though this study has been limited to the North American context, it is easy to see how a historical environmental diplomacy approach would be a beneficial frame for analyzing the other international activities of both countries.[12] Moreover, the history of bilateral environmental and energy relations demonstrates that Canada should loom much larger in the academic literature on American foreign relations. It is still always surprising that Canada, the country which shares the world's longest border with the United States, has been its most important trading partner over the last century, and is its major foreign provider of energy, is so persistently overlooked by those who study historical and contemporary American foreign policy.

The history of Canada-US environmental and energy diplomacy is, as *Natural Allies* has endeavoured to show, in large part responsible for the cooperative relationship and unprecedented affluence the two countries share. But that very peace and prosperity is a double-edged sword: it has naturalized a belief in perpetual abundance and growth that has led to a voracious consumption of resources that is not remotely close to being sustainable. Canada and the United States have made signal contributions to the evolution of international environmental law and transboundary governance, perhaps more than any two other countries. However, perhaps no two countries are, per capita, more responsible for our current planetary crises: climate change, habitat and species collapse, toxic pollutants, and so on. These will disproportionately and unjustly impact the rest of humanity, but even within North America, where affluence will allow many to adapt to those crises, ecological hazards now outweigh external military forces or terrorism as the greatest security threats. Natural security is what is at stake if we continue on our current trajectory.

Notes

INTRODUCTION

1 Arctic sovereignty is a subject area where Canadian diplomatic and security historians have sometimes incorporated environmental history into their approach – see the references of chapter 10 of this book. One publication from that area worth noting here, since it did include a more direct effort to put environmental and international history in conversation, is Meren and Plumptre, "Rights of Passage." In addition, in chapter 6 of his 1992 book on Canada-US relations history, Robert Bothwell focused mostly on energy and environmental issues, which is worth pointing out since Bothwell is a prominent historian of Canadian diplomacy and Canada-US relations. See Bothwell, *Canada and the United States.*

2 The term *nature* is admittedly problematic because of the false separation it implies between humans and the rest of the natural world; I will, however, continue to use that term, along with other terms such as non-human and more-than-human, because to do otherwise becomes too unwieldly.

3 In the Canadian case, the reader is advised to consult the 2016 collection *Powering Up Canada* which has chapters surveying the history of the various energy types. The second part of this collection, the Mineral Regime, is of particular relevance since it looks at coal, hydroelectricity, petroleum, natural gas, and nuclear power. Ruth W. Sandwell, ed., *Powering Up Canada*.

4 McDorman, *Salt Water Neighbors*, 3–4.

5 Lynton Caldwell grouped binational environmental-resource conflicts into three categories: inadvertent, developmental, and latent. Caldwell, "Binational Responsibilities for a Shared Environment."

6 Bothwell, "Thanks for the Fish: Nixon, Kissinger, and Canada," 399.

7 Stacey, *Canada and the Age of Conflict, Vol. 1*, 35. A classic work on Canadian foreign policy in the last two decades of the nineteenth century is Robert Craig Brown's *Canada's National Policy, 1883–1900*. Multi-volume survey histories of general Canadian foreign policy include C.P. Stacey, *Canada and the Age of Conflict* and James Eayrs, *In Defence of Canada*.

8 John McNeill has produced foundational work on international environmental history, such as his *Something New Under the Sun*. Kurkpatrick Dorsey and Mark Lytle outlined a range of methodological and ideological reasons that diplomatic historians have ignored environmental history: the study of diplomatic history has traditionally been very anthropocentric while environmental history is premised on bringing in non-human actors and agencies; environmental history uses more theory; diplomatic historians tend to address subjects that are bounded by borders and nation-states, which often is not the case with environmental history. Additionally, environmental history employs many non-traditional historical sources while diplomatic history has traditionally relied on archival evidence. Granted, the cultural turn in international history has been changing that for some time now, and in the last decade the number of environmental diplomacy studies has grown. Lytle, "An Environmental Approach to American Diplomacy History"; Dorsey, "Dealing with the Dinosaur (and Its Swamp): Putting the Environment in Diplomatic History"; Dorsey and Lytle, "Forum: New Directions in Diplomatic and Environmental History"; Clark, "Making Environmental Diplomacy an Integral Part of Diplomatic History."

9 Publications on the history of American environmental diplomacy include: Dorsey, *Whales and Nations*; Dorsey, *The Dawn of Conservation Diplomacy*; Hamblin, *Arming Mother Nature*; Colby, *Orca*; McNeill and Unger, eds., *Environmental Histories of the Cold War*; Bsumek, Kinkela, and Lawrence, eds., *Nation-States and the Global Environment*; Cioc, *The Game of Conservation*; Kaufmann, *The Environment and International History*.

10 William Willoughby's work from the 1960s and 1970s often focused on natural resources in Canadian-American relations (though without drawing much on the then-emerging field of environmental history): William Willoughby, *The Joint Organizations of Canada and the United States*. In the specific Canada-US environment context, political science and governance collections since 1990 include: Lemco, ed., *The Canada-United States Relationship*; Kay and Wirth, *Environmental Management on*

North America's Borders; Le Prestre and Stoett, eds., *Bilateral Ecopolitics*; Stoett and Temby, eds., *Towards Continental Environmental Policy?*; Brooks and Olive, eds., *Transboundary Environmental Governance Across the World's Longest Border*.

11 Chaloux and Paquin, "Green paradiplomacy in North America."

12 Lumsden, ed., *Close the 49th Parallel, etc.*; Levitt, *Silent Surrender*.

13 Brebner, *North Atlantic Triangle*.

14 Belanger, *Prejudice and Pride*, 38.

15 I align my interpretive approach to an extent with what can be called the "North American school" of Canadian-American relations. This school points to the importance of shared continental outlooks and tendencies, highlights the constant aspects of day-to-day diplomacy and the ballast it provides when politics turns stormy, and frames Canada's turn away from Britain and toward the United States in the mid-twentieth century as the most realistic option. This approach built upon many of the themes of the Carnegie series by stressing Canada US similarities and links. I am a continentalist in the sense that I think the United States has long been Canada's most important ally and partner, I see Canada as more of a North American nation than a British one, and I agree that the quotidian aspects of international relations need to be emphasized. Moreover, this awareness is also personal and subjective: as a Canadian living in the United States, I generally benefit from continental integration and the resulting opportunities. This school's senior historians include Norman Hillmer, Robert Bothwell, J.L. Granatstein, and Greg Donaghy.

16 For recent examples of injecting race, gender, and other neglected topics into Canadian international and transnational history see Dubinsky, Mills, and Rutherford, eds., *Canada and the Third World*; Madokoro, McKenzie, and Meren, eds., *Dominion of Race*; Campbell-Miller, Donaghy, and Barker, eds., *Breaking Barriers*; and the "Rethinking Canada in the World" series at McGill-Queen's University Press.

17 There are many excellent borderlands studies that have been published in recent decades. Some representative surveys and collections include: Stuart, *Dispersed Relations*; Konrad and Nicol, *Beyond Walls*; Bukowczyk et al., *Permeable Border*; Johnson and Graybill, eds., *Bridging National Borders in North America*; Hele, ed., *Lines Drawn upon the Water*; Binnema, "'Most Fruitful Results'"; Evenden and Wynn, "54, 40 or Fight."

18 The term "natural security" has been employed in different ways by a number of scholars. The version of "natural security" advanced here is an elaboration of what I proposed in Macfarlane, "Natural Security: Canada-US Environmental Diplomacy."

CHAPTER ONE

1 Kurkpatrick Dorsey breaks the existing historical literature on early international diplomacy of the environment into three general streams: early fisheries treaties; multilateral wildlife conservation treaties; and pollution control accords. However, water deserves its own separate listing beyond simply being subsumed under "pollution control" water accords since hydroelectricity, dams, and navigation were among the most important transborder issues in the early twentieth century. Dorsey, "Crossing Boundaries," 690.
2 Carroll, *A Good and Wise Measure*; Hoy, *A Line of Blood and Dirt*.
3 On Canadian-American east coast fish diplomacy in the nineteenth century see: Innis, *The Cod Fisheries*; Tallman, "Warships and Mackerel"; Candow and Corbin, *How Deep Is the Ocean*; Payne, *Fishing a Borderless Sea*.
4 Carroll, *A Good and Wise Measure*.
5 Payne, *Fishing a Borderless Sea*.
6 Bird and Heintzelman, "Canada/US Transboundary Energy Governance," 175–6.
7 Lower, *The North American Assault on the Canadian Forest*.
8 Nelles, *The Politics of Development*; Kuhlberg, *In the Power of Government*.
9 Stewart, *The American Response to Canada since 1776*.
10 US Department of State, Foreign Relations of the United States (hereafter FRUS), "Treaty between the United States and Great Britain for the settlement of pending questions between the two countries, concluded at Washington, on the 8th of May, 1871," https://history.state.gov/historicaldocuments/frus1873p2v3/d84.
11 Messamore, "Diplomacy or Duplicity?"
12 Hart, *A Trading Nation*, 72–4.
13 Stewart, *The American Response to Canada Since 1776*, 87.
14 Morse, *The Nature of Gold*.
15 Hillmer and Granatstein, *For Better or For Worse*, 57.
16 This list is from Bothwell, *Your Country, My Country*.
17 Dorsey, *The Dawn of Conservation Diplomacy*.
18 On the first decades of the Department of External Affairs see Hilliker, *Canada's Department of External Affairs, Volume I: The Early Years, 1909–1946*.
19 Foster, *Working for Wildlife*.
20 Campbell, ed., *A Century of Parks Canada, 1911–2011*; Young, MacEachern, and Dilsaver, "From Competition to Cooperation."

21 Colpitts, *Game in the Garden*; Artibise and Stelter, "Conservation Planning and Urban Planning"; Gillis and Roach, "The Beginnings of a Movement."

22 FRUS, "Annual Message of President Transmitted to Congress," 6 December 1910, Document 623: https://history.state.gov/historical documents/frus1910.

23 Gluek, "Programmed Diplomacy"; Willoughby, *The Joint Organizations of Canada and the United States*.

24 On Great Lakes fisheries see Margaret Beattie Bogue, *Fishing the Great Lakes*; see also Kurkpatrick Dorsey, "Part I: The Inland Fisheries Treaty," in *The Dawn of Conservation Diplomacy*.

25 Bogue, *Fishing the Great Lakes*, 244–8. For a sample of this commission's work see: US National Archives and Records Administration II (hereafter NARA II,) RG 0022 – US Fish and Wildlife Service. Office of the Commissioner of Fish and Fisheries. Entry #P44: Records of the Joint Fisheries Commission Relative to the Preservation of the Fisheries in Waters Contiguous to Canada and the United States: 1893–95, Folder: Lake Ontario & St Lawrence River.

26 Dorsey, *The Dawn of Conservation Diplomacy*.

27 On this convention see Busch, *The War against Seals*; Dorsey, *The Dawn of Conservation Diplomacy*.

28 Busch, *The War Against Seals*, 152.

29 Dorsey, *The Dawn of Conservation Diplomacy*.

30 Dorsey, "Protecting the National Interest, 1916–1920," chapter 8 in *The Dawn of Conservation Diplomacy*.

31 Dorsey, "Epilogue: Implications of the Progressive Treaties," in *The Dawn of Conservation Diplomacy*.

32 Dorsey, *The Dawn of Conservation Diplomacy*, 237.

CHAPTER TWO

1 Nancy Langston, *Sustaining Lake Superior*, 45.

2 Osborne and Swainson, chapters 2 and 3 in *The Sault Ste. Marie Canal*.

3 Archives of Ontario (hereafter AO), RG 38, no. 105, Ontario Power Commission, Hydro Electric Power Commission (1 January 1904, to 31 December 1918): Geo Y. Wisner, "Lake Erie Regulation," The Board of Engineers of Deep Waterways (n.d.). See also Arthur M. Woodford, *Charting the Inland Seas*; Neary, "Grey, Bryce, and the Settlement of Canadian-American Differences, 1905–1911."

4 Willoughby, *The Joint Organizations of Canada and the United States*, 64.

5 Perlgut, *Electricity across the Border: the US-Canadian Experience*, 11–12.
6 Macfarlane and Watson, "Hydro Democracy"; Mitchell, *Carbon Democracy*.
7 A decision by the Privy Council in 1898 had given ownership of the beds of all inland waterways to Ontario, though this was complicated by the federal government's jurisdiction over navigation. Armstrong, *The Politics of Federalism*, 73.
8 Grauer, "The Export of Electricity from Canada"; Perlgut, *Electricity across the Border*.
9 Armstrong, *The Politics of Federalism*, 72.
10 Exports continued after Hydro-Québec took over the Les Cèdres station.
11 For a survey of these various crossborder electricity exchanges up to 1970, see J.T. Miller, *Foreign Trade in Gas and Electricity in North America*. On electricity interchanges in the Pacific Northwest see Hirt, *The Wired Northwest*.
12 There were hopes that this canal could serve as a deep-draft route from Chicago to the Gulf of Mexico using the Mississippi River but this never fully materialized.
13 The IJC contends that the Chicago diversion reduced the mean levels of Lakes Michigan and Huron by approximately 2.5 inches, Lake Erie by 1.7 inches, Lake Ontario by 1.2 inches, and Lake Superior by less than an inch. If the diversion reached its 10,000 cfs capacity, about three times its current rate, the impact on the lakes would be proportional. Thus, the early twentieth-century estimate of a half-foot drop is reasonable. International Joint Commission (hereafter IJC), *Report on Further Regulation of the Great Lakes*; IJC, *Report on Great Lakes Diversions and Consumptive Uses*; Woodward, *Charting the Inland Seas*.
14 There are a number of publications on the St Mary–Milk issue, but for those who want an overview start with Heinmiller, "The Boundary Waters Treaty and International Joint Commission in the St. Mary-Milk Basin."
15 See Whorley, "From IWC to BWT: Canada-US Institution Building, 1902–1909"; Gluek, "The Lake Carriers' Association and the Origins of the International Waterways Commission," 27–31.
16 IJC, Docket 64, Niagara Falls Reference, box 114, 64-8-4:1, US Congressional Bills and Proceedings: Reports Upon the Existing Water-Power Situation at Niagara Falls, so far as concerns the Diversion of Water on the American Side, by the American Members of the International Waterways Commission and Captain Charles W. Kutz, Corps of Engi-

neers, US Army, 1906; IJC, Docket 64, Niagara Falls Reference, box 105, 64-1-1-1: References in the Compiled Reports of the International Waterways Commission to the 36,000–20,000 cfs Diversion at Niagara Falls, and to the 10,000 cfs Allowance for the Chicago Drainage Canal.

17 Technically it was titled "Treaty between the United States and Great Britain Relating to Boundary Waters, and Questions Arising between the United States and Canada." The treaty text can be viewed here: https://www.ijc.org/en/boundary-waters-treaty-1909.

18 Cohen, "The Commission from the Inside." For a balanced summary of the IJC see also pages 27–8 of Curtis and Carroll, *Canadian-American Relations*.

19 Thompson and Randall, *Canada and the United States*, 198.

20 See Murray Clamen and Daniel Macfarlane, "The International Joint Commission, Water Levels, and Transboundary Governance in the Great Lakes."

21 On the history of the IJC see Macfarlane and Clamen, eds., *The First Century of the International Joint Commission*. See also Dreisziger, "The International Joint Commission of the United States and Canada, 1895-1920"; Spencer, Kirton, and Nossal, eds., *The International Joint Commission Seventy Years On*; Bloomfield and FitzGerald, *Boundary Waters Problems of Canada and the United States*; Willoughby, *The Joint Organizations of Canada and the United States*. On border waters see also the many contributions to two edited collections: Norman, Cohen, and Bakker, eds., *Water Without Borders?*; Heasley and Macfarlane, eds., *Border Flows*.

CHAPTER THREE

1 Stewart, *The American Response to Canada*, 122.

2 Stamm, *Dead Tree Media*, 86.

3 Watson, "Coal in Canada"; Steward, "Energy Consumption in Canada since Confederation"; Piper and Green, "A Province Powered by Coal."

4 Azzi, *Reconcilable Differences*, 101.

5 Hillmer and Granatstein, *For Better or For Worse*, 99.

6 Drummond and Hillmer, *Negotiating Free Trade*.

7 Hillmer, *O.D. Skelton*, 166; Granatstein, *The Ottawa Men*.

8 Perras, *Franklin Roosevelt and the Origins of the Canadian-American Security Alliance, 1933–1945*.

9 Willoughby, *The Joint Organizations of Canada and the United States*, 66–7.

10 FRUS, "The Canadian Minister (Massey) to the Secretary of State," 6 May 1929, 711.428/1283. Papers relating to the foreign relations of the United States, 1929, Volume II: https://history.state.gov/historical documents/frus1929v02/d37.

11 Taylor III, "The Historical Roots of the Canadian-American Salmon Wars," 168. See also Evenden, *Fish versus Power*; Taylor III, *Making Salmon*; Roos, *Restoring Fraser River Salmon*; Wadewitz, *The Nature of Borders*.

12 Willoughby, *The Joint Organizations of Canada and the United States*, 69. Stacey explores the mechanics and significance of Canada signing the treaty alone in *Canada and the Age of Conflict*, 2:49–56.

13 Willoughby, *The Joint Organizations of Canada and the United States*, 69–70.

14 Willoughby, "Fisheries: Agreements and Arrangements," *The Joint Organizations of Canada and the United States*.

15 Wirth, *Smelter Smoke in North America*.

16 Temby and Munton, "The International Joint Commission and Air Pollution."

17 Dinwoodie, "The politics of international pollution control," 229; Alum, "'An Outcrop of Hell.'"

18 Dinwoodie, "The Politics of International Pollution Control," 229.

19 Wirth, *Smelter Smoke in North America*.

20 *FRUS*, "The Canadian Secretary of State for External Affairs (Bennett) to the American Minister in Canada (Robbins)," 711.4215 Air Pollution/582, General, The British Commonwealth, Vol, 1: https://history.state.gov/historicaldocuments/frus1934v01/d721.

21 Temby and Munton, "The International Joint Commission and Air Pollution: A Tale of Two Cases," 322.

22 Wirth, *Smelter Smoke in North America*, 12.

CHAPTER FOUR

1 Benidickson, *Leveling the Lake*; Luby, *Dammed*; Langston, *Sustaining Lake Superior*.

2 Massell, *Amassing Power*; Massell, *Quebec Hydropolitics*; Stamm, *Dead Tree Media*.

3 Benidickson, "The International Joint Commission and Water Quality in the Bacterial Age," 116.

4 Keller, *The Power Situation during the War*.

5 State Reservation at Niagara, *Thirty-Fifth Annual Report, State Reservation at Niagara, 1918* (Albany, J.B. Lyon, 1919).

6 Keller, *The Power Situation during the War.*
7 Froschauer, *White Gold.*
8 See Armstrong, *The Politics of Federalism*, 76–82.
9 Hirt, *The Wired Northwest*, 168.
10 Martin-Nielsen, "South over the Wires"; Grauer, "The Export of Electricity from Canada," 276.
11 Dales, *Hydroelectricity and Industrial Development.*
12 In 1920, the Federal Power Act created the Federal Power Commission. The FPC became the Federal Energy Regulatory Commission in 1977.
13 Hays, *Conservation and the Gospel of Efficiency*, 239–40; Holmes, *A History of Federal Water Resources Programs, 1800–1960*; Holmes, *History of Federal Water Resources Programs and Policies, 1961–70.*
14 US Senate, "St. Lawrence Waterway. Report of the United States and Canadian Government Engineers on the Improvement of the St. Lawrence River from Montreal to Lake Ontario made to the International Joint Commission (Wooten-Bowden Report)." Supplementary to Senate Document No. 114, 67th Congress (Washington: Government Printing Office, 1922).
15 In 1923 the American Super Power Company applied to the US Federal Power Commission for the right to dam the St Lawrence River, proposing to market two-thirds of the approximately 1 million horsepower in the United States. This was denied, however. Armstrong, *The Politics of Federalism*, 165.
16 Franklin D. Roosevelt Library & Archives, President's Secretary File, Diplomatic Correspondence, Canada 1933-35, Box 25, Letter from Cordell Hull to President Roosevelt, 14 December 1934.
17 Macfarlane and Heasley, "Water, Oil, and Fish."
18 Dwight D. Eisenhower Presidential Library & Archives, Staff Files: Records of John S. Bragdon, St Lawrence Seaway – 1954, Box 69, file: St Lawrence Seaway, Statement of Colonel W.H. Potter, Office Chief of Engineers, US Army, 27 June 1950.
19 Government of the United States, US Congress, "Preservation and Improvement of the Scenic Beauty of the Niagara Falls and Rapids: Message from the President of the United States Transmitting the Final Report of the Special International Niagara Board, Together With an Accompanying Report From the Acting Secretary of State and a Copy of a Letter from the Secretary of War," Washington: US Government Printing Office, 1931.
20 Special International Niagara Board, "Preservation and Improvement of

the Scenic Beauty of the Niagara Falls and Rapids" (Ottawa and Washington: Governments of Canada and the United States, 1931).

21 FRUS, "Secretary of State (Hull) to the Minister in Canada (Robbins), February 21, 1935," No. 638.

22 Sir Adam Beck No. 1 was located downriver from the Falls near Queenston in order to make greater use of the drop of the Niagara Escarpment.

23 Library and Archives Canada (hereafter LAC), RG 25, vol. 2636, file 1268-D-40C: St Lawrence River–Niagara River Treaty Proposals (General Correspondence), 4 January 1938, to 21 December 1940: Memorandum by Norman Marr to Mr Johnston, Re: Possible United States–Canadian Power Interchange Arrangement in connection with St Lawrence Treaty, 3 November 1939.

24 NARA II, RG 59, 23 December 1935 – Memorandum to the Secretary of State. From FDR. 711.42157 SA 29/1375 –1/2.

CHAPTER FIVE

1 Evenden, *Allied Power*; Bothwell, *Nucleus*.

2 Grant, *Polar Imperative*.

3 Government of Canada, Department of External Affairs, in *Documents on Canadian External Relations* (hereafter DCER), "Disposal of Canol Project," DEA/463-N-40, 931, Volume #12-931, chapter XI: Relations with the United States, Part 3, Defence, Section B, https://epe.lac-bac.gc.ca/100/206/301/faitc-aecic/history/2013-05-03/www.international.gc.ca/department/history-histoire/dcer/details-en.asp@intRefid=12063; Diubaldo, "The Canol Project in Canadian-American Relations"; Randall, *United States Foreign Oil Policy Since World War I*.

4 http://www.alaskahighwayarchives.ca/en/chap5/index.php.

5 Hillmer and Granatstein, *For Better or For Worse*, 159.

6 Ibid.

7 Coates and Morrison, *The Alaska Highway in World War II*, 71–95; Piper, *The Industrial Transformation of Subarctic Canada*.

8 Coates and Morrison, *The Alaska Highway in World War II*, 86.

9 In terms of household rather than total national consumption, data from the Dominion Bureau of Statistics figures show that (unlike the United States) Canadians were consuming very little electricity in their homes before the Second World War. See Ruth Sandwell *Canada's Rural Majority* and see her introduction as well as Josh MacFadyen's chapter "Hewers of Wood: A History of Wood Energy in Canada" in *Powering Up Canada*.

10 Unger and Thistle, *Energy Consumption in Canada in the 19th and 20th Centuries*.
11 Evenden, *Allied Power*.
12 The transportation of pulpwood logs was also a motivating factor.
13 LAC, RG 25, vol. 3560, file 1268-K-40C: St Lawrence–Niagara River Treaty between Canada and United States – Additional Diversion of Water at Niagara Falls, pt. 1 (April 24/41 to Dec 8/41): Letter from Wrong to Robertson, 24 April 1941; IJC, Docket 64, Niagara Falls Reference, box 114, file 64-8-5:3, Exchange of Notes Re: Niagara 1941: Exchange of Notes relating to further utilization of water for power purposes at Niagara Falls, 27 November 1941; LAC, RG 25, vol. 3560, file 1268-K-40C: St Lawrence–Niagara River Treaty between Canada and United States – Additional Diversion of Water at Niagara Falls, pt. 2 (Jan 1/42 to April 30/44).
14 Hydro-Electric Power Commission of Ontario (hereafter HEPCO) Memorandum (by Lindsay) to WL Mackenzie King Re: Remedial Works in Niagara River (n.d., 1943).
15 Eisenhower Archives, Staff Files: Records of John S. Bragdon, St Lawrence Seaway – 1954, Box 69, file: St Lawrence Seaway, Statement of Colonel W.H. Potter, Office Chief of Engineers, US Army, 27 June 1950.
16 Granatstein, *How Britain's Weakness Forced Canada into the Arms of the United States*.
17 Bothwell, *Your Country, My Country*, 264. See also Bothwell's *Alliance and Illusion* on Canadian foreign relations for most of the Cold War.
18 Mackenzie, "Shades of Gray?"; Donaghy, ed. *Canada and the Early Cold War, 1943-1957*; Chapnick, *Canada on the UN Security Council*; Dutil, ed., *The Unexpected Louis St. Laurent*. On changing conceptions of the "national interest" in Canadian foreign affairs history see Donaghy and Carroll, eds., *In the National Interest*.
19 "Canada Bars a 'Yes' Role to US; Pearson Sees Unity Despite Friction," *New York Times*, 11 April 1951, page 1.
20 Hart,"The Structure of Protection and Its Impact," chapter 7 in *A Trading Nation*.
21 Aronsen, *American National Security and Economic Relations with Canada, 1945–1954*.
22 For a survey of Canadian environmental history that foregrounds the importance of capitalism, consumption, and subsistence see Murton, *Canadians and Their Natural Environment*.
23 See chapter 5 of Mahant and Mount, *Invisible and Inaudible in Washington*.

24 Aronsen, *American National Security and Economic Relations with Canada*.

25 In addition to the literature on Innis's staples theory, there is a strong Marxist and neo-Marxist streak in Canadian political economy literature pertaining to natural resources from the middle years of the Cold War. For example, see Panitch, *The Canadian State*; Laxer, *The Energy Poker Game*; Clarke-Jones, *A Staple State*.

26 Muirhead, *Dancing Around the Elephant*.

27 Aronsen, *American National Security and Economic Relations with Canada*, 121–3; Bothwell, *Nucleus*.

28 Canada did oppose the American testing of nuclear weapons in the Aleutians. DCER, "Extract from Minutes of Meeting of Board of Directors of Eldorado Mining and Refining (1944) Ltd, December 10th, 1949," Volume #16-848, chapter VIII: Relations with the United States, Part 2, Economic Issues, Section A, Atomic Energy, 848, C.D.H./Vol.-9 https://epe.lac-bac.gc.ca/100/206/301/faitc-aecic/history/2013-05-03/www.international.gc.ca/department/history-histoire/dcer/details-en.asp@intRefid=7869.

29 Aronsen, *American National Security and Economic Relations with Canada*, 115.

30 Mahant and Mount contend that American officials were not so much concerned that most of their nickel came from one country, but that most of it came from one firm: INCO. Mahant and Mount, *Invisible and Inaudible in Washington*, 107.

31 Melissa Clark-Jones argues that US Cold War foreign policy objectives encouraged the type of resource stockpiling that led to these sorts of paper product cartels and monopolies, aided and abetted by the Canadian government. Clark-Jones, *A Staple State*, 105.

32 Beigie and Hero, *Natural Resources in US-Canadian Relations*, 2:20.

33 DCER, "Memorandum from Under-Secretary of State for External Affairs to Secretary of State for External Affairs, Radar Defence System, January 19, 1952," Volume #18-688, chapter VIII, Relations with the United States, Part I, Defence Issues, Section B, Radar Defence System (Pinetree), 688, DEA/50210-040, https://epe.lac-bac.gc.ca/100/206/301/faitc-aecic/history/2013-05-03/www.international.gc.ca/department/history-histoire/dcer/details-en.asp@intRefId=4184.

34 Lackenbauer and Farish, "The Cold War on Canadian Soil."

35 Holmes, *Life with Uncle*. See also Holmes's two-volume *The Shaping of Peace: Canada and the Search for World Order, 1943–1957*; Hilliker and Barry, *Canada's Department of External Affairs, Volume II*; Livingston T.

Merchant, ed., *Neighbours Taken for Granted*. Robert Teigrob argues that ordinary Canadians also pushed the government towards alliance with the United States in *Warming up to the Cold War*.

CHAPTER SIX

1 NARA II, RG 59, Box 3303, 711.42157 SA 29/10-148 to 711.42157 SA 29/10-3048 State Dept Memorandum from Satterthwaite to Hickerson, 22 December 1948. The sections on Niagara Falls in this book are chiefly drawn from Macfarlane, *Fixing Niagara Falls*.

2 The United States was not able to utilize its full complement of the water, as it did not have enough hydroelectric generating facilities in place, so Canada was allowed to use this extra water until PASNY completed its Moses station in the early 1960s. Dwight D. Eisenhower Archives, Staff Files: Records of John S. Bragdon, St Lawrence Seaway – 1954, Box 69, file: St Lawrence Seaway, Proposed F.P.C. Plan for Niagara Power Redevelopment; Government of Canada, Department of External Affairs, "Memorandum from Secretary of State for External Affairs to Cabinet, February 18, 1950," Cabinet Document No. 56 50, in *Documents on Canadian External Relations*, vol. 16 (Ottawa: Minister of Public Works and Government Services Canada, 1997), 974.

3 IJC, Docket 64, Report to the International Joint Commission by the International Falls Engineering Board, "Preservation and Enhancement of Niagara Falls – March 1, 1953."

4 Macfarlane, *Fixing Niagara Falls*.

5 IJC, Docket 64, Niagara Falls Reference, box 110, 64-7-3:3 (3), INBC – Final Report of Construction of Niagara River Remedial Works – 1960/09/30: Construction of Niagara River Remedial Works, Final Report by the International Niagara Board of Control, 30 September 1960.

6 Drescher, *Engineers for the Public Good*, 259.

7 A few years later the two countries requested that the scope be widened to include aspects of public safety at the flanks of the American Falls and the Goat Island flank of the Horseshoe Falls.

8 Drescher, *Engineers for the Public Good*, 264.

9 LAC, RG 25, 86-1-7:1, American Falls (Niagara): Preservation and Enhancement of the American Falls, Final Report of the International Joint Commission to United States and Canada, July 1975.

10 Macfarlane, *Negotiating a River*.

11 Ibid.

12 *FRUS*, "Memorandum by the Under Secretary of State (Webb) to the

President. Subject: Visit of Prime Minister St. Laurent on September 28 to discuss the St. Lawrence Seaway and Power Project, September 27, 1951," 1951, Vol. II, Canada, 916.

13 This section on St Lawrence construction and environmental impact is drawn from Macfarlane, *Negotiating a River*.

14 Macfarlane, "Nature Empowered."

15 IJC, Canadian Section, 68-3-1:2, St Lawrence Power Application, Correspondence, C. McGrath, Joint Report by HEPCO and PASNY, "Assessment of Shoreline Erosion and Marshland Recession Downstream of the St. Lawrence Power Project," March 1983.

16 This section is drawn partly from Hillmer, Macfarlane, and Manulak, "Pearson and Environmental Diplomacy." There are many useful studies of the Columbia River developments including: Swainson, *Conflict over the Columbia*; Waterfield, *Continental Waterboy*; Cosens, ed., *The Columbia River Treaty Revisited*; Sandford, Harford, and O'Riordan, *The Columbia River Treaty*.

17 Lower Bonnington Falls Dam (1898), Upper Bonnington Falls Dam (1907), South Slocan Dam (1928), Corra Linn Dam (1932), Brilliant Dam (1944).

18 Macfarlane, "Environmental Nationalist."

19 Mouat, "The Columbia Exchange." For more detail on the diplomatic negotiations, see also Swainson, *Conflict over the Columbia*.

20 Canadian Departments of External Affairs and National Resources, *The Columbia River Treaty, Protocol, and Related Documents*.

21 Hillmer, Macfarlane, and Manulak, "Pearson and Environmental Diplomacy," 325.

22 Waterfield, *Continental Waterboy*, 116.

23 Moy and O'Riordan, "The International Joint Commission's Unique and Colourful Role in Three Projects in the Pacific Northwest."

24 Armstrong and Nelles, *Monopoly's Moment*, 237–8.

CHAPTER SEVEN

1 Macfarlane, "Hydro Diplomacy."

2 Duncan and Sandwell, "Manufactured and Natural Gas"; Cobban, *Cities of Oil*.

3 Gray, *Forty Years in the Public Interest*; Doern and Gattinger, *Power Switch*.

4 Chastko, "Anonymity and Ambivalence," 171.

5 DCER, "Extract from Memorandum from American Division to Under-Secretary of State for External Affairs, Export of Natural Gas: Westcoast

Transmission Company: FPC Proceedings, March 7th, 1953," Volume #19-814, chapter VIII, Relations with the United States, Part 5, Economic Issues, Section D, Natural Gas, 814, DEA/5420-40, https://epe.lac-bac.gc.ca/100/206/301/faitc-aecic/history/2013-05-03/www.international.gc.ca/department/history-histoire/dcer/details-en.asp@intRefId=2445; Alper, "Transboundary Environmental Governance in the Pacific West."

6 On the TransCanada pipeline controversy see Kilbourn, *Pipeline*. For discussion of other pipeline debates from the 1950s to the 1970s, see McDougall, *Fuels and the National Policy*.

7 Clark-Jones, *A Staple State*; Richards and Pratt, *Prairie Capitalism*.

8 Taylor, *Imperial Standard*.

9 Mahant and Mount, *Invisible and Inaudible in Washington*, 133.

10 Tammy Nemeth, "Canada-US Oil and Gas Relations, 1958 to 1974," 48.

11 The term "exemptionalism" was coined by R.D. Cuff and J.L. Granatstein in their book *Canadian-American Relations in Wartime from the Great War to the Cold War*.

12 Muirhead, chapters 1 and 2 in *Dancing Around the Elephant*.

13 For detailed studies of Canadian-American relations in the 1960s, see works such as McKercher, *Camelot and Canada*; Donaghy, *Tolerant Allies*; Cavell and Touhey, *Reassessing the Rogue Tory*. On anti-Americanism see Granatstein, *Yankee Go Home?*

14 Nemeth, "Canada-US Oil and Gas Relations, 1958 to 1974." For an overview of petroleum liquids in Canada, see Steve Penfold's chapter in *Powering Up Canada*.

15 Nemeth, "Canada-US Oil and Gas Relations, 1958 to 1974," 246.

16 Nemeth, "From Conflict to Cooperation," 155–6.

17 Gordan, *Coal and Canada-US Energy Relations*, 11.

18 Watson, "Coal in Canada."

19 Azzi, *Walter Gordon and the Rise of Canadian Nationalism*. On bilateral trade from Diefenbaker to Trudeau see Muirhead, *Dancing Around the Elephant*.

20 Anastakis, *Auto Pact*.

CHAPTER EIGHT

1 Lynton Caldwell presciently made this point in his chapter "Transboundary Conflicts: Resources and Environment."

2 Jennifer Read, "Origin of the Great Lakes Water Quality Agreement"; DCER, "Memorandum from Secretary of State for External Affairs to Prime Minister, Pollution of Boundary Waters, March 23rd, 1955," Vol-

ume #21-460, chapter IV: Relations with the United States, Part 5, International Joint Commission, Section A, Cross-Border Pollution, 460, DEA/8010-40: https://epe.lac-bac.gc.ca/100/206/301/faitc-aecic/history/2013-05-03/www.international.gc.ca/department/history-histoire/dcer/details-en.asp@intRefId=1520.

3 Scarpino, "Addressing Cross-Border Pollution of the Great Lakes after World War II," 120; Kehoe, *Cleaning Up the Great Lakes*.

4 Botts and Muldoon, *Evolution of the Great Lakes Water Quality Agreement*.

5 On federalism and environmental policy since the 1960s, see Harrison, *Passing the Buck*; Weibust, *Green Leviathan*.

6 Krantzberg, "The Great Lakes Remedial Action Plan"; John H. Hartig and M. Munawar, eds., *Ecosystem-Based Management of Laurentian Great Lakes Areas of Concern*.

7 Fletcher, *From Love Canal to Environmental Justice*; Harrison and Hoberg, *Risk, Science, and Politics*.

8 The 1994 contingency plan was updated in 2009. For more details on this plan see: LAC & Environmental Protection Agency (EPA), "Canada-United States Joint Inland Pollution Contingency Plan," 1 June 2022, https://www.epa.gov/sites/default/files/2014-08/documents/us_can_jcp_eng.pdf.

9 IJC, *Report on Further Regulation of the Great Lakes*.

10 IJC, *Report on Further Regulation of the Great Lakes*; International Joint Commission, *Report on Great Lakes Diversions and Consumptive Uses*.

11 IJC, *Great Lakes Diversions and Consumptive Uses: Final Report*.

12 IJC, *Levels Reference Study: Great Lakes-St. Lawrence River Basin*.

13 Gaden, Brant, and Lambe, "Why a Great Lakes Fishery Commission?"

14 Tanner, *Something Spectacular*.

15 See Alexander, *Pandora's Locks*.

16 Alexander, *Pandora's Locks*, xix.

CHAPTER NINE

1 Perlgut, *Electricity across the Border*, 11.

2 Hirt, *The Wired Northwest*, 312.

3 Cohn, *The Grid*, 152.

4 For a summary of interconnections as of 1975 see Perlgut, *Electricity Across the Border*.

5 Several points in this paragraph are derived from Froschauer, *White Gold*.

6 Brandson and Olson, "The International Joint Commission and Mid-

Continent Water Issues." For a survey of transborder prairie issues see Heinmiller, "Transboundary Water Governance in the Prairie Region."

7 Carroll, *Environmental Diplomacy*, 175.

8 IJC, *Transboundary Implications of the Garrison Diversion Unit.*

9 The Rafferty-Alameda saga is best known because of its association with environmental assessment policy. On Rafferty-Alameda see Hood, *Against the Flow*; Redekop, *Dams of Contention*; https://ijc.org/en/srb/who/mandate

10 Carroll, *Environmental Diplomacy*, 195–6.

11 Waldram, *As Long as the Rivers Run*; Martin and Hoffman, eds., *Power Struggles*; Froschauer, "Nelson River Power (Manitoba)," chapter 6 in *White Gold.*

12 Carroll, *Environmental Diplomacy*, 192.

13 Van Huizen, "Building a Green Dam."

14 Dilsaver and Wyckoff, "Agency Culture, Cumulative Causation and Development in Glacier National Park, Montana."

15 Peyton, "Corporate Ecology"; Alper, "Transboundary Environmental Governance in the Pacific West."

16 Kenny, "The International Joint Commission and Hydro-power Development on the Northeastern Borderlands, 1945–1970."

17 Ibid.

18 Camp, "Tellico Dam, Dickey Dam, and Endangered Species Law in the United States during the 1970s."

19 See Carroll, "Oil and the Coastline," chapter 4 in *Environmental Diplomacy*; for a survey of pressing Canada-US environmental issues in the mid-1970s, including Eastport, see Lemarquand and Scott, "Canada-United States Environmental Relations."

20 Carroll, *Environmental Diplomacy*, 105.

21 Desbiens, *Power from the North*; McCutcheon, *Electric Rivers.*

CHAPTER TEN

1 Beigie and Hero, *Natural Resources in US-Canadian Relations, Volume I*; Beigie and Hero, *Natural Resources in US-Canadian Relations, Volume II*; John Carroll's book *Environmental Diplomacy*. Curtis and Carroll's chapter "Transboundary Environmental and Resource Issues" in Norman Hillmer's 1989 edited collection *Partners Nevertheless* could be seen as the first focused attention on environmental diplomacy to appear in a book on the history of Canadian-American relations. This chapter was in turn drawn from Curtis and Carroll's 1984 book *Canadian-American Relations.*

2 In the 1990s, Lemco, *The Canada-United States Relationship*; chapter 6 of Bothwell, *Canada and the United States*. Continuing this transboundary environmental governance emphasis into the twenty-first century, we see showcases of work by various scholars in collections such as *Bilateral Ecopolitics: Continuity and Change in Canadian-American Environmental Relations*; *Transboundary Environmental Governance across the World's Longest Border*; *Towards Continental Environmental Policy?* Authors continued this trend into the twenty-first century, including John Carroll, Lynton Caldwell, George Hoberg, Alan Schwartz, Debora VanNijnatten, Ian Rowlands, Bruce Doern, Don Munton, and Peter Stoett.

3 Hillmer, Macfarlane, and Manulak, "Pearson and Environmental Diplomacy." On Canadian international history during the Pearson years see works such as John English's *Shadow of Heaven*; McKercher and Perras, eds., *Mike's World: Lester B. Pearson and Canadian External Affairs*.

4 The American environmental movement certainly influenced Canadian environmentalism in both direct and indirect ways. Marilyn Dubasak expands on the institutional differences between the two countries in her book *Wilderness Preservation*.

5 See Morton's chapter "The Relevance of Canadian Historians"; Worster, "Wild, Tame, and Free: Comparing Canadian and US Views of Nature." On the links between the environment and identity in Canada and the United States see also Harris, "The Myth of the Land in Canadian Nationalism"; Kline, *Beyond the Land Itself*; Berger, "The Truth North Strong and Free"; Alteymer, "Three Ideas of Nature in Canada, 1893–1914"; Miller, *Nature's Nation*; Kaufmann, "Naturalizing the Nation"; Campbell, *Shaped by the West Wind*; MacEachern, "A Little Essay on Big: Towards a History of Canada's Size"; Hillmer and Chapnick, eds., *Canadas of the Mind*.

6 Michael Manulak argues that Canada's contributions to the 1972 UN Conference on the Human Environment were shaped by its concerns for the Arctic Waters Pollution Prevention Act. Manulak, "Multilateral Solutions to Bilateral Problems." On the general American influence on Canadian environmental policy see Hoberg, "Sleeping with the Elephant."

7 On Trudeau's foreign policies see Granatstein and Bothwell, *Pirouette* and John English's biography of Trudeau. On the Department of External Affairs during the Trudeau (and Clark) years, see Hilliker, Halloran, and Donaghy, *Canada's Department of External Affairs, Volume III*.

8 Thompson and Randall, *Canada and the United States*, 247.

9 Chastko, chapter 8 in *Developing Alberta's Oil Sands*.

10 Uslaner, "Energy Policy and Federalism in the United States and Canada."
11 Mitchell, *Carbon Democracy*.
12 Bothwell, *Canada and the United States*, 120.
13 Doern and Toner, *The Politics of Energy*.
14 Bonder, "Herb Gray and the Founding of the Foreign Investment Review Agency."
15 The "A" in the acronym NORAD now stood for North American *Aerospace* Defence Command.
16 Nemeth, "From Conflict to Cooperation," 150.
17 Nemeth, "Continental Drift: Energy Policy and Canadian-American Relations."
18 Ashworth, "Continuity and Change in the US Decision-Making Process," 92.
19 Before the end of the century the Alberta line was expanded, but the international stretch remained on hold. In the twenty-first century there was movement towards completing a liquified natural gas export pipeline, called the Alaska Pipeline Project.
20 Kirkey, "Moving Alaskan Oil to Market."
21 On the Manhattan and Northwest Passage, Kirkey "The Arctic Waters Pollution Prevention Initiatives"; Kirton and Munton, "The Manhattan Voyages and their Aftermath."
22 Lackenbauer and Kikkert, "Building on 'Shifting Sands.' There are many recent studies of the Arctic sovereignty question by Whitney Lackenbauer, Elizabeth B. Elliot-Meisel, Rob Huebert, Peter Kikkert, Adam Lajeunnese, Heather Nicol, Shelagh Grant, John English, and others.
23 See chapters 4–6 in Beigie and Hero, *Natural Resources in US-Canadian Relations, Volume II*.
24 Bratt, *The Politics of CANDU Exports*.
25 McIntyre, *Uranium, Nuclear Power, and Canada-US Energy Relations*; Baker Fox, Hero, and Nye, eds., *Canada and the United States*.
26 Hero and Beigie, *Natural Resources in US-Canadian Relations*, Vol II, 546.

CHAPTER ELEVEN

1 Gotlieb, "Canadian Diplomatic Initiatives: The Law of the Sea." The following section on the Law of the Sea draws from Hillmer, Macfarlane, and Manulak, "Pearson and Environmental Diplomacy."
2 Ibid., 144–7.

3 Canada and the United States also signed the Agreement on Reciprocal Fisheries of 1970. McDorman, *Salt Water Neighbors*, 82.

4 Ibid., 49.

5 Canada did not become a party to the UNCLOS until 2003. McDorman, *Salt Water Neighbors*, 87.

6 Riddell-Dixon, *Canada and the International Seabed*; Morell, *The Law of the Sea*.

7 The Special Negotiator also outlined treaties on west coast fishing, but these too failed to gain traction. McDorman, *Salt Water Neighbors*, 119.

8 Doran, *Forgotten Partnership*, 181. It is worth noting that Doran devotes two chapters to environmental and energy issues in this book.

9 Barry, "The US Senate and the Collapse of the East Coast Fisheries Agreement."

10 Marshall, "Defining Maritime Boundaries"; Cook, "Lobster Boat Diplomacy."

11 DCER, "Memorandum from Secretary of State for External Affairs to Cabinet, North Pacific Fur Seals Conference, November 18, 1955," Volume #21-490, chapter IV: Relations with the United States, Part 7, Pelagic Sealing, 490, PCO, Cabinet Document No. 229-55: https://epe.lac-bac.gc.ca/100/206/301/faitc-aecic/history/2013-05-03/www.international.gc.ca/department/history-histoire/dcer/details-en.asp@intRefId=1551.

12 Along with Japan, Canada and the United States also signed the North Pacific Fisheries Convention in 1952, which addressed other fish in addition to salmon.

13 For the text of the Pacific Salmon Treaty see; Pacific Salmon Commission, "Treaty Between the Government of Canada and the Government of the United States of American Concerning Pacific Salmon," February 2022: https://www.psc.org/about-us/history-purpose/pacific-salmon-treaty/. For scholarly work on the treaty see McDorman, *Salt Water Neighbors*; Roos, *Restoring Fraser River Salmon*; Rogers and Stewart, "Prisoners of their Histories"; Jensen, "The United States-Canada Pacific Salmon Interception Treaty."

14 Taylor, "The Historical Roots of the Canadian-American Salmon Wars," 175.

15 Ibid.

16 On the 1997 dispute see Samuel Barkin, "The Pacific Salmon Dispute and Canada-US Environmental Relations." Since the 1980s British Columbia and Washington State have collaborated on protecting aspects of the transboundary Salish Sea ecosystem, such as salmon, water quality, and tankers moving fossil fuels, highlighted by a 1992

Environmental Cooperation Agreement. This was followed by a joint statement of cooperation on sustainability goals by Environment Canada and the EPA. Donald Alper, "Transboundary Environmental Governance in the Pacific West."

17 For more information on this treaty see NOAA Fisheries, "Pacific Hake/Whiting Treaty," https://www.fisheries.noaa.gov/west-coast/laws-and-policies/pacific-hake-whiting-treaty (accessed 5 December 2022).

18 DCER, "Memorandum from Under-Secretary of State for External Affairs to Secretary of State for External Affairs, Great Lakes Fisheries Convention, September 14, 1954," Volume #20-599, chapter V: Relations with the United States, Part 5, Great Lakes Fisheries Convention, 599, DEA/9130-40: https://epe.lac-bac.gc.ca/100/206/301/faitc-aecic/history/2013-05-03/www.international.gc.ca/department/history-histoire/dcer/details-en.asp@intRefId=774.

19 Taylor, ed., *Great Lakes Fisheries Policy and Management*.

20 Song, Temby, Krantzberg, and Hickey, "Institutional Features of US Canadian Transboundary Fisheries Governance"; Gaden and Krueger, "Multi-jurisdictional Governance of the Shared Great Lakes Fishery."

21 On the transnational approach to endangered species see Olive, *Land, Stewardship, and Legitimacy*.

22 Boardman, "Multi-level Environmental Governance in North America: Migratory Birds and Biodiversity"; Robert Wilson, *Seeking Refuge*.

23 The text of the 1987 Porcupine Caribou Herd agreement can he found here: Environment and Climate Change Canada, "Compendium of Canada's Engagement in International Environmental Agreements and Instruments: Agreement between the Government of Canada and the Government of the United States on the Conservation of the Porcupine Caribou Herd," https://www.canada.ca/content/dam/eccc/documents/pdf/international-affairs/compendium/2020/batch-4/canada-united-states-conservation-porcupine-caribou-herd.pdf (accessed 25 January 2021); see also: Don Russell and Anne Gunn (Shadow Lake Environmental Inc.), "Vulnerability analysis of the Porcupine Caribou Herd to potential development of the 1002 lands in the Arctic National Wildlife Refuge, Alaska," Report prepared for: Environment Yukon, Canadian Wildlife Service, and GNWT Department of Environment and Natural Resources, 3 February 2019, https://yukon.ca/sites/yukon.ca/files/env/env-vulnerability-analysis-porcupine-caribou-herd-potential-development-anwr.pdf (accessed 25 January 2021).

24 Temby and Munton, "The International Joint Commission and Air Pollution."

25 The two federal governments had been moving towards air pollution regulations during the IJC investigation: the 1970 US Clean Air Act and the 1971 Canadian Clean Air Act. Owen Temby, "Control and Suppression in Sarnia's Chemical Valley during the 1960s."
26 Temby and Munton, "The International Joint Commission and Air Pollution."
27 See chapter 10 of Carroll's *Environmental Diplomacy* for more on these issues. The Poplar River coal plant in Saskatchewan, which was previously discussed in the context of water quality, was also addressed with the bilateral monitoring system established in 1980, and included technological changes to the Poplar plant to reduce emissions.
28 Schwartz, "The Canada-US environmental relationship," 239.
29 Munton, "Transboundary Air Pollution: Dependence and Interdependence," 76; Munton, "Acid Rain Politics in North America."
30 Clarkson, *Uncle Sam and Us*, 193.
31 Munton, "Transboundary Air Pollution: Dependence and Interdependence," 79; Temby and O'Connor, "Property, Technology, and Environmental Policy"; Mulroney, *Memoirs*, 498–500; May, "Brian Mulroney and the environment," 386.
32 Azzi, *Reconcilable Differences*, 222–3; Smith, "Shades of Grey in Canada's Greening during the Mulroney Era," 75.
33 McGrath and Milnes, eds, *Age of the Offered Hand*.
34 Munton, "Transboundary Air Pollution: Dependence and Interdependence."
35 Munton, "Transboundary Air Pollution: Dependence and Interdependence"; Don Munton, "Acid Rain and Transboundary Air Quality in Canadian-American Relations."
36 For biennial progress reports on the Air Quality Agreement see: EPA, "US-Canada Air Quality Agreement Progress Reports," https://www.epa.gov/airmarkets/us-canada-air-quality-agreement-progress-reports (accessed 4 December 2022).
37 Smith, "Shades of Grey in Canada's Greening during the Mulroney Era," 80.
38 Benedick, *Ozone Diplomacy*.
39 Handley, "Exports of Waste From the United States to Canada."
40 For more detail see US EPA, *Waste Shipments Between the United States and Canada* (Washington: US EPA, 2007), 5.

CHAPTER TWELVE

1 Stanford, "A Cure for Dutch Disease."
2 Hoberg, "Canadian-American Environmental Relations"; Doern, *Green Diplomacy*; Doern, Auld, Stoney, "International Environmental Policy: Canada-US Relations and Global Agreements," chapter 3 in *Green-Lite*.
3 There are many books the reader can consult on the 1988 free trade negotiations, such as: Dymond and Robertson, *Decision at Midnight*; Ritchie, *Wrestling with the Elephant*; Doern and Tomlin, *Faith and Fear*; Gotlieb, *The Washington Diaries: 1983–1991*.
4 US Energy Information Adminstration, "Petroleum & Other Liquids" (30 November 2022): https://www.eia.gov/dnav/pet/hist/LeafHandler.ashx?n=PET&s=MTTIMUSCA1&f=A.
5 Froschauer, *White Gold*, 48. Monica Gattinger contends that prior to the 1990s the electric supply industry in Canada and the United States was regulated mainly as a "natural monopoly" with the various segments owned and operated by single vertically integrated utilities. Monica Gattinger, "Canada-United States Electricity Relations," 8.
6 Froschauer, *White Gold*, 47.
7 The general literature on NAFTA negotiations includes Tomlin and Cameron, *The Making of NAFTA*; Robert, *Negotiating NAFTA*.
8 Boyd, *Unnatural Law*.
9 John Carroll makes this point in his chapter "Environment, Free Trade, and Canada-US Relations," in Lemco, *The Canada-United States Relationship*. For an opposing view see Kirton, "Managing Canada's US Relations through NAFTA's Trade-Environment Regime."
10 Hajdu, "The Canada-US Softwood Lumber Dispute"; Hart and Dymond, "The Cul-de-sac of Softwood Lumber."
11 Daowei, *The Softwood Lumber War*.
12 Hart, *A Trading Nation*; Barichello, Josling, and Sumner, "Agricultural Trade Relations between Canada and the United States."
13 Dempsey, *Great Lakes For Sale – Updated Edition*.
14 NARA II, RG 0076, Boundary and Claims Commissions and Arbitrations Department of State/US Embassy, Canada. Entry #P 97: Individual Claims Files of the Lake Ontario Claims Tribunal 1965–1968; Murray Clamen and Daniel Macfarlane, "Plan 2014."
15 VanNijnatten and Johns, "The International Joint Commission and the Evolution of the Great Lakes Water Quality Agreement"; Johns, "Transboundary Environmental Governance and Water Pollution in the Great Lakes Region."

16 VanNijnatten and Stoett, "Continental Counter-Invasion." In the early twenty-first century, the IJC began experimenting with the International Watersheds Initiative for many of the transborder waterbodies covered in this book. These involved the creation of watershed boards, which were to be ecosystem-based and bring in a wider variety of stakeholders to the decision-making process, including First Nations.

17 Olive, "Biodiversity without Borders?," 139.

18 Brandson and Olson, "The International Joint Commission and Mid-Continent Water Issues"; Paris, "The Devils Lake Dispute between Canada and the United States."

19 Brandson and Olson, "The International Joint Commission and Mid-Continent Water Issues," 230.

20 This list is chiefly drawn from Stephen Brooks, "Canada-United States Environmental Relations During the Trudeau-Trump Years." See also Peter Stoett's chapter on environmental relations during the Trump-Trudeau period: Stoett, "Fairweather Friends?" Recent surveys of bilateral US-Canada environment and energy relations can be found in two edited collections: *Transboundary Environmental Governance across the World's Longest Border* and *Towards Transboundary Environmental Policy?*

21 After a period of sixty years either country was free to leave the treaty or renegotiate its terms, with advance warning required.

CHAPTER THIRTEEN

1 Azzi and Hillmer, "Intolerant Allies." For an overview of energy and environment in Canada-US relations after 9/11 see Clarkson, *Does North America Exist?*; Hale, *So Near Yet So Far*. Books on Canada-US relations in this period by political scientists include: Bow and Lennox, *An Independent Foreign Policy for Canada*; Gattinger and Hale, eds., *Borders and Bridges*; Anderson and Sands, eds., *Forgotten Partnership Redux*.

2 Meng, "The Impacts of Fracking on the Environment."

3 Urquhart, *Costly Fix*; Szeman, *On Petrocultures*.

4 Insko, "The 2010 Marshall, Michigan Tar Sands Oil Spill."

5 Kheraj, "A History of Long-Distance Oil Spills in Canada," 188.

6 Ibid.

7 Cohen, "From Public Good to Private Exploitation," 29.

8 Froschauer, *White Gold*, 44.

9 Gattinger, "From Government to Governance in the Energy Sector."

10 Saunders, "Canada-US Energy Issues," 2; Doern and Gattinger, "US

Influences: FERC and Alternative Energy Regulatory Models," chapter 3 in *Power Switch*.

11 Rabe, "Beyond Kyoto."

12 Smith, "Shades of Grey in Canada's Greening during the Mulroney Era," 178.

13 On Canadian climate change policies see Harrison, "The Road Not Taken"; VanNijnatten, "From the International Joint Commission to Copenhagen"; Lachapelle, Borick, and Rabe, "Public Attitudes toward Climate Science and Climate Policy in Federal Systems: Canada and the United States Compared"; Macdonald, *Carbon Province, Hydro Province*; MacNeil, *Thirty Years of Failure*. On the development of American climate policy in the decade in the twenty-first century see works such as Rahm, *Climate Change Policy in the United States*; Rabe, ed., *Greenhouse Governance*; Sweet, *Climate Diplomacy from Rio to Paris*; Gupta, *The History of Global Climate Governance*.

14 CBC News, "Mulroney Honoured for Environmental Record," 20 April 2006, https://www.cbc.ca/news/canada/mulroney-honoured-for-environmental-record-1.616580.

15 Harrison, *Passing the Buck*.

16 VanNijnatten and Lopez-Vallejo Olvero, "Canada-United States Relations and a Low Carbon Economy for North America," 206.

17 Selin and VanDeveer, "Canadian-US Cooperation"; Selin and VanDeveer, *Changing Climates in North American Politics*; Chaloux, "The Implementation of the Western Climate Initiative."

18 MacNeil, *Thirty Years of Failure*.

19 Klein, *A Good War*.

20 English, *Ice and Water*.

21 Huebert, "Canada-United States Arctic Environmental Policies."

CONCLUSION

1 For statistics on carbon emissions see: Our World in Data, "Where in the World Do People Emit Most CO_2?," https://ourworldindata.org/per-capita-co2 (accessed 11 June 2021).

2 At the 2006 G8 Summit, Canadian prime minister Stephen Harper called Canada an "emerging energy superpower." Quoted in Duane Bratt, "Tools and Levers."

3 McNeill and Engelke, *The Great Acceleration*.

4 Debora VanNijnatten calls this "environmental interoperability" in reference to the extensive network of governance officials, agencies, and

institutions, many at the middling or subnational levels, that had been built up, and which serve to insulate many environmental issues from the ups and downs of other political aspects of the bilateral relationship. VanNijnatten, "Canadian-American Environmental Relations." See also Brunet-Jailly, "The Emergence of Cross-Border Regions and Canadian-United States Relations"; Schwartz, "The Canada-US Environmental Relationship," 446.

5 For statistics on recent Canadian energy exports to the United States see: US Energy Information Adminstration, "Canada Is the Largest Source of US Energy Imports," 5 June 2020, https://www.eia.gov/todayinenergy/detail.php?id=43995.

6 Recent statistics on Canadian petroleum exports are taken from: Canadian Association of Petroleum Producers, "Markets: Canada and the US," https://www.capp.ca/energy/markets/ (accessed 20 March 2022).

7 Rowlands, "US-Canadian Subnational Electricity Relations."

8 Canadian Electricity Association, "The Integrated Electricity System: Sustainable Electricity as the Foundation for Economic Recovery in North America."

9 US Energy Information Adminstration, "Canada Is the Largest Source."

10 Bird and Heintzelman, "Canada/US Transboundary Energy Governance"; Rowlands, "US-Canadian Subnational Electricity Relations"; Rowlands, "North American Integration and 'Green' Electricity," 336; see also the chapter titled "Shared Energy, Shared Energies? Engaged American Policies" in Hale, *So Near Yet So Far*.

11 Song, Temby, Krantzberg, and Hickey, "Institutional Features of US-Canadian Transboundary Fisheries Governance."

12 Such an approach would be particularly beneficial for Canada since American scholars have been more active in detailing the history of their country's environmental diplomacy abroad. The following are obvious issues that would benefit from an environmental diplomacy approach: Canadian mining companies abroad; Canada's role in contributing to nuclear weapons, and then efforts to limit their tests and proliferation; the ecological side-effects of Canadian peace-keeping efforts in Asia and Africa; the environmental impacts of Canada's globalized trade regimes; Canadian positions on multilateral environmental agreements such as the Montreal Protocol or Kyoto Accord.

Bibliography

ARCHIVAL AND PRIMARY SOURCES

Archives of Ontario (AO)
CBC News
Documents on Canadian External Relations (DCER)
Dwight D. Eisenhower Presidential Library & Archives
Franklin D. Roosevelt Library & Archives
Hydro-Electric Power Commission of Ontario (HEPCO)
International Joint Commission (IJC)
Library and Archives Canada (LAC)
New York State Archives (NYSA)
New York State, State Reservation at Niagara
New York Times
US Department of State, Foreign Relations of the United States (FRUS)
US Environmental Protection Agency (EPA)
US Congress
US National Archives and Records Administration II (NARA II)
US Senate

SECONDARY SOURCES

Alexander, Jeff. *Pandora's Locks: The Opening of the Great Lakes-St. Lawrence Seaway*. Lansing: Michigan State University Press, 2009.

Alper, Donald. "Transboundary Environmental Governance in the Pacific West." In *Transboundary Environmental Governance across the World's Longest Border*, edited by Stephen Brooks and Andrea Olive, 137–74. Lansing: Michigan State University Press, 2018.

Altmeyer, George. "Three Ideas of Nature in Canada, 1893-1914." *Journal of Canadian Studies* 11(1976): 21–36. DOI: 10.3138/jcs.11.3.21.

Alum, James R. "'An Outcrop of Hell': History, Environment, and the Politics of the Trail Smelter Dispute." In *Transboundary Harm in International Law: Lessons from the Trail Smelter Arbitration*, edited by Rebecca Bratspies and Russell Miller, 13–26. New York: Cambridge University Press, 2006.

Anastakis, Dimitry. *Auto Pact: Creating a Borderless North American Auto Industry, 1960–1971*. Toronto: University of Toronto Press, 2005.

– *Autonomous State: The Struggle for a Canadian Auto Industry from OPEC to Free Trade*. Toronto: University of Toronto Press, 2013.

Anderson, Greg, and Christopher Sands, eds. *Forgotten Partnership Redux: Canada-US Relations*. Amherst, NY: Cambria Press, 2011.

Armstrong, Christopher. *The Politics of Federalism: Ontario's Relations with the Federal Government, 1867–1942*. Toronto: University of Toronto Press, 1981.

Armstrong, Christopher, and H.V. Nelles. *Monopoly's Moment: The Organization and Regulation of Canadian Utilities, 1830–1930*. Philadelphia: Temple University Press, 1986.

Aronsen, Lawrence. *American National Security and Economic Relations with Canada, 1945–1954*. New York: Praeger, 1997.

Artibise, Alan F.J., and Gilbert A. Stelter. "Conservation Planning and Urban Planning: The Canadian Commission of Conservation in Historical Perspective." In *Planning for Conservation: An International Perspective*, edited by R.J.P. Cain, 17–36. London: Mansell, 1981.

Ashworth, John. "Continuity and Change in the US Decision-Making Process." In *Natural Resources in US-Canadian Relations, Volume I: The Evolution of Policies and Issues*, edited by Carl E. Beigie and Alfred O. Hero, Jr, 65–100. New York: Routledge, 1980.

Azzi, Stephen. *Reconcilable Differences: A History of Canada-US Relations*. New York: Oxford University Press, 2014.

– *Walter Gordon and the Rise of Canadian Nationalism*. Montreal: McGill-Queen's University Press, 1999.

Azzi, Stephen and Norman Hillmer. "Intolerant Allies: Canada and the George W. Bush Administration, 2001–2005." *Diplomacy and Statecraft* 27, no. 4 (December 2016): 726–45. https://doi.org/10.1080/09592296.2016.1238704.

Barichello, Richard, Timothy Josling, and Daniel A. Sumner. "Agricultural Trade Relations between Canada and the United States," Working Paper Number 2004-03. Vancouver: Food and Resource Economics, University of British Columbia, January 2004.

Barkin, Samuel. "The Pacific Salmon Dispute and Canada-US Environmental Relations." In *Bilateral Ecopolitics: Continuity and Change in Canadian-American Environmental Relations*, edited by Philippe Le Prestre and Peter Stoett, 197–210. New York: Routledge, 2006.

Barry, Donald. "The US Senate and the Collapse of the East Coast Fisheries Agreement." *Dalhousie Review* 62, no. 3 (1982): 495–503.

Beigie, Carle E., and Alfred O. Hero, Jr. *Natural Resources in US-Canadian Relations, Volume I: The Evolution of Policies and Issues*. New York: Routledge, 1980.

– *Natural Resources in US-Canadian Relations, Volume II: Patterns and Trends in Resource Supplies and Policies*. New York: Routledge, 1980.

Belanger, Damien Claude. *Prejudice and Pride: Canadian Intellectuals Confront the United States*. Toronto: University of Toronto Press, 2011.

Benedick, Richard Elliot. *Ozone Diplomacy: New Directions in Safeguarding the Planet*. Cambridge, MA: Harvard University Press, 1991.

Benidickson, Jamie. "The International Joint Commission and Water Quality in the Bacterial Age." In *The First Century of the International Joint Commission*, edited by Daniel Macfarlane and Murray Clamen, 115–42. Calgary: University of Calgary Press, 2020.

– *Leveling the Lake: Transboundary Resource Management in the Lake of the Woods Watershed*. Vancouver: UBC Press, 2019.

Berger, Carl. "The Truth North Strong and Free." In *Nationalism in Canada*, edited by Peter Russell, 3–26. Toronto: University of Toronto Press, 1967.

Binnema, Theodore. "'Most Fruitful Results': Transborder Approaches to Canadian-American Environmental History." In *A Companion to American Environmental History*, edited by Douglas C. Sackman, 615–34. Malden, MA: Blackwell, 2010.

Bird, Stephen, and Martin Heintzelman, "Canada/US Transboundary Energy Governance." In *Transboundary Environmental Governance across the World's Longest Border*, edited by Stephen Brooks and Andrea Olive, 175–200. Lansing: Michigan State University Press, 2018.

Bloomfield, L.M., and G.F. FitzGerald. *Boundary Waters Problems of Canada and the United States*. Toronto: Carswell, 1958.

Boardman, Robert. "Multi-level Environmental Governance in North America: Migratory Birds and Biodiversity." In *Bilateral Ecopolitics: Continuity and Change in Canadian-American Environmental Relations*, edited by Philippe Le Prestre and Peter Stoett, 179–96. New York: Routledge, 2006.

Bogue, Margaret Beattie. *Fishing the Great Lakes: An Environmental History, 1783–1933*. Madison: University of Wisconsin Press, 2000.

Bonder, Jennifer. "Herb Gray and the Founding of the Foreign Investment

Review Agency." In *People, Politics, and Purpose: Biography and Canadian Political History*, edited by Greg Donaghy and Whitney Lackenbauer, 175–98. Vancouver: UBC Press, 2023.

Bothwell, Robert. *Alliance and Illusion: Canada and the World, 1945–1984*. Vancouver: UBC Press, 2008.

– *Canada and the United States: The Politics of Partnership*. Toronto: University of Toronto Press, 1992.

– *Nucleus: The History of Atomic Energy of Canada Limited*. Toronto: University of Toronto Press, 1989.

– "Thanks for the Fish: Nixon, Kissinger, and Canada." In *Nixon in the World*, edited by Fredrik Logevall and Andrew Preston, 326–45. New York: Oxford University Press, 2008.

– *Your Country, My Country: A Unified History of the United States and Canada*. Oxford, UK: Oxford University Press, 2015.

Botts, Lee, and Paul Muldoon. *Evolution of the Great Lakes Water Quality Agreement*. Lansing: Michigan State University Press, 2005.

Bow, Brian, and Patrick Lennox. *An Independent Foreign Policy for Canada?* Toronto: University of Toronto Press, 2008.

Boyd, David R. *Unnatural Law: Rethinking Canadian Environmental Law and Policy*. Vancouver: UBC Press, 2003.

Brandson, Norman, and Allen Olson. "The International Joint Commission and Mid-Continent Water Issues: The Garrison Diversion, Red River, Devils Lake, and the Northwest Area Water Supply Project." In *The First Century of the International Joint Commission*, edited by Daniel Macfarlane and Murray Clamen, 215–38. Calgary: University of Calgary Press, 2020.

Bratt, Duanne. *The Politics of CANDU Exports*. Toronto: University of Toronto Press, 2006.

– "Tools and Levers: Energy as an Instrument of Canadian Foreign Policy." In *Canada Among Nations 2008: 100 Years of Canadian Foreign Policy*, edited by Robert Bothwell and Jean Daudelin, 209–31. Montreal: McGill-Queen's University Press, 2009.

Brebner, John Bartlet. *North Atlantic Triangle: The Interplay of Canada, the United States, and Great Britain*. New York: Columbia University Press, 1958.

Brooks, Stephen. "Canada-United States Environmental Relations During the Trudeau-Trump Years: A Story of Divergence and Resilience." *American Review of Canadian Studies* 50:1 (2020): 48–65. DOI: 10.1080/02722011.2020.1742998.

Brooks, Stephen, and Andrea Olive, eds. *Transboundary Environmental Governance Across the World's Longest Border*. Lansing: Michigan State University Press, 2018.

Brown, Robert Craig. *Canada's National Policy, 1883–1900: A Study in Canadian-American Relations*. Princeton, NJ: Princeton University Press, 1964.

Brunet-Jailly, Emmanuel. "The Emergence of Cross-Border Regions and Canadian-United States Relations." In *Cities and Global Governance: New Sites for International Relations*, edited by Mark Amen, Noah J. Toly, Patricia Mccarney, and Klaus Segbers, 83–104. London, UK: Routledge, 2011.

Bsumek, Erika Maria, David Kinkela, and Mark Atwood Lawrence, eds. *Nation-States and the Global Environment: New Approaches to International Environmental History*. New York: Oxford University Press, 2013.

Bukowczyk, John et al. *Permeable Border: The Great Lakes Basin as Transnational Region, 1650–1990*. Pittsburgh, PA: University of Pittsburgh Press, 2005.

Busch, Briton Cooper. *The War Against Seals: A History of the North American Seal Fishery*, rev. ed. Montreal: McGill-Queen's University Press, 1987.

Caldwell, Lynton. "Binational Responsibilities for a Shared Environment." In *Canada and the United States: Enduring Friendship, Persistent Stress*, edited by Charles F. Doran and John H. Sigler, 203–30. Englewood Cliffs, NJ: Prentice-Hall, 1985.

– "Transboundary Conflicts: Resources and Environment." In *The Canada-United States Relationship: The Politics of Energy and Environmental Coordination*, edited by Jonathan Lemco, 15–40. London, UK: Praeger, 1992.

Camp, Michael. "Tellico Dam, Dickey Dam, and Endangered Species Law in the United States during the 1970s." In *Energy in the Americas: Critical Reflections on Energy and History*, edited by Amelie Kiddle, 151–78. Calgary: University of Calgary Press, 2021.

Campbell, Claire Elizabeth, ed. *A Century of Parks Canada, 1911–2011*. Calgary: University of Calgary Press, 2011.

– *Shaped by the West Wind: Nature and History in Georgian Bay*. Vancouver: UBC Press, 2005.

Campbell-Miller, Jill, Greg Donaghy, and Stacey Barker, eds. *Breaking Barriers, Shaping Worlds: Canadian Women and the Search for Global Order*. Vancouver: UBC Press, 2021.

Canadian Electricity Association. "The Integrated Electricity System: Sustainable Electricity as the Foundation for Economic Recovery in North America." Ottawa: CEA, April 2010.

Canadian Departments of External Affairs and National Resources. *The Columbia River Treaty, Protocol, and Related Documents*. Ottawa: Queen's Printer, 1964.

Candow, James, and Carol Corbin. *How Deep Is the Ocean? Historical Essays on Canada's Atlantic Fishery*. Sydney, NS: University College of Cape Breton Press, 1997.

Carroll, Francis M. *A Good and Wise Measure: The Search for the Canadian-American Boundary, 1783–1842*. Toronto: University of Toronto Press, 2001.

Carroll, John. "Environment, Free Trade, and Canada-US Relations," in *The Canada-United States Relationship: The Politics of Energy and Environmental Coordination*, edited by Jonathan Lemco, 81–92. Westport, CN: Praeger, 1992.

– *Environmental Diplomacy: An Examination and a Prospective of Canadian-US Transboundary Environmental Relations*. Ann Arbor: University of Michigan Press, 1983.

Cavell, Janice, and Ryan M. Touhey. *Reassessing the Rogue Tory: Canadian Foreign Relations in the Diefenbaker Era*. Vancouver: UBC Press, 2019.

Chaloux, Annie. "The Implementation of the Western Climate Initiative: How North American States and Provinces Lead International Climate Negotiations." *International Negotiation* 22 (2017): 239–58. DOI: 10.1163/15718069-22021112.

Chaloux, Annie, and Stephane Paquin. "Green Paradiplomacy in North America." In *Sustainable Development and Subnational Governments: Policy Making and Multi-level Interactions*, edited by H. Bruyninckx et al., 217–36. New York: Palgrave Macmillan, 2012.

Chapnick, Adam. *Canada on the UN Security Council: A Small Power on a Large Stage*. Vancouver: UBC Press, 2019.

Chastko, Paul. "Anonymity and Ambivalence: The Canadian and American Oil Industry and the Emergence of Continental Oil." *Journal of American History* 99, no. 1 (2012): 166–76. https://doi.org/10.1093/jahist/jas049.

– *Developing Alberta's Oil Sands: From Karl Clark to Kyoto*. Calgary: University of Calgary Press, 2004.

Cioc, Mark. *The Game of Conservation: International Treaties to Protect the World's Migratory Animals*. Athens: Ohio University Press, 2009.

Clamen, Murray, and Daniel Macfarlane. "The International Joint Commission, Water Levels, and Transboundary Governance in the Great Lakes." *Journal of Policy Research* 32, no. 1 (January 2015): 40–59. https://doi.org/10.1111/ropr.12107.

– "Plan 2014: The Historical Evolution of Lake Ontario-St. Lawrence River Regulation." *Canadian Water Resources Journal/Revue canadienne des ressources hydriques* 43, no. 4 (December 2018): 416–31. https://doi.org/10.1080/07011784.2018.1475263.

Clark, John G. "Making Environmental Diplomacy an Integral Part of Diplomatic History." *Diplomatic History* 21, no. 3 (1997): 453–60. https://doi.org/10.1111/1467-7709.00080

Clarke-Jones, Melissa. *A Staple State: Canadian Industrial Resources in Cold War*. Toronto: University of Toronto Press, 1987.

Clarkson, Stephen. *Does North America Exist? Governing the Continent after NAFTA and 9/11*. Toronto: University of Toronto Press, 2008.

– *Uncle Sam and Us: Globalization, Neoconservatism, and the Canadian State*. Toronto: University of Toronto Press, 2002.

Coates, Kenneth S., and William R. Morrison. *The Alaska Highway in World War II: The US Army of Occupation in Canada's Northwest*. Norman: University of Oklahoma Press, 2015.

Cobban, Timothy. *Cities of Oil: Municipalities and Petroleum Manufacturing in Southern Ontario, 1860–1960*. Toronto: University of Toronto Press, 2013.

Cohen, Marjorie Griffin. "From Public Good to Private Exploitation: GATS and the Restructuring of Canadian Utilities." *Canadian-American Public Policy* 48 (December 2001): 1–79.

Cohen, Maxwell. "The Commission from the Inside." In *The International Joint Commission Seventy Years On*, edited by Robert Spencer, John Kirton, and Kim Richard Nossal, 106–23. Toronto: Centre for International Studies, University of Toronto, 1981.

Cohn, Julie. *The Grid: Biography of an American Technology*. Cambridge, MA: MIT Press, 2017.

Colby, Jason. *Orca: How We Came to Know and Love the Ocean's Greatest Predator*. New York: Oxford University Press, 2018.

Colpitts, George. *Game in the Garden: A Human History of Wildlife in Western Canada to 1940*. Vancouver: UBC Press, 2002.

Cook, Beverly. "Lobster Boat Diplomacy: The Canada-US Grey Zone." *Marine Policy* 29 (2005): 385–90. DOI: 10.1016/j.marpol.2004.05.010.

Cosens, Barbara, ed. *The Columbia River Treaty Revisited: Transboundary River Governance in an Age of Uncertainty*. Corvallis: Oregon State University Press, 2012.

Cuff, R.D., and J.L. Granatstein. *Canadian-American Relations in Wartime from the Great War to the Cold War*. Toronto: Hakkert, 1975.

Curtis, Kenneth M., and John E. Carroll. *Canadian-American Relations: The Promise and the Challenge*. Toronto: D.C. Heath and Company, 1983.

– "Transboundary Environmental and Resource Issues." In *Partners Nevertheless: Canadian-American Relations in the Twentieth Century*, edited by Norman Hillmer, 194–205. Toronto: Copp Clark Pittman, 1989.

Dales, John H. *Hydroelectricity and Industrial Development: Quebec, 1898–1940*. Cambridge, MA: Harvard University Press, 1957.

Daowei, Zhang. *The Softwood Lumber War: Politics, Economics, and the Long US-Canada Trade Dispute*. Washington, DC: Resources for the Future, 2007.

Dempsey, Dave. *Great Lakes For Sale – Updated Edition*. Traverse City, MI: Mission Point Press, 2021.

Desbiens, Caroline. *Power from the North: Territory, Identity, and the Culture of Hydroelectricity in Quebec*. Vancouver: UBC Press, 2013.

Dilsaver, Lary M., and William Wyckoff, "Agency Culture, Cumulative Causation and Development in Glacier National Park, Montana." *Journal of Historical Geography* 25, 1 (1999): 75–92. https://doi.org/10.1006/jhge.1998.0108.

Dinwoodie, D.H. "The Politics of International Pollution Control: The Trail Smelter Case." *International Journal* 27, no. 2 (Spring 1972): 219–35. https://doi.org/10.1177/002070207202700204.

Diubaldo, Richard J. "The Canol Project in Canadian-American Relations." *Historical Papers* (Canadian Historical Association) 12, no. 1 (1977): 178–95.

Doern, G. Bruce. *Green Diplomacy: How Environmental Policy Decisions Are Made*. Toronto: C.D. Howe Institute, 1993.

Doern, G. Bruce, Graeme Auld, and Christopher Stoney. *Green-Lite: Complexity in Fifty Years of Canadian Environmental Policy, Governance, and Democracy*. Montreal: McGill-Queen's University Press, 2015.

Doern, G. Bruce, and Monica Gattinger. *Power Switch: Energy Regulatory Governance in the Twenty-First Century*. Toronto: University of Toronto Press, 2003.

Doern, G. Bruce, and Brian W. Tomlin. *Faith and Fear: The Free Trade Story*. Toronto: Stoddart, 1991.

Doern, G. Bruce, and Glen Toner. *The Politics of Energy: The Development and Implementation of the NEP*. New York: Routledge, 1985.

Donaghy, Greg, ed. *Canada and the Early Cold War, 1943–1957*. Ottawa: Department of Foreign Affairs and International Trade, 1998.

– *Tolerant Allies: Canada and the United States, 1963–1968*. Montreal: McGill-Queen's University Press, 2002.

Donaghy, Greg, and Michael Carroll, eds. *In The National Interest: Canadian Foreign Policy and the Department of Foreign Affairs and International Trade, 1909–2009*. Calgary: University of Calgary Press, 2011.

Doran, Charles. *Forgotten Partnership: US-Canada Relations Today*. Baltimore, MD: Johns Hopkins University Press, 1985.

Dorsey, Kurkpatrick. "Crossing Boundaries: The Environment in International Relations." In *The Oxford Handbook of Environmental History*, edited by Andrew C. Isenberg, 688–715. Oxford: Oxford University Press, 2014.

– *The Dawn of Conservation Diplomacy: US-Canadian Wildlife Protection Treaties in the Progressive Era*. Seattle: University of Washington Press, 1998.

– "Dealing with the Dinosaur (and Its Swamp): Putting the Environment in Diplomatic History." *Diplomatic History* 29, no. 4 (September 2005): 573–87. https://doi.org/10.1111/j.1467-7709.2005.00507.x.

– *Whales and Nations: Environmental Diplomacy on the High Seas*. Seattle: University of Washington Press, 2014.

Dorsey, Kurkpatrick, and Mark Lytle. "Forum: New Directions in Diplomatic and Environmental History." *Diplomatic History* 32, no. 4 (September 2008): 517–646. https://doi.org/10.1111/j.1467-7709.2008.00710.x.

Dreisziger, N.F. "The International Joint Commission of the United States and Canada, 1895–1920: A Study in Canadian-American Relations." Doctoral dissertation, University of Toronto, 1974.

Drescher, Nuala. *Engineers for the Public Good: A History of the Buffalo District, US Army Corps of Engineers*. Washington, DC: US Army Corps of Engineers, 1999.

Drummond, Ian, and Norman Hillmer. *Negotiating Free Trade: The United Kingdom, the United States, Canada and the Trade Agreements of 1938*. Waterloo, ON: Wilfrid Laurier University Press, 1989.

Dubasak, Marilyn. *Wilderness Preservation: A Cross-Cultural Comparison of Canada and the United States*. New York: Garland Publishing, 1991.

Dubinsky, Karen, Sean Mills, and Scott Rutherford, eds. *Canada and the Third World: Overlapping Histories*. Toronto: University of Toronto Press, 2016.

Duncan, Colin A.M., and Ruth Sandwell, "Manufactured and Natural Gas." In *Powering Up Canada: The History of Power, Fuel, and Energy From 1600*, edited by Ruth W. Sandwell, 300–28. Montreal: McGill-Queen's University Press, 2016.

Dutil, Patrice, ed. *The Unexpected Louis St. Laurent: Politics and Policies for a Modern Canada*. Vancouver: UBC Press, 2020.

Dymond, Bill, and Colin Robertson. *Decision at Midnight: Inside the Canada-US Free Trade Negotiations*. Vancouver: UBC Press, 1994.

Eayrs, James. *In Defence of Canada*. Toronto: University of Toronto Press, 1964.

English, John. *Ice and Water: Politics, Peoples, and the Arctic Council*. Toronto: Penguin Random House Canada, 2013.

– *Just Watch Me: The Life of Pierre Elliott Trudeau: 1968–2000*. Toronto: Knopf Canada, 2009.
– *Shadow of Heaven: The Life of Lester Pearson, 1949–1972*. Toronto: Lester & Orpen Dennys, 1989.
Evenden, Matthew. *Allied Power: Mobilizing Hydro-Electricity during Canada's Second World War*. Toronto: University of Toronto Press, 2015.
– *Fish versus Power: An Environmental History of the Fraser River*. New York: Cambridge University Press, 2004.
Evenden, Matthew, and Graeme Wynn. "54, 40 or Fight: Writing Within and Across Borders in North American Environmental History." In *Nature's End*, edited by Sverker Sorlin and Paul Warde, 215–46. London: Palgrave Macmillan, 2009.
Fletcher, Thomas L. *From Love Canal to Environmental Justice: The Politics of Hazardous Waste on the Canada-US Border*. Peterborough, ON: Broadview Press, 2003.
Foster, Janet. *Working for Wildlife: The Beginning of Preservation in Canada*, 2nd ed. Toronto: University of Toronto Press, 1998.
Fox, Annette Baker, Alfred O. Hero, Jr, and Joseph S. Nye, eds. *Canada and the United States: Transnational and Transgovernmental Relations*. New York: Columbia University Press, 1976.
Froschauer, Karl. *White Gold: Hydroelectric Power in Canada*. Vancouver: UBC Press, 1999.
Gaden, Marc, and Charles C. Krueger, "Multi-jurisdictional Governance of the Shared Great Lakes Fishery: Can a Nonbinding Agreement Work?" In *Transboundary Environmental Governance across the World's Longest Border*, edited by Stephen Brooks and Andrea Olive, 51–76. Lansing: Michigan State University Press, 2018.
Gaden, Marc, Cory Brant, and Robert Lambe, "Why a Great Lakes Fishery Commission? The Seven-Decade Pursuit of a Canada-US Fishery Treaty." *Journal of Great Lakes Research* 47, supplement 1 (December 2021): 11–23. https://doi.org/10.1016/j.jglr.2021.01.003.
Gattinger, Monica. *Canada-United States Electricity Relations: Test-Bed for North American Policy Making*, No. 77. Orono, MN: Canadian-American Center, University of Maine, 2011.
– "From Government to Governance in the Energy Sector: The State of the Canada-US Energy Relationship." *American Review of Canadian Studies* 35, no. 2 (2005): 321–52. https://doi.org/10.1080/02722010509481375.
Gattinger, Monica, and Geoffrey Hale, eds. *Borders and Bridges: Canada's Policy Relations in North America*. Toronto: Oxford University Press, 2010.
Gillis, Peter, and Thomas R. Roach. "The Beginnings of a Movement: The

Montreal Congress and its Aftermath, 1880–1896." In *Consuming Canada: Readings in Environmental History*, edited by Chad Gaffield and Pam Gaffield, 131–51. Toronto: Copp Clark Limited, 1995.

Gluek, Alvin C., Jr. "The Lake Carriers' Association and the Origins of the International Waterways Commission." *The Inland Seas: Quarterly Journal of the Great Lakes Historical Society* 37 (1981): 27–31.

– "Programmed Diplomacy: The Settlement of the North American Fisheries Question, 1907–12." *Acadiensis* 6, no. 1 (1976): 43–70.

Gordan, Richard L. *Coal and Canada-US Energy Relations*. Montreal: C.D. Howe Research Institute and National Planning Association, 1976.

Gotlieb, A.E. "Canadian Diplomatic Initiatives: The Law of the Sea." In *"Freedom and Change": Essays in Honour of Lester B. Pearson*, edited by Michael G. Fry, 136–51. Toronto: McClelland and Stewart, 1975.

Gotlieb, Allan. *The Washington Diaries: 1983–1991*. Toronto: McClelland and Stewart, 2006.

Granatstein, J.L. *How Britain's Weakness Forced Canada into the Arms of the United States*. Toronto: University of Toronto Press, 1989.

– *The Ottawa Men: The Civil Service Mandarins, 1936–1957*. Toronto: University of Toronto Press, 1982.

– *Yankee Go Home? Canadians and Anti-Americanism*. Toronto: HarperCollins, 1996.

Granatstein, J.L., and Robert Bothwell. *Pirouette: Pierre Trudeau and Canadian Foreign Policy*. Toronto: University of Toronto Press, 1991.

Grant, Shelagh. *Polar Imperative: A History of Arctic Sovereignty in North America*. Toronto: Macmillan, 2011.

Grauer, A.E.D. "The Export of Electricity from Canada." In *Canadian Issues: Essays in Honour of Henry F. Angus*, edited by R.M. Clark, 248–85. Toronto: University of Toronto Press, 1961.

Gray, Earle. *Forty Years in the Public Interest: A History of the National Energy Board*. Vancouver: Douglas and McIntyre, 2000.

Gupta, Joyeeta. *The History of Global Climate Governance*. Cambridge, UK: Cambridge University Press, 2014.

Hajdu, Csaba. "The Canada-US Softwood Lumber Dispute: A Brief History." The Fraser Institute. March 2010. http://www.fraserinstitute.org/publicationdisplay.aspx?id=15843&terms=softwood+lumber.

Hale, Geoffrey. *So Near Yet So Far: The Public and Hidden Worlds of Canada-US Relations*. Vancouver: UBC Press, 2012.

Hamblin, Jacob. *Arming Mother Nature: The Birth of Catastrophic Environmentalism*. New York: Oxford University Press, 2013.

Handley, F. "Exports of Waste From the United States to Canada: The How and Why." *Environmental Law Report*, 20 ELR 10061 (1990): 10061–6.

Harris, Cole. "The Myth of the Land in Canadian Nationalism." In *Nationalism in Canada*, edited by Peter Russell, 27–43. Toronto: McGraw-Hill, 1966.

Harrison, Kathryn. *Passing the Buck: Federalism and Canadian Environmental Policy*. Vancouver: UBC Press, 1996.

– "The Road Not Taken: Climate Change Policy in Canada and the United States." *Global Environmental Politics* 7, no. 4 (November 2007): 92–117. https://doi.org/10.1162/glep.2007.7.4.92.

Harrison, Kathryn, and George Hoberg. *Risk, Science, and Politics: Regulating Toxic Substances in Canada and the United States*. Montreal: McGill-Queen's University Press, 1994.

Hart, Michael. *A Trading Nation: Canadian Trade Policy from Colonialism to Globalization*. Vancouver: UBC Press, 2003.

Hart, Michael, and Bill Dymond. "The Cul-de-sac of Softwood Lumber." *Policy Options* (November 2005). https://policyoptions.irpp.org/magazines/canada-us-trade-tensions/the-cul-de-sac-of-softwood-lumber/.

Hartig, John H. and M. Munawar, eds. *Ecosystem-Based Management of Laurentian Great Lakes Areas of Concern: Three Decades of US-Canadian Cleanup and Recovery*. Lansing: Michigan State University Press, 2021.

Hays, Samuel. *Conservation and the Gospel of Efficiency: The Progressive Conservation Movement, 1890–1920*. Pittsburgh, PA: University of Pittsburgh Press, 1959.

Heasley, Lynne, and Daniel Macfarlane, eds. *Border Flows: A Century of the Canadian-American Water Relationship*. Calgary: University of Calgary Press, 2016.

Heinmiller, B. Timothy. "The Boundary Waters Treaty and International Joint Commission in the St. Mary-Milk Basin." In *The First Century of the International Joint Commission*, edited by Daniel Macfarlane and Murray Clamen, 143–64. Calgary: University of Calgary Press, 2020.

– "Transboundary Water Governance in the Prairie Region." In *Transboundary Environmental Governance across the World's Longest Border*, edited by Stephen Brooks and Andrea Olive, 113–36. Lansing: Michigan State University Press, 2018.

Hele, Karl S., ed. *Lines Drawn upon the Water: First Nations and the Great Lakes Borders and Borderlands*. Waterloo, ON: Wilfrid Laurier University Press, 2008.

Hilliker, John. *Canada's Department of External Affairs, Volume I: The Early Years, 1909–1946*. Montreal: McGill-Queen's University Press, 1990.

Hilliker, John, and Donald Barry. *Canada's Department of External Affairs, Volume II: Coming of Age, 1946–1948*. Montreal: McGill-Queen's University Press, 1995.

Hilliker, John, Mary Halloran, and Greg Donaghy. *Canada's Department of External Affairs, Volume III: Innovation and Adaptation, 1968–1984*. Toronto: University of Toronto Press, 2017.

Hillmer, Norman. *O.D. Skelton: A Portrait of Canadian Ambition*. Toronto: University of Toronto Press, 2016.

Hillmer, Norman and Adam Chapnick, eds. *Canadas of the Mind: The Making and Unmaking of Canadian Nationalisms in the Twentieth Century*. Montreal: McGill-Queen's University Press, 2007.

Hillmer, Norman, and J.L. Granatstein. *For Better or For Worse: Canada and the United States into the Twenty-First Century*. Toronto: Thomson Nelson, 2007.

Hillmer, Norman, Daniel Macfarlane, and Michael Manulak. "Pearson and Environmental Diplomacy." In *Mike's World: Lester B. Pearson and Canadian External Affairs*, edited by Asa McKercher and Galen Roger Perras, 320–41. Vancouver: UBC Press, 2017.

Hirt, Paul. *The Wired Northwest: The History of Electric Power, 1870s–1970s*. Lawrence: University Press of Kansas, 2012.

Hoberg, George. "Canadian-American Environmental Relations: A Strategic Framework." In *Canadian Environmental Policy: Context and Cases*, edited by Debora VanNijnatten and Robert Boardman, 171–89. New York: Oxford University Press, 2002.

– "Sleeping with the Elephant: American Influence on Canadian Environmental Regulation." *Journal of Public Policy* 11, no. 1 (1991): 107–31. https://doi.org/10.1017/S0143814X00004955.

Holmes, Beatrice. *A History of Federal Water Resources Programs, 1800–1960*. Washington, DC: US Department of Agriculture, 1972.

– *History of Federal Water Resources Programs and Policies, 1961–70*. Washington, DC: US Department of Agriculture, 1969.

Holmes, John W. *Life with Uncle: The Canadian-American Relationship*. Toronto: University of Toronto Press, 1981.

– *The Shaping of Peace: Canada and the Search for World Order, 1943–1957*. Vol. 1. Toronto: University of Toronto Press, 1979.

Hood, George N. *Against the Flow: Rafferty-Alameda and the Politics of the Environment*. Saskatoon, SK: Fifth House Publishers, 1994.

Hoy, Benjamin. *A Line of Blood and Dirt: Creating the Canada-United States Border Across Indigenous Lands*. New York: Oxford University Press, 2021.

Huebert, Rob. "Canada-United States Arctic Environmental Policies." In

Bilateral Ecopolitics: Continuity and Change in Canadian-American Environmental Relations, edited by Philippe Le Prestre and Peter Stoett, 115–32. New York: Routledge, 2006.

Innis, Harold. *The Cod Fisheries: The History of an International Economy*. New Haven, CT: Yale University Press, 1940.

Insko, Jeffrey. "The 2010 Marshall, Michigan Tar Sands Oil Spill." In *Encyclopedia of Water: Science, Technology, and Society*, edited by Patricia Maurice, 2679–84. Hoboken, NJ: Wiley, 2019.

Jensen, Thomas C. "The United States-Canada Pacific Salmon Interception Treaty: An Historical and Legal Overview." *Environmental Law* 16, no. 3 (1986): 363–422.

Johns, Carolyn. "Transboundary Environmental Governance and Water Pollution in the Great Lakes Region." In *Transboundary Environmental Governance across the World's Longest Border*, edited by Stephen Brooks and Andrea Olive, 77–112. Lansing: Michigan State University Press, 2018.

Johnson, Benjamin, and Andrew Graybill, eds. *Bridging National Borders in North America: Transnational and Comparative Histories*. Durham, NC: Duke University Press, 2010.

Kaufmann, Eric. "Naturalizing the Nation: The Rise of Naturalistic Nationalism in the United States and Canada." *Comparative Studies in Society and History* 40 (1998): 666–95. https://doi.org/10.1017/S0010417598001698

Kaufmann, Scott. *The Environment and International History*. New York: Bloomsbury Academic, 2018.

Kay, Richard, and John D. Wirth. *Environmental Management on North America's Borders*. College Station: Texas A & M University Press, 1998.

Kehoe, Terence. *Cleaning Up the Great Lakes: From Cooperation to Confrontation*. Dekalb: Northern Illinois University Press, 1997.

Keller, Col. Charles. *The Power Situation during the War*. Washington, DC: US Government Printing Office, 1921.

Kenny, James. "The International Joint Commission and Hydro-power Development on the Northeastern Borderlands, 1945–1970." In *The First Century of the International Joint Commission*, edited by Daniel Macfarlane and Murray Clamen, 165–94. Calgary: University of Calgary Press, 2020.

Kheraj, Sean. "A History of Long-Distance Oil Spills in Canada." *Canadian Historical Review* 101, no. 2 (June 2020): 161–91. DOI: 10.3138/chr.2019-0005.

Kilbourn, William. *Pipeline: TransCanada and the Great Debate, A History of Business and Politics*. Toronto: Clarke Irwin, 1970.

Kirkey, Christopher. "The Arctic Waters Pollution Prevention Initiatives:

Canada's Response to an American Challenge." *International Journal of Canadian Studies* 13 (Spring 1996): 41–59.

– "Moving Alaskan Oil to Market: Canadian National Interests and the Trans-Alaska Pipeline, 1968–73." *American Review of Canadian Studies* 27, no. 4 (2007): 492–522. https://doi.org/10.1080/02722019709481139.

Kirton, John. "Managing Canada's US Relations through NAFTA's Trade-Environment Regime." In *Bilateral Ecopolitics: Continuity and Change in Canadian-American Environmental Relations*, edited by Philippe Le Prestre and Peter Stoett, 17–50. New York: Routledge, 2006.

Kirton, John, and Don Munton. "The Manhattan Voyages and Their Aftermath." In *Politics of the Northwest Passage*, edited by Franklyn Griffiths, 67–97. Montreal: McGill-Queen's University Press, 1987.

Klein, Seth. *A Good War: Mobilizing Canada for the Climate Emergency*. Toronto: ECW Press, 2020.

Kline, Marcia B. *Beyond the Land Itself: Views of Nature in Canada and the United States*. Cambridge, MA: Harvard University Press, 1970.

Konrad, Victor, and Heather N. Nicol. *Beyond Walls: Re-inventing the Canada-United States Borderlands*. London, UK: Ashgate, 2008.

Krantzberg, Gail. "The Great Lakes Remedial Action Plan: A Historical and Contemporary Description and Analysis." In *The First Century of the International Joint Commission*, edited by Daniel Macfarlane and Murray Clamen, 367–94. Calgary: University of Calgary Press, 2020.

Kuhlberg, Mark. *In the Power of the Government: The Rise and Fall of Newsprint in Ontario, 1894–1932*. Toronto: University of Toronto Press, 2015.

Lachapelle, Erick, Christopher P. Borick, and Barry Rabe. "Public Attitudes toward Climate Science and Climate Policy in Federal Systems: Canada and the United States Compared." *Review of Policy Research* 29, no. 3 (May 2012): 335–58. https://doi.org/10.1111/j.1541-1338.2012.00563.x.

Lackenbauer, Whitney, and Matthew Farish. "The Cold War on Canadian Soil: Militarizing a Northern Environment," *Environmental History* 12, no. 4 (October 2007): 921–50. https://doi.org/10.1093/envhis/12.4.920.

Lackenbauer, Whitney, and Peter Kikkert. "Building on 'Shifting Sands': The Canadian Armed Forces, Sovereignty, and the Arctic, 1968–72." In *Canada and Arctic Sovereignty and Security: Historical Perspectives*, edited by P.W. Lackenbauer, 284–308. Calgary: Centre for Military and Strategic Studies/University of Calgary Press, 2011.

Langston, Nancy. *Sustaining Lake Superior: An Extraordinary Lake in a Changing World*. New Haven, CN: Yale University Press, 2017.

Laxer, James. *The Energy Poker Game: The Politics of the Continental Resources Deal*. Toronto: New Press, 1970.

– *Oil and Gas*. Toronto: Lorimer, 1983.

Lemarquand, David, and Anthony D. Scott. "Canada-United States Environmental Relations." *Proceedings of the Academy of Political Science* 32, no. 2 (1976): 149–63.

Lemco, Jonathan, ed. *The Canada-United States Relationship: The Politics of Energy and Environmental Coordination*. London, UK: Praeger, 1992.

Le Prestre, Philippe, and Peter Stoett, eds. *Bilateral Ecopolitics: Continuity and Change in Canadian-American Environmental Relations*. New York: Routledge, 2006.

Levitt, Kari. *Silent Surrender: The Multinational Corporation in Canada*. Toronto: MacMillan, 1970.

Lower, A.R.M. *The North American Assault on the Canadian Forest: A History of the Lumber Trade between Canada and the United States*. Toronto: Ryerson Press, 1938.

Luby, Brittany. *Dammed: The Politics of Loss and Survival in Anishnaabe Territory*. Winnipeg: University of Manitoba Press, 2020.

Lumsden, Ian ed. *Close the 49th Parallel, etc.: The Americanization of Canada*. Toronto: University of Toronto Press, 1970.

Lytle, Mark H. "An Environmental Approach to American Diplomacy History." *Diplomatic History* 20, no. 2 (April 1996): 279–300. https://doi.org/10.1111/j.1467-7709.1996.tb00628.x.

Macdonald, Douglas. *Carbon Province, Hydro Province: The Challenge of Canadian Energy and Climate Federalism*. Toronto: University of Toronto Press, 2020.

MacEachern, Alan. "A Little Essay on Big: Towards a History of Canada's Size." In *Big Country, Big Issues: Canada's Environment, Culture, and History*, edited by Nadine Klopfer and Christof Mauch, 6–15. *RCC Perspectives* 4 (2011).

MacFadyen, Joshua. "Hewers of Wood: A History of Wood Energy in Canada." In *Powering Up Canada: The History of Power, Fuel, and Energy from 1600*, edited by Ruth W. Sandwell, 129–60. Montreal: McGill-Queen's University Press, 2016.

Macfarlane, Daniel. "Environmental Nationalist: Andrew McNaughton and Canada-US Relations in the Cold War." *International Journal* 76, no. 1 (2021): 129–44. https://doi.org/10.1177/00207020211994513.

– *Fixing Niagara Falls: Environment, Energy, and Engineers at the World's Most Famous Waterfall*. Vancouver: UBC Press, 2020.

– "Hydro Diplomacy: Canada-US Hydroelectricity Exports and Regulations Prior to the NEB." *American Review of Canadian Studies* 51, no. 4

(December 2021): 508–32. https://doi.org/10.1080/02722011.2021.1997335.

– "Natural Security: Canada-US Environmental Diplomacy." In *Undiplomatic History: The New Study of Canada and the World*, edited by Asa McKercher and Philip Van Huizen. Montreal: McGill-Queen's University Press, 2019.

– "Nature Empowered: Hydraulic Models and the Engineering of Niagara Falls." *Technology and Culture* 61, no. 1 (January 2020): 109–43. DOI: 10.1353/tech.2020.0031

– *Negotiating a River: Canada, the US, and the Creation of the St. Lawrence Seaway*. Vancouver: UBC Press, 2014.

Macfarlane, Daniel, and Murray Clamen, eds. *The First Century of the International Joint Commission*. Calgary: University of Calgary Press, 2020.

Macfarlane, Daniel, and Lynne Heasley. "Water, Oil, and Fish: The Chicago River as a Transnational Matrix of Place." In *City of Lake and Prairie: Chicago's Environmental History*, edited by Kathleen Brosnan, Will Barnett, and Ann Keating, 91–104. Pittsburgh, PA: University of Pittsburgh Press, 2020.

Macfarlane, Daniel, and Andrew Watson. "Hydro Democracy: Water Power and Political Power in Ontario." *Scientia Canadensis* 40, no. 1 (2018): 1–18. DOI: 10.7202/1048923ar.

Mackenzie, Hector. "Shades of Gray? 'The Foundations of Canadian Policy in World Affairs' in Context." *American Review of Canadian Studies* 37, no. 4 (2007): 459–73. https://doi.org/10.1080/02722010709481812.

MacNeil, Robert. *Thirty Years of Failure: Understanding Canadian Climate Policy*. Toronto: Fernwood, 2019.

Madokoro, Laura, Francine McKenzie, and David Meren, eds. *Dominion of Race: Rethinking Canada's International History*. Vancouver: UBC Press, 2017.

Mahant, Edelgard, and Graeme S. Mount. *Invisible and Inaudible in Washington: American Policies Toward Canada During the Cold War*. Vancouver: UBC Press, 1999.

Manulak, Michael W. "Multilateral Solutions to Bilateral Problems: The 1972 Stockholm Conference and Canadian Foreign Environmental Policy." *International Journal* 70, no. 1 (2015): 4–22. https://doi.org/10.1177/0020702014546338.

Marshall, Joan. "Defining Maritime Boundaries: 'The Murky Hand of History's Oversight' in the Gulf of Maine." *The Canadian Geographer* 48, no. 3 (2004): 266–86. https://doi.org/10.1111/j.0008-3658.2004.00060.x.

Martin, Thibault, and Steven Hoffman, eds. *Power Struggles: Hydro*

Development and First Nations in Manitoba and Quebec. Winnipeg: University of Manitoba Press, 2008.

Martin-Nielsen, Janet. "South over the Wires: Hydro-electricity Exports from Canada, 1900–1925." *Water History* 1 (2009): 109–29. DOI:10.1007/S12685-009-0011-6.

Massell, David. *Amassing Power: J.B. Duke and the Saguenay River, 1897–1927*. Montreal: McGill-Queen's University Press, 2000.

– *Quebec Hydropolitics: The Peribonka Concessions of the Second World War*. Montreal: McGill-Queen's University Press, 2011.

May, Elizabeth. "Brian Mulroney and the Environment." In *Transforming the Nation: Canada and Brian Mulroney*, edited by Raymond B. Blake, 381–92. Montreal: McGill-Queen's University Press, 2007.

McCutcheon, Sean. *Electric Rivers: The Story of the James Bay Project*. Montreal: Black Rose, 1991.

McDorman, Ted. *Salt Water Neighbors*. New York: Oxford University Press, 2009.

McDougall, John N. *Fuels and the National Policy*. Toronto: Butterworth and Co., 1982.

McGrath, James, and Arthur Milnes, eds. *Age of the Offered Hand: The Cross-Border Partnership between President George H.W. Bush and Prime Minister Brian Mulroney: A Documentary History*. Kingston, ON: School of Policy Studies, 2009.

McIntyre, Hugh C. *Uranium, Nuclear Power, and Canada-US Energy Relations*. Montreal and Washington, DC: Canadian-American Committee, 1978.

McKercher, Asa. *Camelot and Canada: Canadian-American Relations in the Kennedy Era*. Toronto: Oxford University Press, 2016.

McKercher, Asa, and Galen Perras, eds. *Mike's World: Lester B. Pearson and Canadian External Affairs*. Vancouver: UBC Press, 2017.

McNeill, John. *Something New under the Sun: An Environmental History of the Twentieth Century World*. New York: Norton, 2000.

McNeill, John R., and Corinna R. Unger, eds. *Environmental Histories of the Cold War*. New York: Cambridge University Press, 2010.

McNeill, J.R., and Peter Engelke. *The Great Acceleration: An Environmental History of the Anthropocene since 1945*. Cambridge, MA: Harvard University Press, 2016.

Meng, Qingmin. "The Impacts of Fracking on the Environment: A Total Environmental Study Paradigm." *Science of the Total Environment* 580 (February 2017): 953–7. https://doi.org/10.1016/j.scitotenv.2016.12.045.

Merchant, Livingston T., ed. *Neighbours Taken for Granted: Canada and the United States*. New York: Frederick A. Praeger, 1965.

Meren, David and Bora Plumptre. "Rights of Passage: The Intersecting of Environmentalism, Arctic Sovereignty, and Law of the Sea, 1986–1982." *Journal of Canadian Studies/Revue d'études canadiennes* 47, no. 1 (Winter 2013): 167–96. DOI: 10.3138/jcs.47.1.167.

Messamore, Barbara. "Diplomacy or Duplicity? Lord Lisgar, John A. Macdonald, and the Treaty of Washington, 1871." *Journal of Imperial and Commonwealth History* 32, no. 2 (2004): 29–53. https://doi.org/10.1080/0308653041000170039o.

Miller, John T., Jr. *Foreign Trade in Gas and Electricity in North America: A Legal and Historical Study*. New York: Praeger, 1970.

Miller, Perry. *Nature's Nation*. Cambridge, MA: Belknap Press, 1967.

Mitchell, Timothy. *Carbon Democracy: Political Power in the Age of Oil*. London, UK: Verso, 2013.

Morell, J.B. *The Law of the Sea: An Historical Analysis of the 1982 Treaty and Its Rejection by the United States*. London, UK: McFarland and Company, 1992.

Morse, Kathryn. *The Nature of Gold: An Environmental History of the Klondike Gold Rush*. Seattle: University of Washington Press, 2003.

Morton, W.L. *The Canadian Identity*. Madison: University of Wisconsin Press, 1962.

Mouat, Jeremy. "The Columbia Exchange: A Canadian Perspective on the Negotiations." In *The Columbia River Treaty Revisited: Transboundary River Governance in an Age of Uncertainty*, edited by Barbara Cosens, 14–42. Corvallis: Oregon State University Press, 2012.

Moy, Richard, and Jonathan O'Riordan. "The International Joint Commission's Unique and Colourful Role in Three Projects in the Pacific Northwest." In *The First Century of the International Joint Commission*, edited by Daniel Macfarlane and Murray Clamen, 239–83. Calgary: University of Calgary Press, 2020.

Muirhead, Bruce. *Dancing Around the Elephant: Creating a Prosperous Canada in an Era of American Dominance, 1957–1973*. Toronto: University of Toronto Press, 2007.

Mulroney, Brian. *Memoirs: 1939–1993*. Toronto: Penguin Random House, 2007.

Munton, Don. "Transboundary Air Pollution: Dependence and Interdependence." In *Bilateral Ecopolitics: Continuity and Change in Canadian-American Environmental Relations*, edited by Philippe Le Prestre and Peter Stoett, 73–92. New York: Routledge, 2006.

– "Acid Rain and Transboundary Air Quality in Canadian-American Relations." *American Review of Canadian Studies* 27 (1997): 327–58. https://doi.org/10.1080/02722019709481554.

– "Acid Rain Politics in North America: From Conflict to Cooperation to Collusion." In *Acid in the Environment*, edited by Gerald Visgilio and Diana Whitelaw, 175–201. New York: Springer, 2007.

Murton, Jamie. *Canadians and Their Natural Environment: A History*. New York: Oxford University Press, 2021.

Neary, Peter. "Grey, Bryce, and the Settlement of Canadian-American Differences, 1905–1911." *Canadian History Review* 49, no. 4 (1968): 357–80. DOI: 10.3138/chr-049-04-02.

Nelles, H.V. *The Politics of Development: Forest, Mines and Hydro-Electric Power in Ontario, 1849–1941*. Toronto: Macmillan, 1974.

Nemeth, Tammy. "Canada-US Oil and Gas Relations, 1958 to 1974." Doctoral dissertation, University of British Columbia, 2007.

– "Continental Drift: Energy Policy and Canadian-American Relations." In *Diplomatic Departures: The Conservative Era in Canadian Foreign Policy, 1984–1993*, edited by Nelson Michaud and Kim Richard Nossal, 59–70. Vancouver: UBC Press, 2001.

– "From Conflict to Cooperation: Canada's US Oil and Gas Policy from the 1970s to the 1980s." In *Transnationalism: Canada-United States History into the Twenty-First Century*, edited by Michael Behiels and Reginald Stuart, 149–80. Montreal: McGill-Queen's University Press, 2010.

Norman, Emma S., Alice Cohen, and Karen Bakker, eds. *Water without Borders? Canada, the United States, and Shared Waters*. Toronto: University of Toronto Press, 2013.

Olive, Andrea. "Biodiversity without Borders? Acknowledging and Overcoming Obstacles in the Transboundary Governance of Endangered Species." In *Towards Continental Environmental Policy? North American Transnational Environmental Networks, and Governance*, edited by Peter Stoett and Owen Temby, 131–55. Albany, NY: SUNY Press, 2017.

– *Land, Stewardship, and Legitimacy: Endangered Species Policy in Canada and the United States*. Toronto: University of Toronto Press, 2014.

Osborne, Brian S., and Donald Swainson. *The Sault Ste. Marie Canal: A Chapter in the History of Great Lakes Transport*. Ottawa: Government of Canada, 1986.

Panitch, Leo. *The Canadian State: Political Economy and Political Power*. Toronto: University of Toronto Press: 1977.

Paris, Roland. *The Devils Lake Dispute between Canada and the United States: Lessons for Canadian Government Officials*. Ottawa: Centre for International Policy Studies, University of Ottawa, February 2008.

Payne, Brian. *Fishing a Borderless Sea: Environmental Territorialism in the North Atlantic, 1818–1910*. East Lansing: Michigan State University Press, 2010.

Penfold, Steve. In *Powering Up Canada: The History of Power, Fuel, and Energy from 1600*, edited by Ruth W. Sandwell, 274–99. Montreal: McGill-Queen's University Press, 2016.

Perlgut, Mark. *Electricity across the Border: the US-Canadian Experience*. New York: C.D. Howe Research Institute, 1978.

Perras, Galen. *Franklin Roosevelt and the Origins of the Canadian-American Security Alliance, 1933–1945: Necessary, but Not Necessary Enough*. Westport, CN: Praeger, 1998.

Peyton, Jonathan. "Corporate Ecology: B.C Hydro's Stikine-Iskut Project and the Unbuilt Environment." *Journal of Historical Geography* 37, no. 3 (July 2011): 358–69. https://doi.org/10.1016/j.jhg.2011.01.006.

Piper, Liza. *The Industrial Transformation of Subarctic Canada*. Vancouver: UBC Press, 2009.

Piper, Liza, and Heather Green. "A Province Powered by Coal: The Renaissance of Coal Mining in Late Twentieth-Century Alberta." *Canadian Historical Review* 98, no. 3 (Fall 2017): 532–67. DOI: 10.3138/chr.4248.

Rabe, Barry. "Beyond Kyoto: Climate Change Policy in Multilevel Governance Systems." *Governance: An International Journal of Policy, Administration and Institutions* 20, no. 3 (2007): 423–44. https://doi.org/10.1111/j.1468-0491.2007.00365.x.

– ed. *Greenhouse Governance: Addressing Climate Change in America*. Washington, DC: Brookings Institute Press, 2010.

Rahm, Dian. *Climate Change Policy in the United States: The Science, the Politics and the Prospects for Change*. London, UK: McFarland, 2014.

Randall, Stephen. *United States Foreign Oil Policy Since World War I*. Montreal: McGill-Queen's University Press, 2005.

Read, Jennifer. "Origin of the Great Lakes Water Quality Agreement: Concepts and Structures." In *The First Century of the International Joint Commission*, edited by Daniel Macfarlane and Murray Clamen, 347–66. Calgary: University of Calgary Press, 2020.

Redekop, Bill. *Dams of Contention: The Rafferty-Alameda Story and the Birth of Canadian Environmental Law*. Winnipeg: Heartland Associates, 2012.

Richards, John, and Larry Pratt. *Prairie Capitalism: Power and Influence in the New West*. Toronto: McClelland and Stewart, 1979.

Riddell-Dixon, Elizabeth. *Canada and the International Seabed: Domestic Determinants and External Constraints*. Montreal: McGill-Queen's University Press, 1989.

Ritchie, Gordon. *Wrestling with the Elephant: The Inside Story of the Canada-US Trade Wars*. Toronto: Macfarlane, Walter and Ross, 1997.

Robert, Maryse. *Negotiating NAFTA: Explaining the Outcome in Culture, Textiles, Autos, and Pharmaceuticals*. Toronto: University of Toronto Press, 2000.

Rogers, Raymond A., and Catherine Stewart. "Prisoners of their Histories: Canada-US Conflicts in the Pacific Salmon Fishery." *American Review of Canadian Studies*, 27, no. 2 (1997): 253–69. https://doi.org/10.1080/02722019709481499.

Roos, John F. *Restoring Fraser River Salmon: A History of the International Pacific Salmon Fisheries Commission, 1937–1985*. Vancouver: Pacific Salmon Commission, 1991.

Rowlands, Ian. "North American Integration and 'Green' Electricity." In *Bilateral Ecopolitics: Continuity and Change in Canadian-American Environmental Relations*, edited by Philippe Le Prestre and Peter Stoett, 211–24. New York: Routledge, 2006.

– "US-Canadian Subnational Electricity Relations." In *Towards Continental Environmental Policy? North American Transnational Environmental Networks and Governance*, edited by Peter Stoett and Owen Temby, 334–56. Albany, NY: SUNY Press, 2017.

Sandford, Robert, Deborah Harford, and Jon O'Riordan. *The Columbia River Treaty: A Primer*. Victoria, BC: Rocky Mountain Books, 2014.

Sandwell, Ruth W. *Canada's Rural Majority: Households, Environments, and Economies, 1870–1940*. Toronto: University of Toronto Press, 2016.

– ed. *Powering Up Canada: The History of Power, Fuel, and Energy from 1600*. Montreal: McGill-Queen's University Press, 2016.

Saunders, J. Owen. "Canada-US Energy Issues: Electricity and Regulatory Sovereignty." In *Canada and the New American Empire*, 2004. https://www.uvic.ca/research/centres/globalstudies/publications/publicationsdb/pubs/canada-us-energy-issues-electric-id-98.php.

Scarpino, Philip. "Addressing Cross-Border Pollution of the Great Lakes after World War II: The Canada-Ontario Agreement and the Great Lakes Water Quality Agreement." In *Transnationalism: Canada-United States History into the Twenty-First Century*, edited by Michael Behiels, and Reginald Stuart, 115–32. Montreal: McGill-Queen's University Press, 2010.

Schwartz, Alan M. "The Canada-US Environmental Relationship: Calm Waters but Slow Sailing." *International Journal* 60, 2 (Spring 2005): 437–38. DOI: 10.2307/40204301.

Selin, Henrik, and Stacy D. VanDeveer. "Canadian-US Cooperation: Regional Climate Change Action in the Northeast." In *Bilateral Ecopolitics: Continuity and Change in Canadian-American Environmental Relations*, edited by Philippe Le Prestre and Peter Stoett, 93–114. New York: Routledge, 2006.

– *Changing Climates in North American Politics: Institutions, Policymaking and Multilevel Governance.* Cambridge, MA: The MIT Press, 2009.

Smith, Heather. "Shades of Grey in Canada's Greening during the Mulroney Era." In *Diplomatic Departures: The Conservative Era in Canadian Foreign Policy, 1984–1993*, edited by Nelson Michaud and Kim Richard Nossal, 71–83. Vancouver: UBC Press, 2001.

Song, Andrew, Owen Temby, Gail Krantzberg, and Gordon M. Hickey. "Institutional Features of US-Canadian Transboundary Fisheries Governance: Organization and Networks, Formal and Informal." In *Towards Continental Environmental Policy? North American Transnational Environmental Networks, and Governance*, edited by Peter Stoett and Owen Temby, 156–79. Albany, NY: SUNY Press, 2017.

Special International Niagara Board. *Preservation and Improvement of the Scenic Beauty of the Niagara Falls and Rapids*. Ottawa and Washington, DC: Governments of Canada and the United States, 1931.

Spencer, Robert, John Kirton, and Kim Richard Nossal, eds. *The International Joint Commission Seventy Years On*. Toronto: University of Toronto Centre for International Studies, 1981.

Stacey, C.P. *Canada and the Age of Conflict, Vol. 1: 1867–1921*. Toronto: University of Toronto Press, 1984.

– *Canada and the Age of Conflict, Volume 2: 1921–1948, The Mackenzie King Era*. Toronto: University of Toronto Press, 1981.

Stamm, Michael. *Dead Tree Media: Manufacturing the Newspaper in Twentieth Century North America*. Baltimore, MD: Johns Hopkins University Press, 2018.

Stanford, Jim. *A Cure for Dutch Disease: Active Sector Strategies for Canada's Economy, Alternative Federal Budget Technical Paper*. Ottawa: Canadian Center for Policy Alternatives, 2012.

Steward, F.R. "Energy Consumption in Canada since Confederation." *Energy Policy* 6, no. 3 (1978): 239–45. https://doi.org/10.1016/0301-4215(78)90056-3.

Stewart, Gordon T. *The American Response to Canada since 1776*. Lansing: Michigan State University Press, 1992.

Stoett, Peter J. "Fairweather Friends? Canada-United States Environmental Relations in the Days of Trump and the Era of Climate Change." In *Canada-US Relations: Sovereignty or Shared Institutions?*, edited by David Carment and Christopher Sands, 105–124. London, UK: Palgrave Macmillan, 2019. https://doi.org/10.1007/978-3-030-05036-8_6.

Stoett, Peter and Owen Temby, eds. *Towards Continental Environmental Policy? North American Transnational Environmental Networks and Governance*. Albany, NY: SUNY Press, 2017.

Stuart, Reginald C. *Dispersed Relations: Americans and Canadians in Upper North America*. Baltimore, MD: Johns Hopkins University Press, 2007.

Swainson, Neil A. *Conflict over the Columbia: The Canadian Background to an Historic Treaty*. Montreal: McGill-Queen's University Press, 1979.

Sweet, William. *Climate Diplomacy from Rio to Paris: The Effort to Contain Global Warming*. New Haven, CT: Yale University Press, 2016.

Szeman, Imre. *On Petrocultures: Globalization, Culture, and Energy*. Morgantown: West Virginia University Press, 2019.

Tallman, Robert. "Warships and Mackerel: The North Atlantic Fisheries in Canadian-American Relations, 1867–1877." Doctoral dissertation, University of Maine, 1971.

Tanner, Howard. *Something Spectacular: My Great Lakes Salmon Story*. Lansing: Michigan State University Press, 2018.

Taylor, Graham D. *Imperial Standard: Imperial Oil, Exxon, and the Canadian Oil Industry from 1880*. Calgary: University of Calgary Press, 2019.

Taylor, William W. *Great Lakes Fisheries Policy and Management: A Binational Perspective*. Lansing: Michigan State University Press, 2012.

Taylor, Joseph, III. *Making Salmon: An Environmental History of the Northwest Fisheries Crisis*. Seattle: University of Washington Press, 2001.

– "The Historical Roots of the Canadian-American Salmon Wars." In *Parallel Destinies: Canadian-American Relations West of the Rockies*, edited by Kenneth Coates and John Findlay, 155–80. Seattle: University of Washington Press, 2002.

Teigrob, Robert. *Warming up to the Cold War: Canada and the United States Coalition of the Willing, from Hiroshima to Korea*. Toronto: University of Toronto Press, 2009.

Temby, Owen. "Control and Suppression in Sarnia's Chemical Valley during the 1960s." *Enterprise and Society*, 21, no. 2 (2020): 1–33. DOI: https://doi.org/10.1017/eso.2019.35.

Temby, Owen, and Don Munton. "The International Joint Commission and Air Pollution: A Tale of Two Cases." In *The First Century of the International Joint Commission*, edited by Daniel Macfarlane and Murray Clamen, 313–46. Calgary: University of Calgary Press, 2020.

Temby, Owen, and Ryan O'Connor. "Property, Technology, and Environmental Policy: The Politics of Acid Rain in Ontario, 1978–1985." *Journal of Policy History* 27, no. 4 (2015): 636–69. DOI: https://doi.org/10.1017/S0898030615000299.

Thompson, John Herd, and Stephen J. Randall. *Canada and the United States: Ambivalent Allies*, 4th ed. Athens: University of Georgia Press, 2008.

Tomlin, Brian, and Max Cameron. *The Making of NAFTA: How the Deal Was Done*. Ithaca, NY: Cornell University Press, 2000.

Unger, Richard W., and John Thistle. *Energy Consumption in Canada in the 19th and 20th Centuries: A Statistical Outline*. Rome: Consiglio Nazionale delle Ricerche, Instituto di Studi sulle Società del Mediterraneo, 2013.

Urquhart, Ian. *Costly Fix: Power, Politics, and Nature in the Tar Sands*. Toronto: University of Toronto Press, 2018.

Uslaner, Eric M. "Energy Policy and Federalism in the United States and Canada." In *The Canada-United States Relationship: The Politics of Energy and Environmental Coordination*, edited by Jonathan Lemco, 41–64. London, UK: Praeger, 1992.

Van Huizen, Philip. "Building a Green Dam: Environmental Modernism and the Canadian-American Libby Dam Project." *Pacific Historical Review* 79, no. 3 (August 2010): 418–53. https://doi.org/10.1525/phr.2010.79.3.418.

VanNijnatten, Debora. "Canadian-American Environmental Relations: Interoperability and Politics." *The American Review of Canadian Studies* 34, no. 4 (Winter 2004): 649–64. https://doi.org/10.1080/02722010409481693.

– "From the International Joint Commission to Copenhagen: Partnership in Environmental Management in a North American Regional Context." In *Forgotten Partnership Redux*, edited by Greg Anderson and Christopher Sands, 507–34. Amherst, NY: Cambria Press, 2011.

VanNijnatten, Debora and Carolyn Johns. "The International Joint Commission and the Evolution of the Great Lakes Water Quality Agreement: Accountability, Progress Reporting, and Measuring Performance." In *The First Century of the International Joint Commission*, edited by Daniel Macfarlane and Murray Clamen, 395–430. Calgary: University of Calgary Press, 2020.

VanNijnatten, Debora, and Marcela Lopez-Vallejo Olvero. "Canada-United States Relations and a Low Carbon Economy for North America." In *Transboundary Environmental Governance across the World's Longest Border*, edited by Stephen Brooks and Andrea Olive, 201–26. Lansing: Michigan State University Press, 2018.

VanNijnatten, Debora, and Peter Stoett. "Continental Counter-Invasion: Invasive Species Management in North America." In *Towards Continental Environmental Policy? North American Transnational Environmental Networks and Governance*, edited by Peter Stoett and Owen Temby, 180–202. Albany, NY: SUNY Press, 2017.

Wadewitz, Lissa. *The Nature of Borders: Salmon and Boundaries in the Salish Sea*. Seattle: University of Washington Press, 2012.

Waldram, James. *As Long as the Rivers Run: Hydroelectric Development and Native Communities*. Winnipeg: University of Manitoba Press, 1993.

Waterfield, Donald. *Continental Waterboy: The Columbia River Controversy*. Toronto: Clarke, Irwin, 1970.

Watson, Andrew. "Coal in Canada." In *Powering Up Canada: The History of Power, Fuel, and Energy from 1600*, edited by Ruth W. Sandwell, 213–50. Montreal: McGill-Queen's University Press, 2016.

Weibust, Inger. *Green Leviathan: The Case for a Federal Role in Environmental Policy*. New York: Routledge, 2009.

Whorley, David. "From IWC to BWT: Canada-US Institution Building, 1902–1909." In *The First Century of the International Joint Commission*, edited by Daniel Macfarlane and Murray Clamen, 35–70. Calgary: University of Calgary Press, 2020.

Willoughby, William. *The Joint Organizations of Canada and the United States*. Toronto: University of Toronto Press, 1979.

Wilson, Robert. *Seeking Refuge: Birds and Landscapes of the Pacific Flyway*. Seattle: University of Washington Press, 2010.

Wirth, John D. *Smelter Smoke in North America: The Politics of Transborder Pollution*. Lawrence: University Press of Kansas, 2000.

Woodward, Arthur M. *Charting the Inland Seas: A History of the US Lake Survey*. Detroit, MI: US Army Corps of Engineers, Detroit District, 1991.

Worster, Donald. "Wild, Tame, and Free: Comparing Canadian and US Views of Nature." In *Parallel Destinies: Canadian-American Relations West of the Rockies*, edited by Kenneth Coates and John Findlay, 246–73. Seattle: University of Washington Press, 2002.

Young, Terence, Alan MacEachern, and Lary Dilsaver. "From Competition to Cooperation: A History of Canada-US National Park Relations." *Environment and History* 27, no. 4 (November 2021): 607–34. DOI: https://doi.org/10.3197/096734019X15631846928783.

Index

The letters t and f following a page number denote tables and figures, respectively.

www.ingramcontent.com/pod-product-compliance
Lightning Source LLC
LaVergne TN
LVHW090902230826
846271LV00024BA/136